SCIENCE FICTION

The characters and most of the likenesses in this book are based on historical figures, and we've tried to give a true account of their lives and work. But though based on fact, this book is in equal measures history and historical fiction. Real events interweave with those we imagined for dramatic purposes, and documented quotes blend with our interpretations of thoughts and actions. We hope you'll consult the references for the stories and then let us know what you think about these fascinating scientists.

Dignifying Science
Stories About Women Scientists

Third Edition: April, 2009

ISBN 978-0-9788037-3-5
Library of Congress Control Number: 2003091534

 Special thanks to Sara for unpaid editing, Steve and Linda for unpaid art direction, and Kat for both, as well as for ~~un~~requited love.

A General Tektronics Labs book.

G.T. Labs
P.O. Box 8145
Ann Arbor, MI 48107

info@gt-labs.com
www.gt-labs.com

5 4 3 2 1

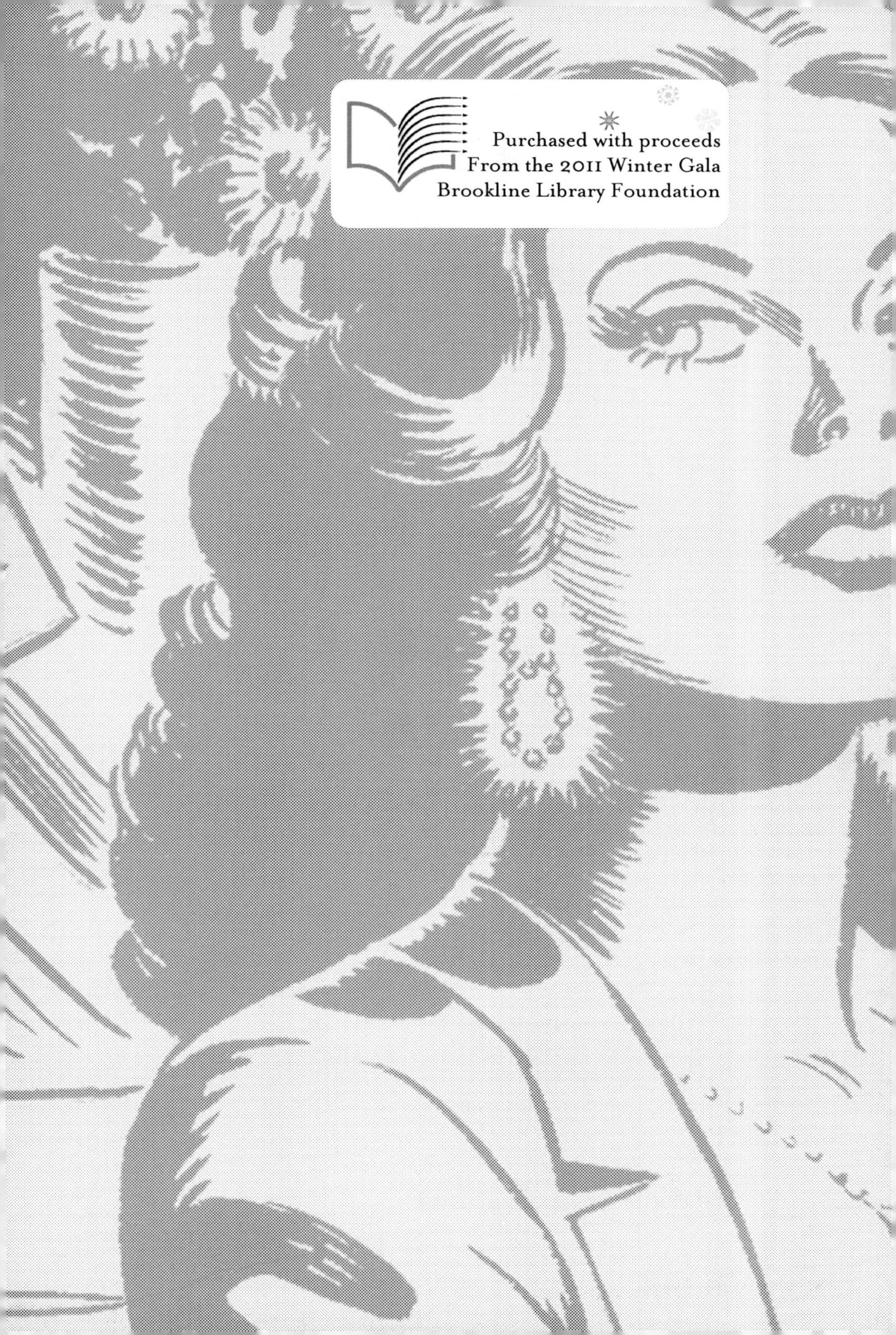

DIGNIFYING SCIENCE

Stories about women scientists written by Jim Ottaviani and illustrated by Donna Barr, Stephanie Gladden, Roberta Gregory, Lea Hernandez, Carla Speed McNeil, Linda Medley, Marie Severin, Jen Sorensen, and Anne Timmons, with covers by Mary Fleener and Ramona Fradon.

OTHER BOOKS FROM G.T. LABS

SAFECRACKER: A TWO-FISTED SCIENCE COMIC

TWO-FISTED SCIENCE: STORIES ABOUT SCIENTISTS

WILD PERSON IN THE WOODS

"TALKING" ORANGUTANS IN BORNEO (FOR THE ORANGUTAN FOUNDATION
INTERNATIONAL)

FALLOUT: J. ROBERT OPPENHEIMER, LEO SZILARD, AND THE POLITICAL SCIENCE OF THE
ATOMIC BOMB

SUSPENDED IN LANGUAGE: NIELS BOHR'S LIFE, DISCOVERIES, AND THE CENTURY
HE SHAPED

BONE SHARPS, COWBOYS, AND THUNDER LIZARDS:
EDWARD DRINKER COPE, OTHNIEL CHARLES MARSH, AND THE GILDED AGE
OF PALEONTOLOGY

WIRE MOTHERS: HARRY HARLOW AND THE SCIENCE OF LOVE

LEVITATION: PHYSICS AND PSYCHOLOGY IN THE SERVICE OF DECEPTION

ALSO

CHARLES R. KNIGHT: AUTOBIOGRAPHY OF AN ARTIST

TABLE OF CONTENTS

PROLOGUE: MARIE SKLODOVSKA

PROLOGUE: MARIE SKLODOVSKA

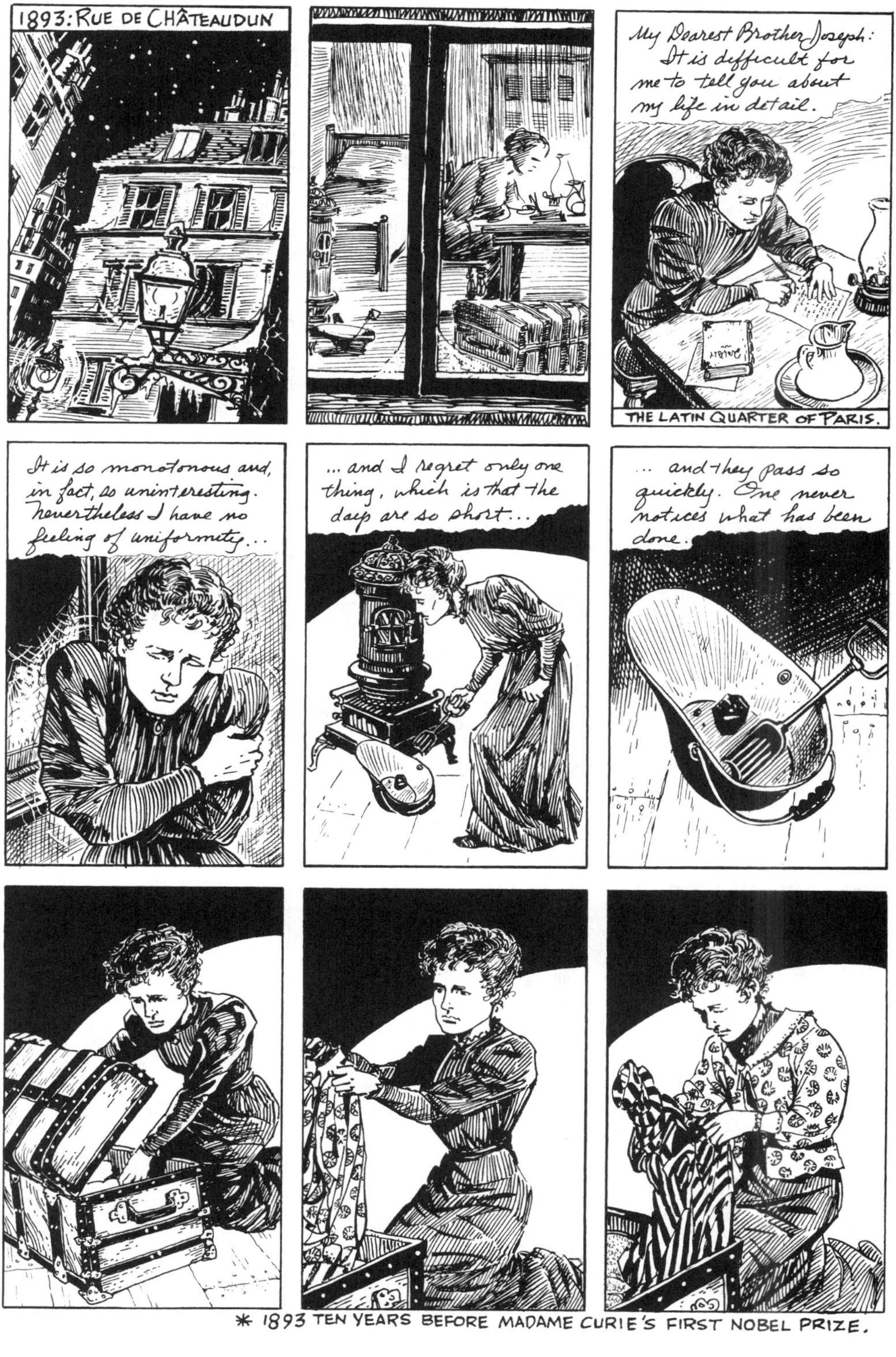
1893: RUE DE CHÂTEAUDUN
My Dearest Brother Joseph: It is difficult for me to tell you about my life in detail.
THE LATIN QUARTER OF PARIS.
It is so monotonous and, in fact, so uninteresting. Nevertheless I have no feeling of uniformity...
... and I regret only one thing, which is that the days are so short...
... and they pass so quickly. One never notices what has been done.

* 1893 TEN YEARS BEFORE MADAME CURIE'S FIRST NOBEL PRIZE.

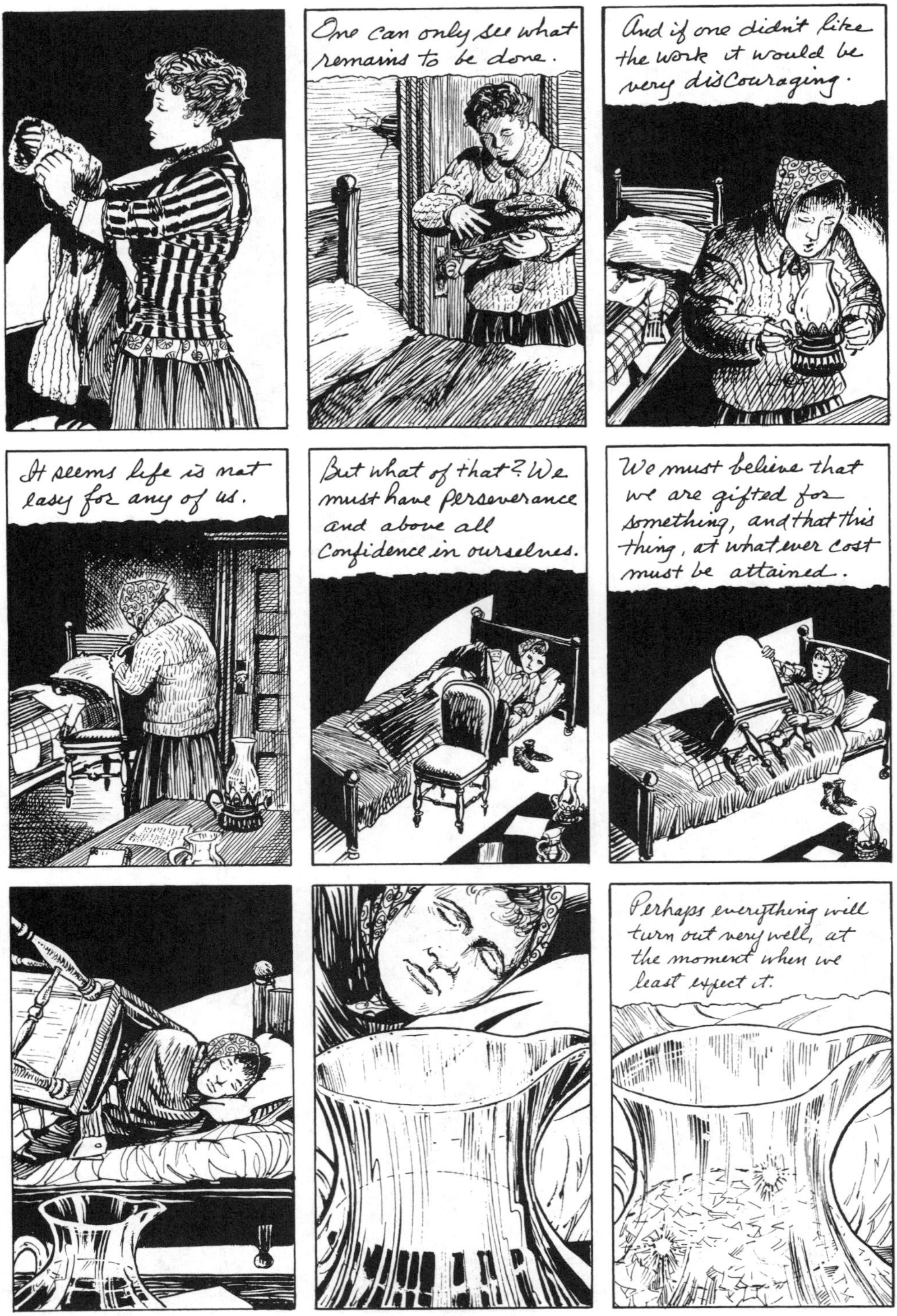
One can only see what remains to be done.
And if one didn't like the work it would be very disCouraging.
It seems life is not easy for any of us.
But what of that? We must have Perseverance and above all Confidence in ourselves.
We must believe that we are gifted for something, and that this thing, at whatever cost must be attained.
Perhaps everything will turn out very well, at the moment when we least expect it.

HEDY LAMARR

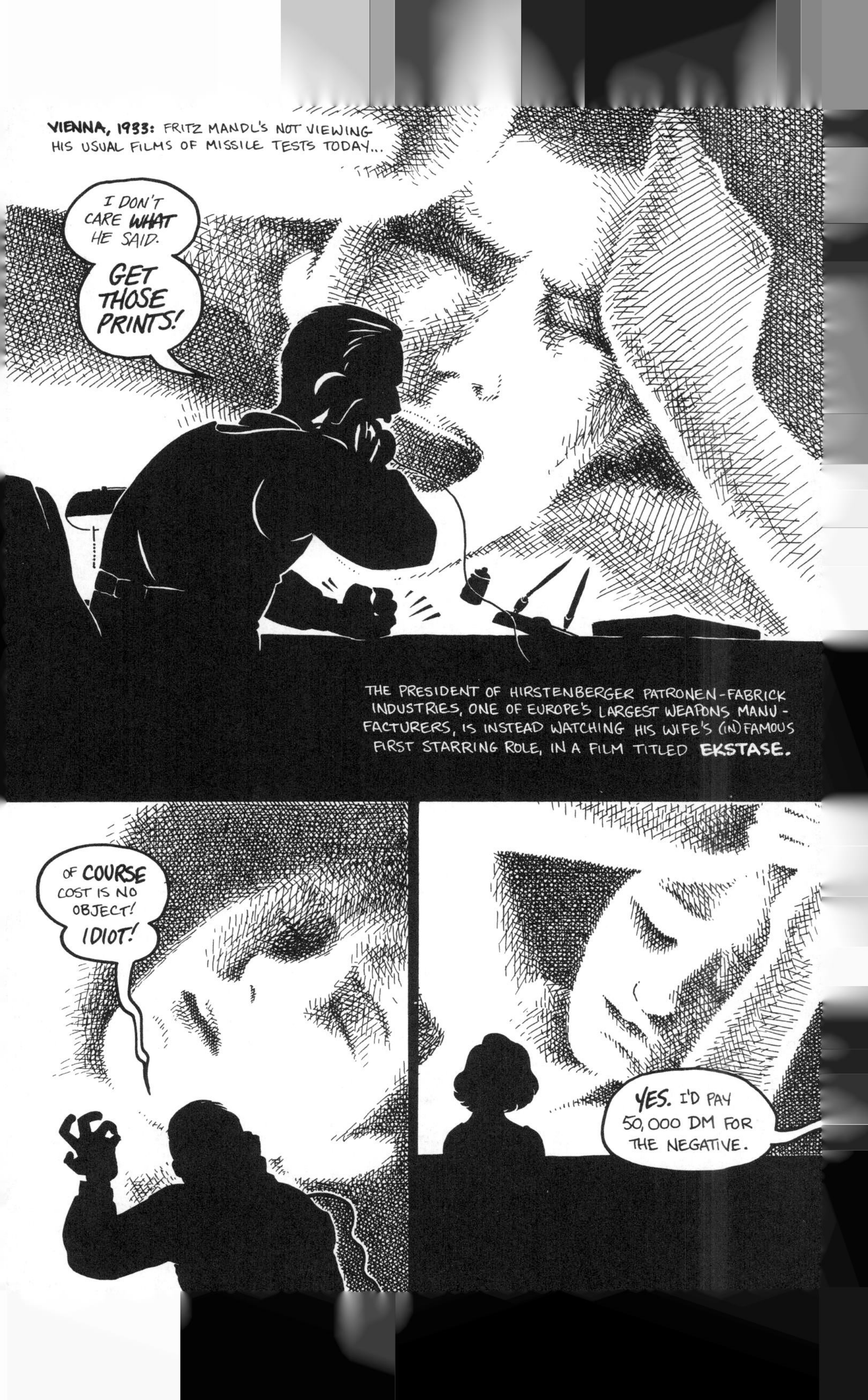
VIENNA, 1933: FRITZ MANDL'S NOT VIEWING HIS USUAL FILMS OF MISSILE TESTS TODAY...
I DON'T CARE WHAT HE SAID. GET THOSE PRINTS!
THE PRESIDENT OF HIRSTENBERGER PATRONEN-FABRICK INDUSTRIES, ONE OF EUROPE'S LARGEST WEAPONS MANU-FACTURERS, IS INSTEAD WATCHING HIS WIFE'S (IN)FAMOUS FIRST STARRING ROLE, IN A FILM TITLED EKSTASE.
OF COURSE COST IS NO OBJECT! IDIOT!
YES. I'D PAY 50,000 DM FOR THE NEGATIVE.

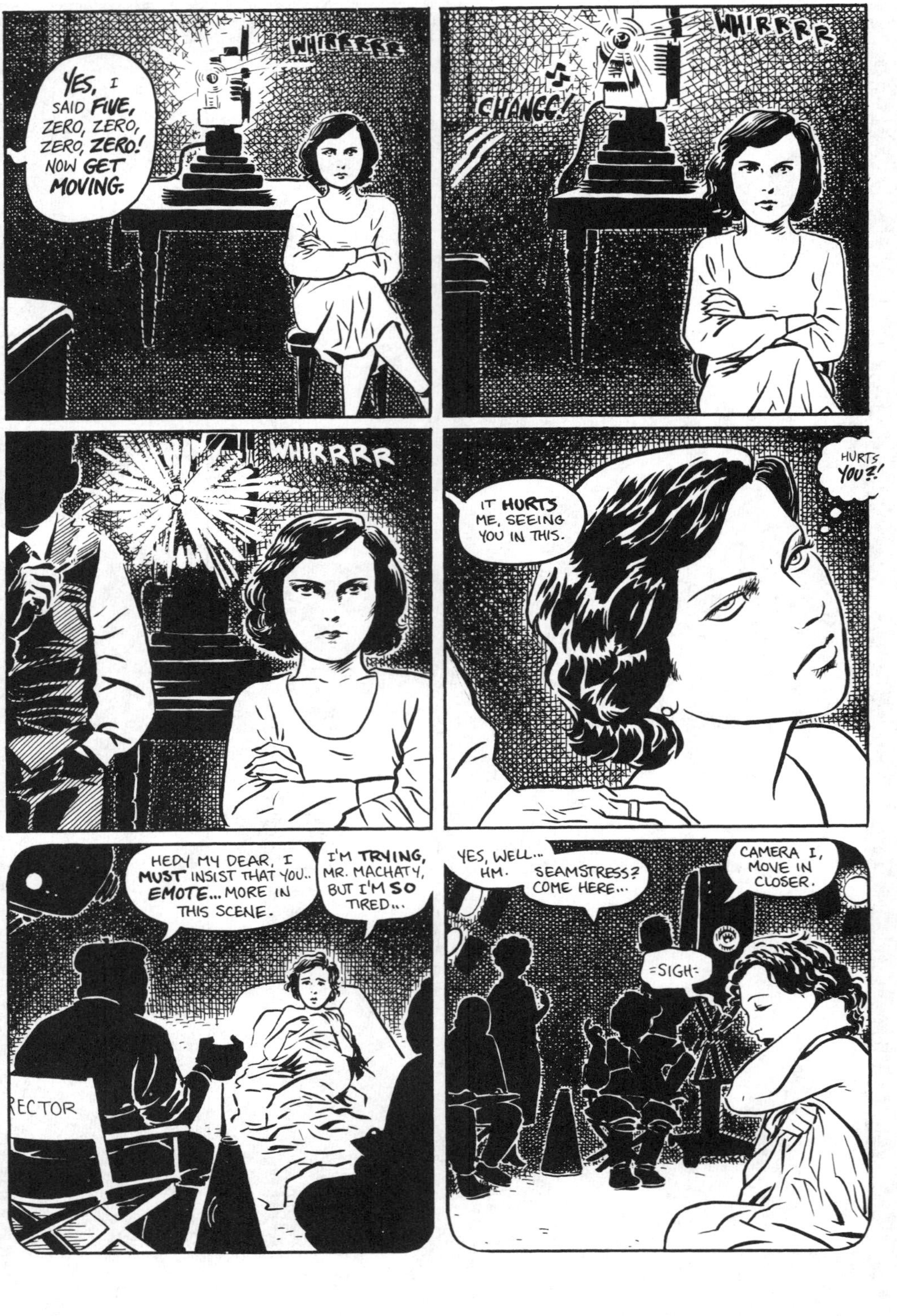
YES, I SAID FIVE, ZERO, ZERO, ZERO, ZERO! NOW GET MOVING.
WHIRRRRR
CHANGG!
WHIRRRR
WHIRRRR
IT HURTS ME, SEEING YOU IN THIS.
HURTS YOU?!
HEDY MY DEAR, I MUST INSIST THAT YOU.. EMOTE... MORE IN THIS SCENE.
I'M TRYING, MR. MACHATY, BUT I'M SO TIRED...
RECTOR
YES, WELL... HM.
SEAMSTRESS? COME HERE...
CAMERA I, MOVE IN CLOSER.
=SIGH=

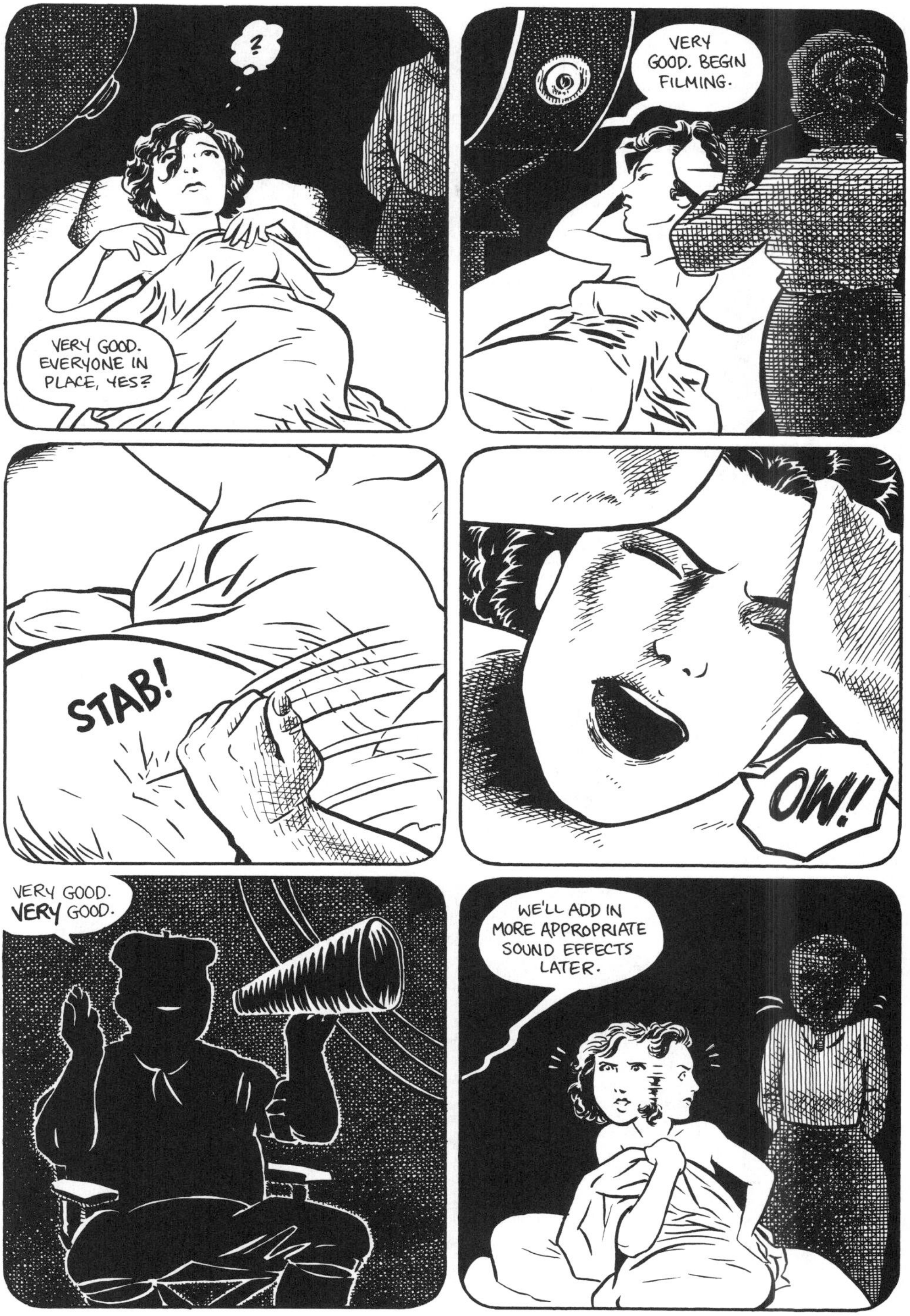
?
VERY GOOD. EVERYONE IN PLACE, YES?
VERY GOOD. BEGIN FILMING.
STAB!
OW!
VERY GOOD. **VERY** GOOD.
WE'LL ADD IN MORE APPROPRIATE SOUND EFFECTS LATER.

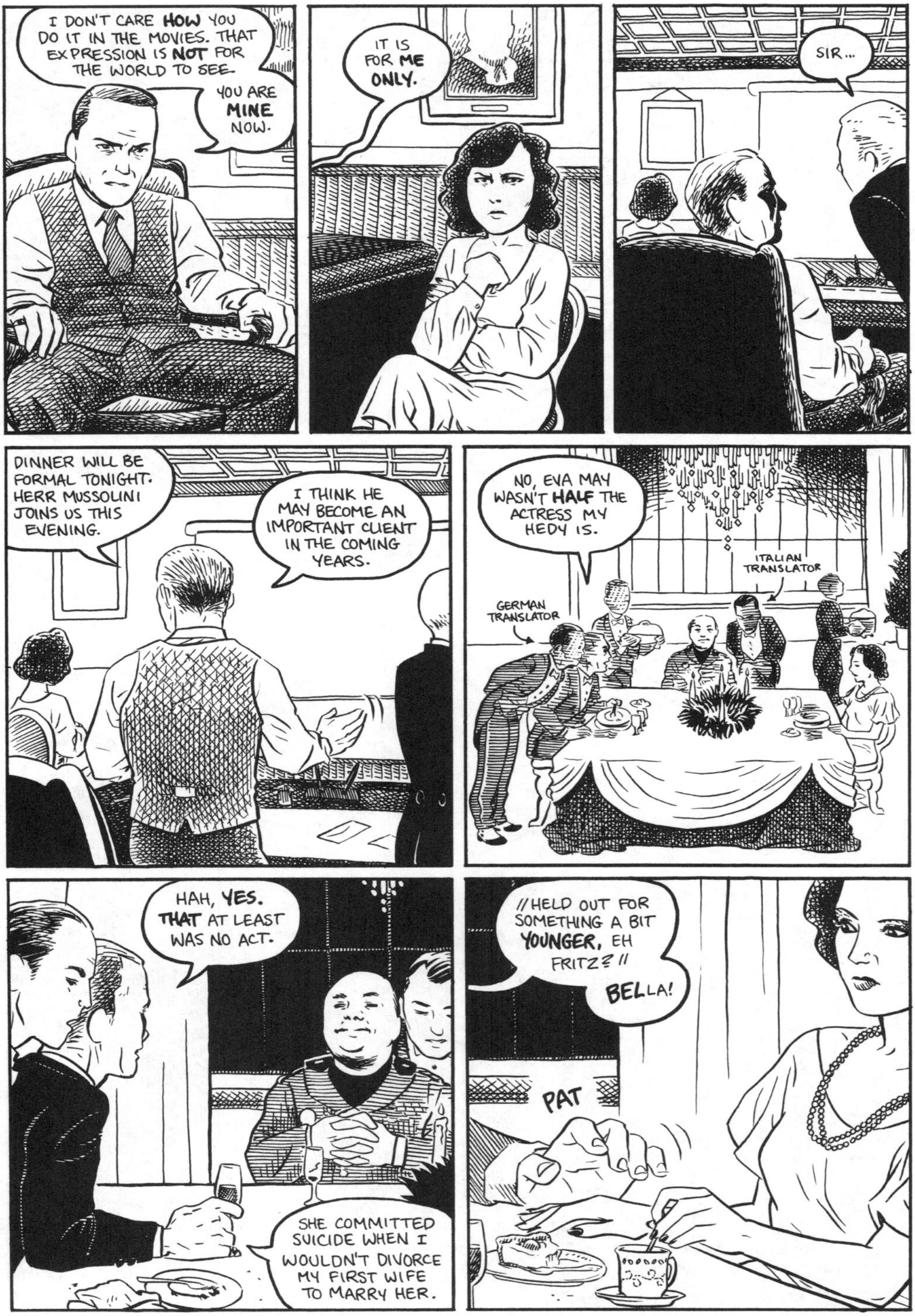
I DON'T CARE HOW YOU DO IT IN THE MOVIES. THAT EXPRESSION IS NOT FOR THE WORLD TO SEE.
YOU ARE MINE NOW.
IT IS FOR ME ONLY.
SIR...
DINNER WILL BE FORMAL TONIGHT. HERR MUSSOLINI JOINS US THIS EVENING.
I THINK HE MAY BECOME AN IMPORTANT CLIENT IN THE COMING YEARS.
NO, EVA MAY WASN'T HALF THE ACTRESS MY HEDY IS.
ITALIAN TRANSLATOR
GERMAN TRANSLATOR
HAH, YES. THAT AT LEAST WAS NO ACT.
SHE COMMITTED SUICIDE WHEN I WOULDN'T DIVORCE MY FIRST WIFE TO MARRY HER.
//HELD OUT FOR SOMETHING A BIT YOUNGER, EH FRITZ?//
BELLA!
PAT

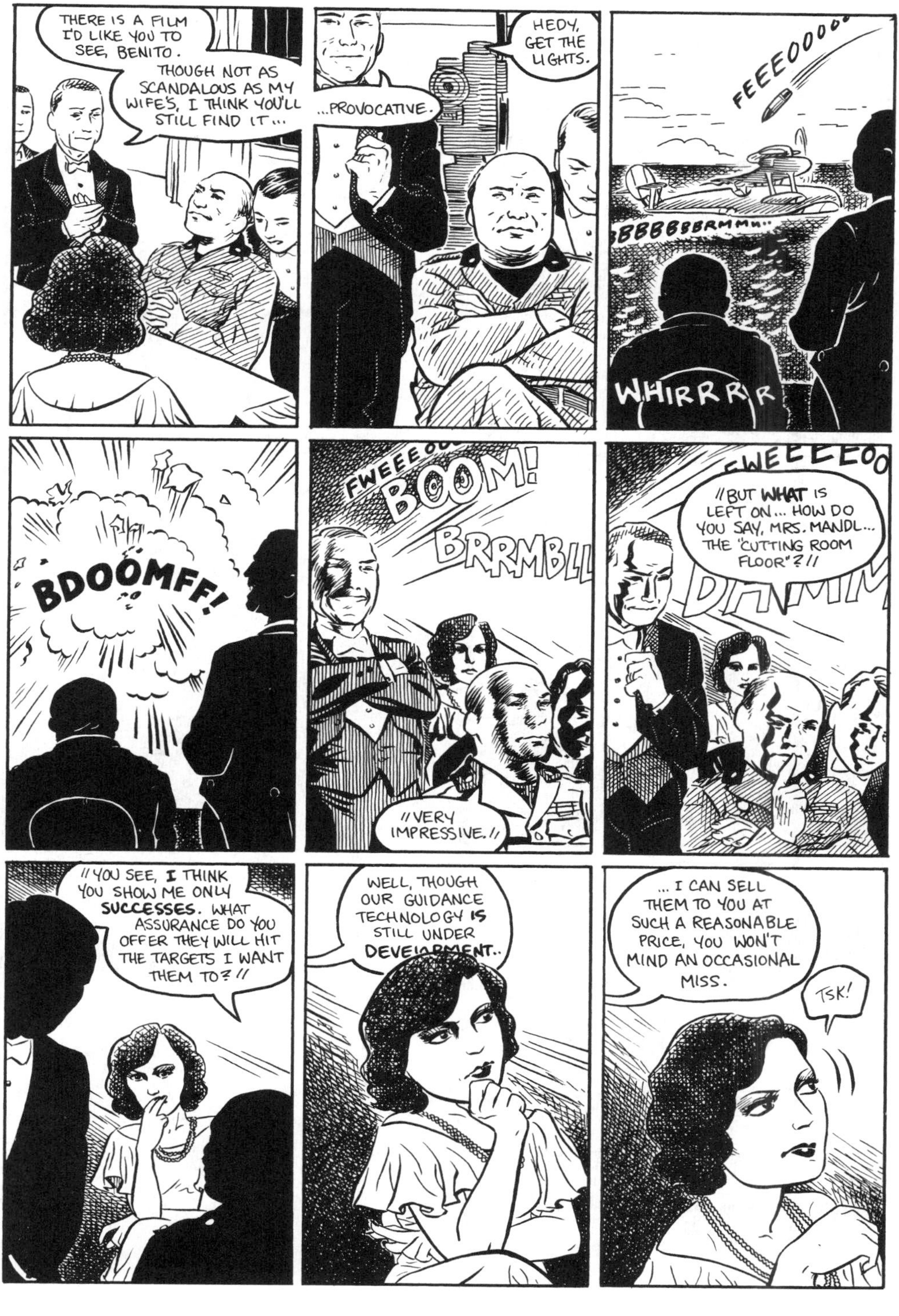
THERE IS A FILM I'D LIKE YOU TO SEE, BENITO.
THOUGH NOT AS SCANDALOUS AS MY WIFE'S, I THINK YOU'LL STILL FIND IT...
...PROVOCATIVE.
HEDY, GET THE LIGHTS.
FEEEOOOO...
BBBBBBBRMMM...
WHIRRRR
BDOOMFF!
FWEEE
BOOM!
BRRMBLL
//VERY IMPRESSIVE.//
FWEEEEOO
//BUT WHAT IS LEFT ON... HOW DO YOU SAY, MRS. MANDL... THE "CUTTING ROOM FLOOR"?//
//YOU SEE, I THINK YOU SHOW ME ONLY SUCCESSES. WHAT ASSURANCE DO YOU OFFER THEY WILL HIT THE TARGETS I WANT THEM TO?//
WELL, THOUGH OUR GUIDANCE TECHNOLOGY IS STILL UNDER DEVELOPMENT..
...I CAN SELL THEM TO YOU AT SUCH A REASONABLE PRICE, YOU WON'T MIND AN OCCASIONAL MISS.
TSK!

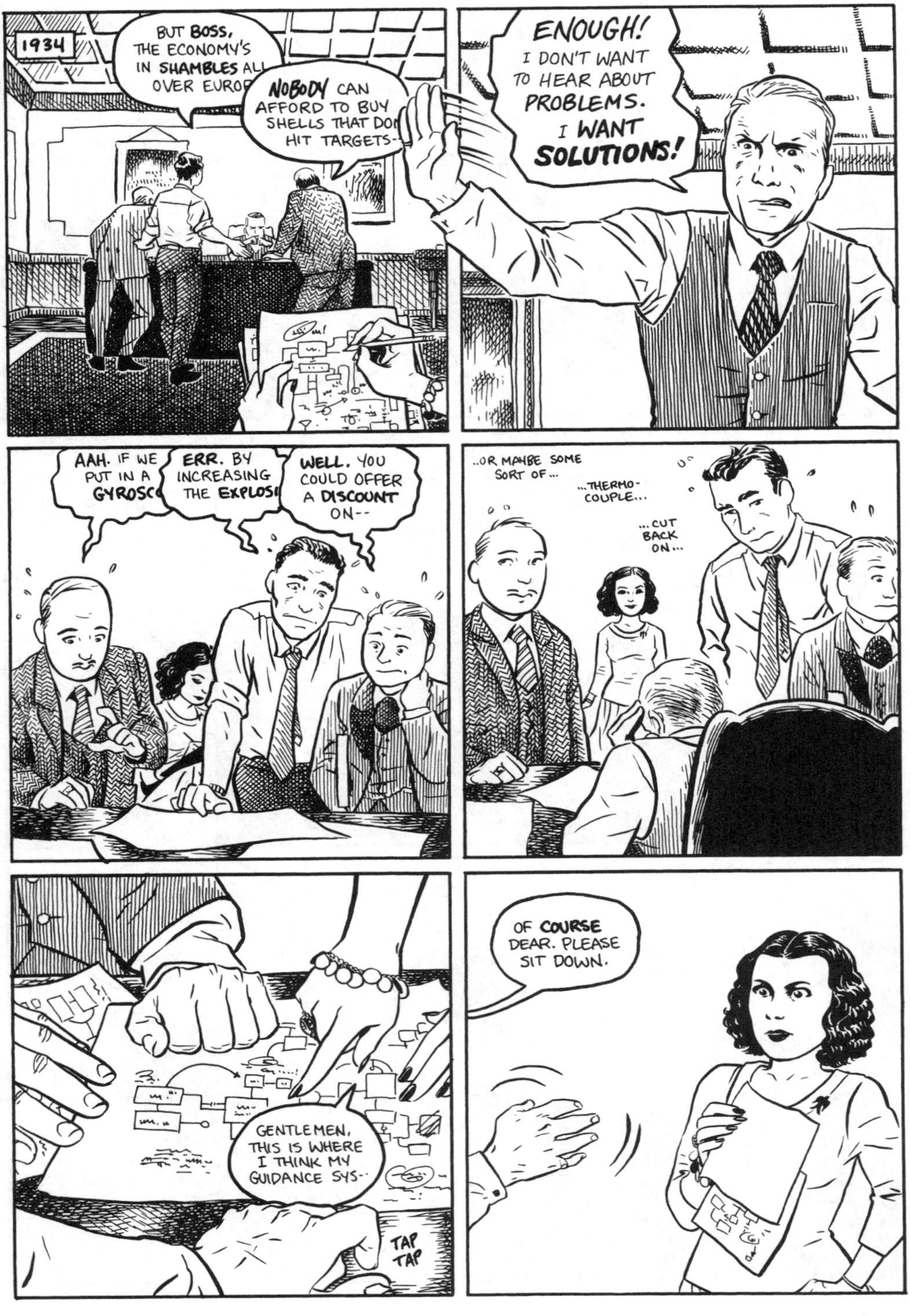
1934
BUT BOSS, THE ECONOMY'S IN SHAMBLES ALL OVER EUROP
NOBODY CAN AFFORD TO BUY SHELLS THAT DON HIT TARGETS--
ENOUGH! I DON'T WANT TO HEAR ABOUT PROBLEMS. I WANT SOLUTIONS!
AAH. IF WE PUT IN A GYROSC
ERR. BY INCREASING THE EXPLOSI
WELL. YOU COULD OFFER A DISCOUNT ON--
...OR MAYBE SOME SORT OF...
...THERMO-COUPLE...
...CUT BACK ON...
GENTLEMEN, THIS IS WHERE I THINK MY GUIDANCE SYS--
TAP TAP
OF COURSE DEAR. PLEASE SIT DOWN.

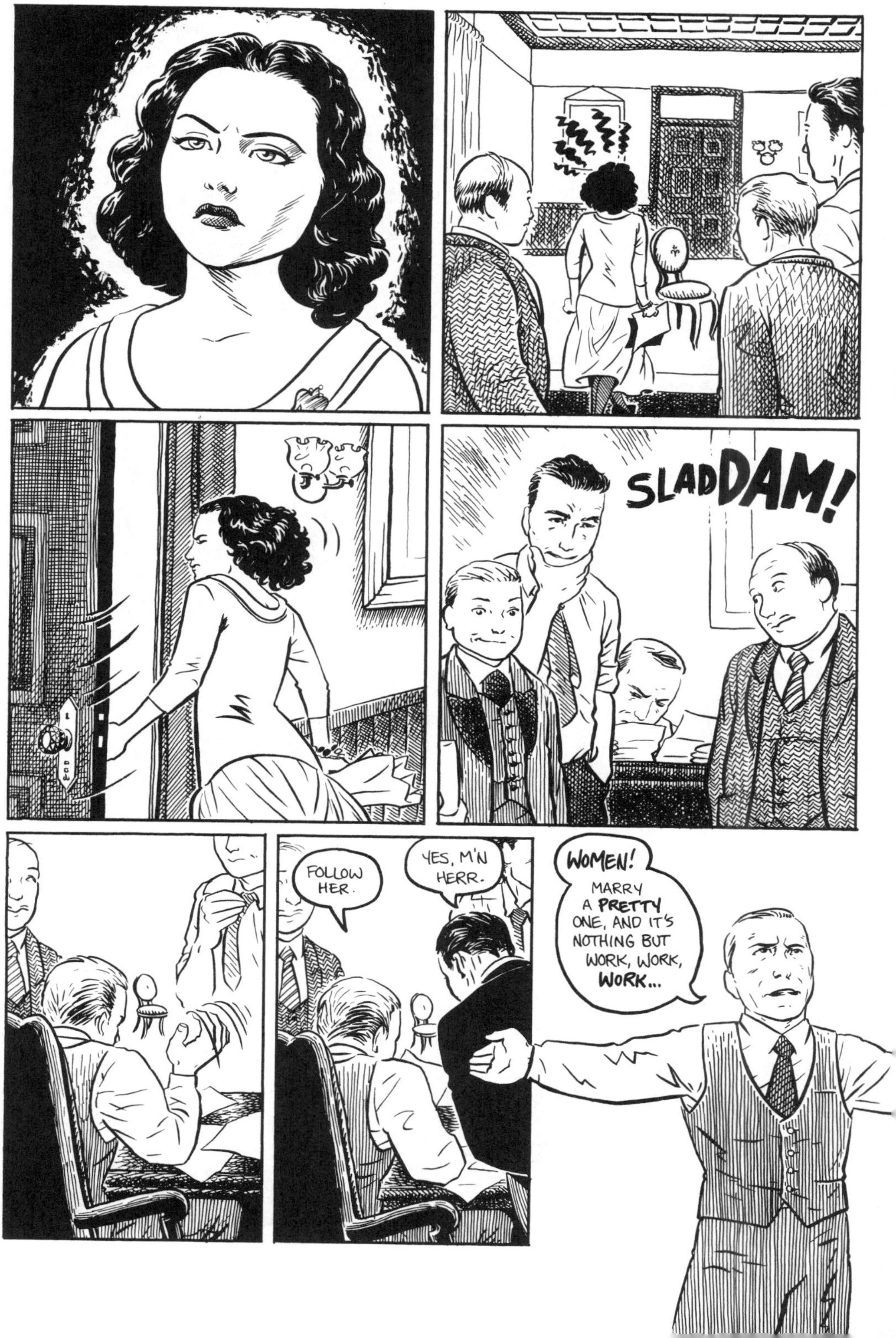
SLADDAM!
FOLLOW HER.
YES, M'N HERR.
WOMEN! MARRY A PRETTY ONE, AND IT'S NOTHING BUT WORK, WORK, WORK...

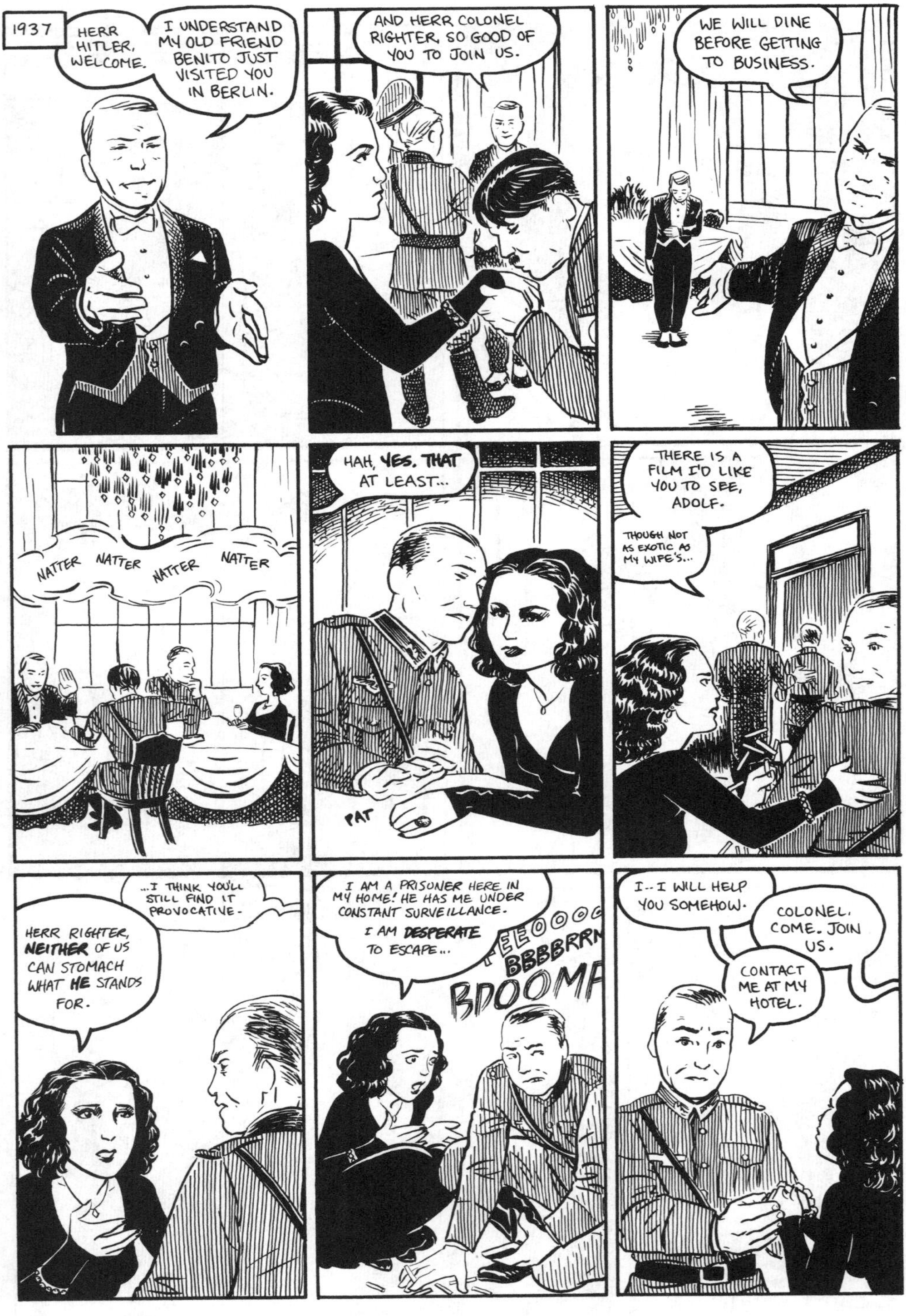
1937
HERR HITLER, WELCOME.
I UNDERSTAND MY OLD FRIEND BENITO JUST VISITED YOU IN BERLIN.
AND HERR COLONEL RIGHTER, SO GOOD OF YOU TO JOIN US.
WE WILL DINE BEFORE GETTING TO BUSINESS.
NATTER NATTER NATTER NATTER
HAH, YES. THAT AT LEAST...
PAT
THERE IS A FILM I'D LIKE YOU TO SEE, ADOLF.
THOUGH NOT AS EXOTIC AS MY WIFE'S...
...I THINK YOU'LL STILL FIND IT PROVOCATIVE.
HERR RIGHTER, NEITHER OF US CAN STOMACH WHAT HE STANDS FOR.
I AM A PRISONER HERE IN MY HOME! HE HAS ME UNDER CONSTANT SURVEILLANCE.
I AM DESPERATE TO ESCAPE...
FEEOOOO
BBBBRRN
BDOOMA
I-- I WILL HELP YOU SOMEHOW.
COLONEL. COME. JOIN US.
CONTACT ME AT MY HOTEL.

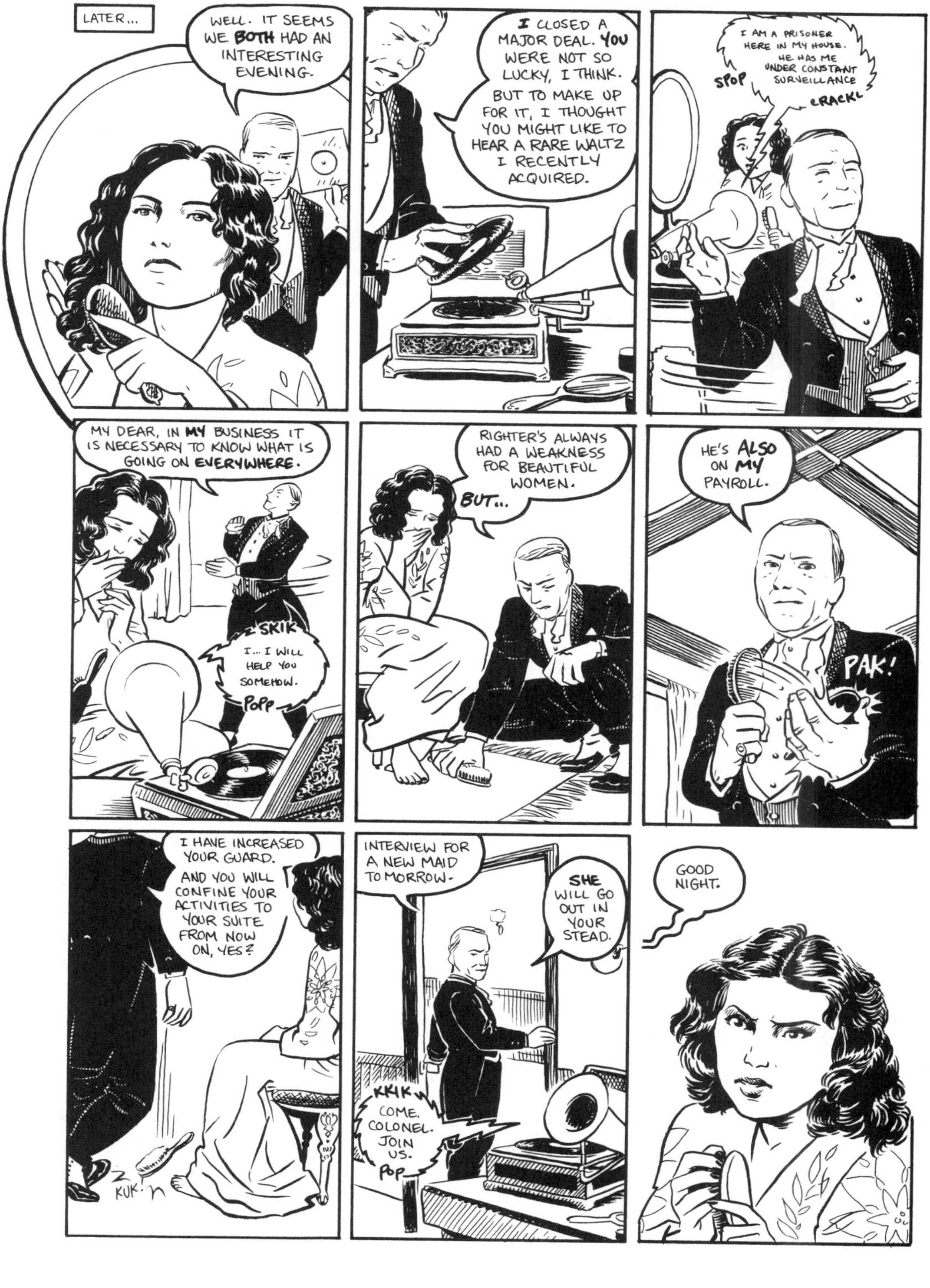
LATER...
WELL. IT SEEMS WE BOTH HAD AN INTERESTING EVENING.
I CLOSED A MAJOR DEAL. YOU WERE NOT SO LUCKY, I THINK.
BUT TO MAKE UP FOR IT, I THOUGHT YOU MIGHT LIKE TO HEAR A RARE WALTZ I RECENTLY ACQUIRED.
I AM A PRISONER HERE IN MY HOUSE. HE HAS ME UNDER CONSTANT SURVEILLANCE
SPOP
CRACKL
MY DEAR, IN MY BUSINESS IT IS NECESSARY TO KNOW WHAT IS GOING ON EVERYWHERE.
SKIK
I... I WILL HELP YOU SOMEHOW.
POPP
RIGHTER'S ALWAYS HAD A WEAKNESS FOR BEAUTIFUL WOMEN.
BUT...
HE'S ALSO ON MY PAYROLL.
PAK!
I HAVE INCREASED YOUR GUARD.
AND YOU WILL CONFINE YOUR ACTIVITIES TO YOUR SUITE FROM NOW ON, YES?
KUK
INTERVIEW FOR A NEW MAID TOMORROW.
SHE WILL GO OUT IN YOUR STEAD.
KKIK
COME. COLONEL. JOIN US.
POP
GOOD NIGHT.

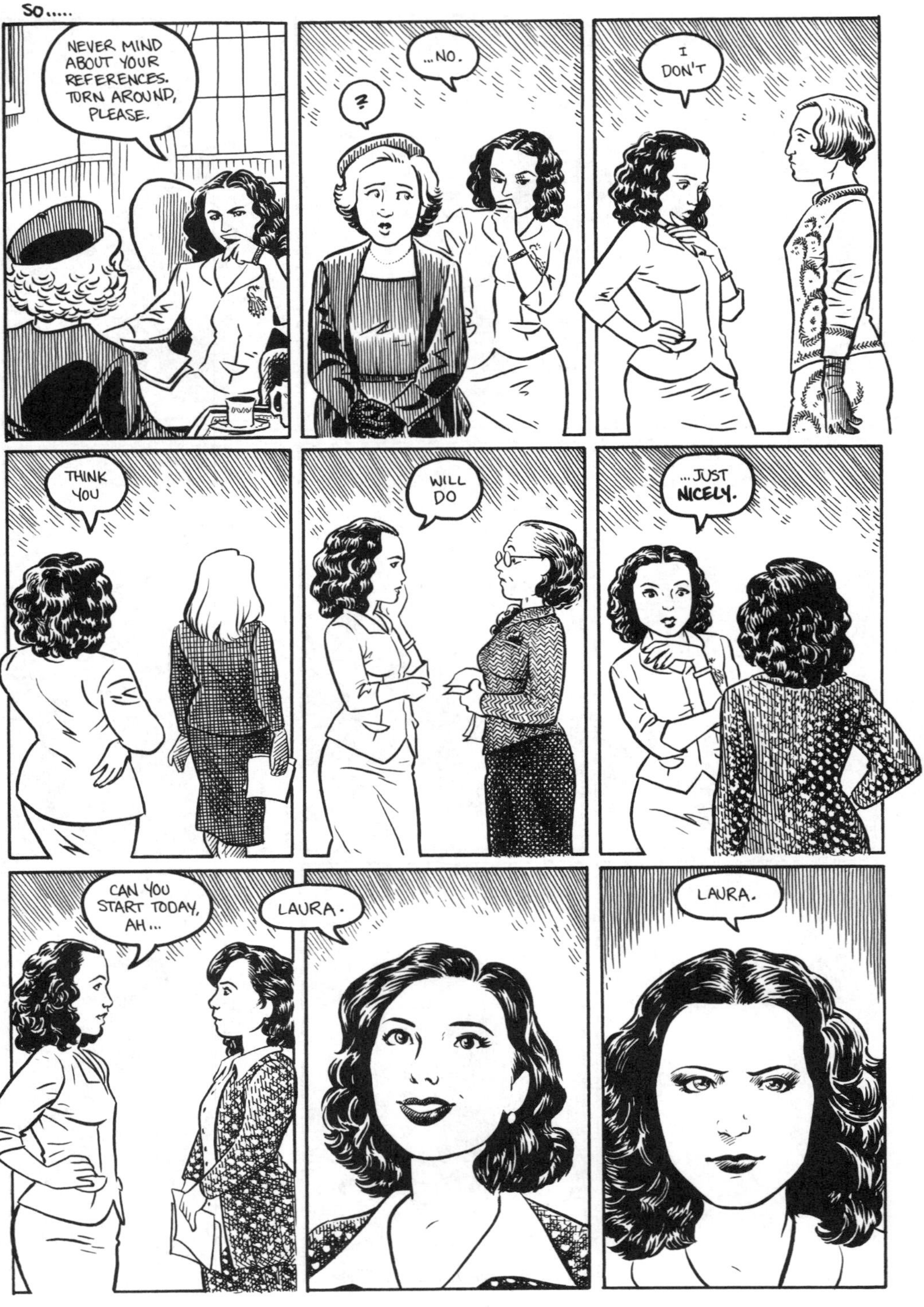
SO.....
NEVER MIND ABOUT YOUR REFERENCES. TURN AROUND, PLEASE.
?
...NO.
I DON'T
THINK YOU
WILL DO
...JUST NICELY.
CAN YOU START TODAY, AH...
LAURA.
LAURA.

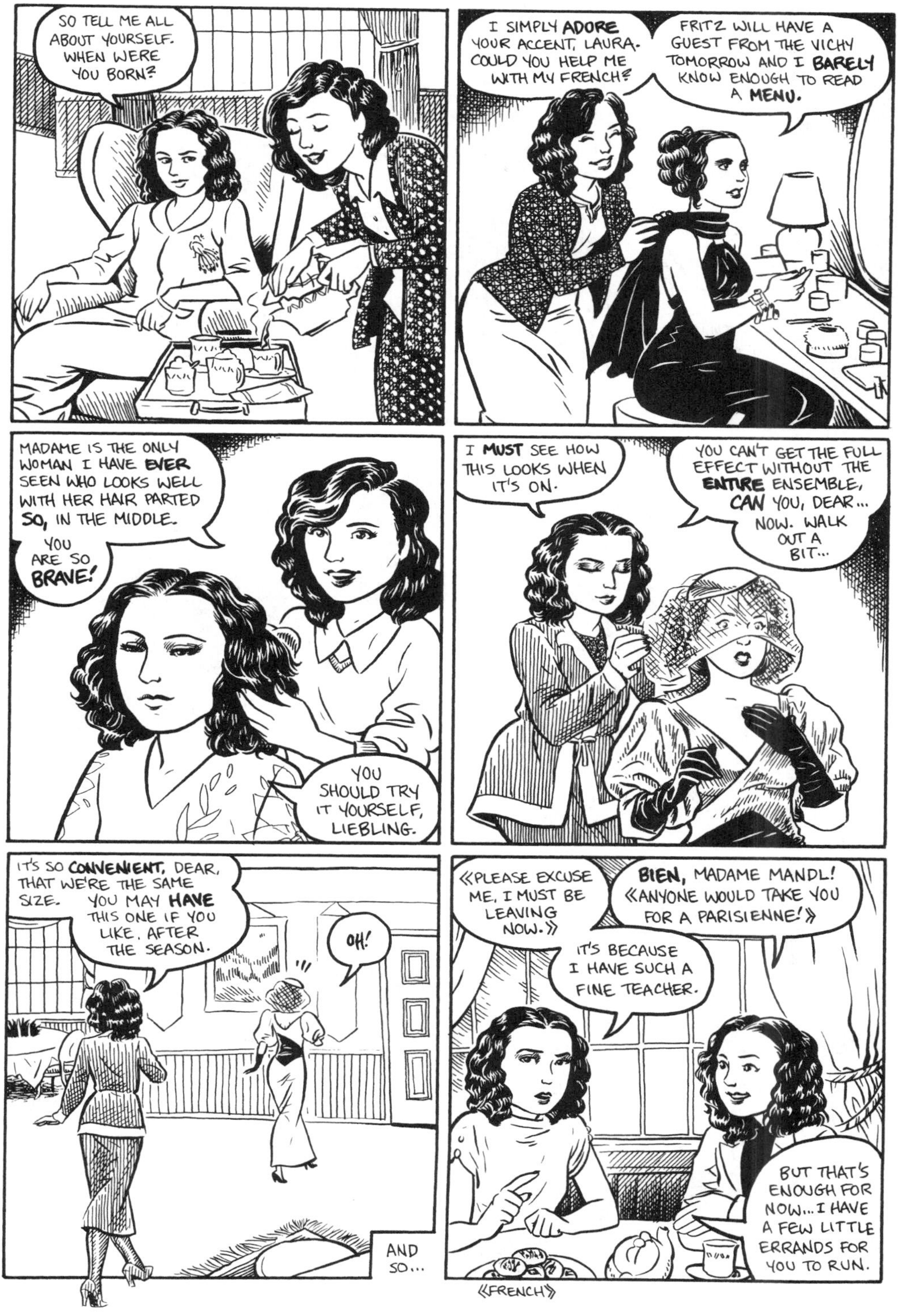
SO TELL ME ALL ABOUT YOURSELF. WHEN WERE YOU BORN?
I SIMPLY ADORE YOUR ACCENT, LAURA. COULD YOU HELP ME WITH MY FRENCH?
FRITZ WILL HAVE A GUEST FROM THE VICHY TOMORROW AND I BARELY KNOW ENOUGH TO READ A MENU.
MADAME IS THE ONLY WOMAN I HAVE EVER SEEN WHO LOOKS WELL WITH HER HAIR PARTED SO, IN THE MIDDLE.
YOU ARE SO BRAVE!
YOU SHOULD TRY IT YOURSELF, LIEBLING.
I MUST SEE HOW THIS LOOKS WHEN IT'S ON.
YOU CAN'T GET THE FULL EFFECT WITHOUT THE ENTIRE ENSEMBLE, CAN YOU, DEAR... NOW. WALK OUT A BIT...
IT'S SO CONVENIENT, DEAR, THAT WE'RE THE SAME SIZE.
YOU MAY HAVE THIS ONE IF YOU LIKE. AFTER THE SEASON.
OH!
AND SO...
«PLEASE EXCUSE ME, I MUST BE LEAVING NOW.»
BIEN, MADAME MANDL! «ANYONE WOULD TAKE YOU FOR A PARISIENNE!»
IT'S BECAUSE I HAVE SUCH A FINE TEACHER.
BUT THAT'S ENOUGH FOR NOW... I HAVE A FEW LITTLE ERRANDS FOR YOU TO RUN.

«FRENCH»

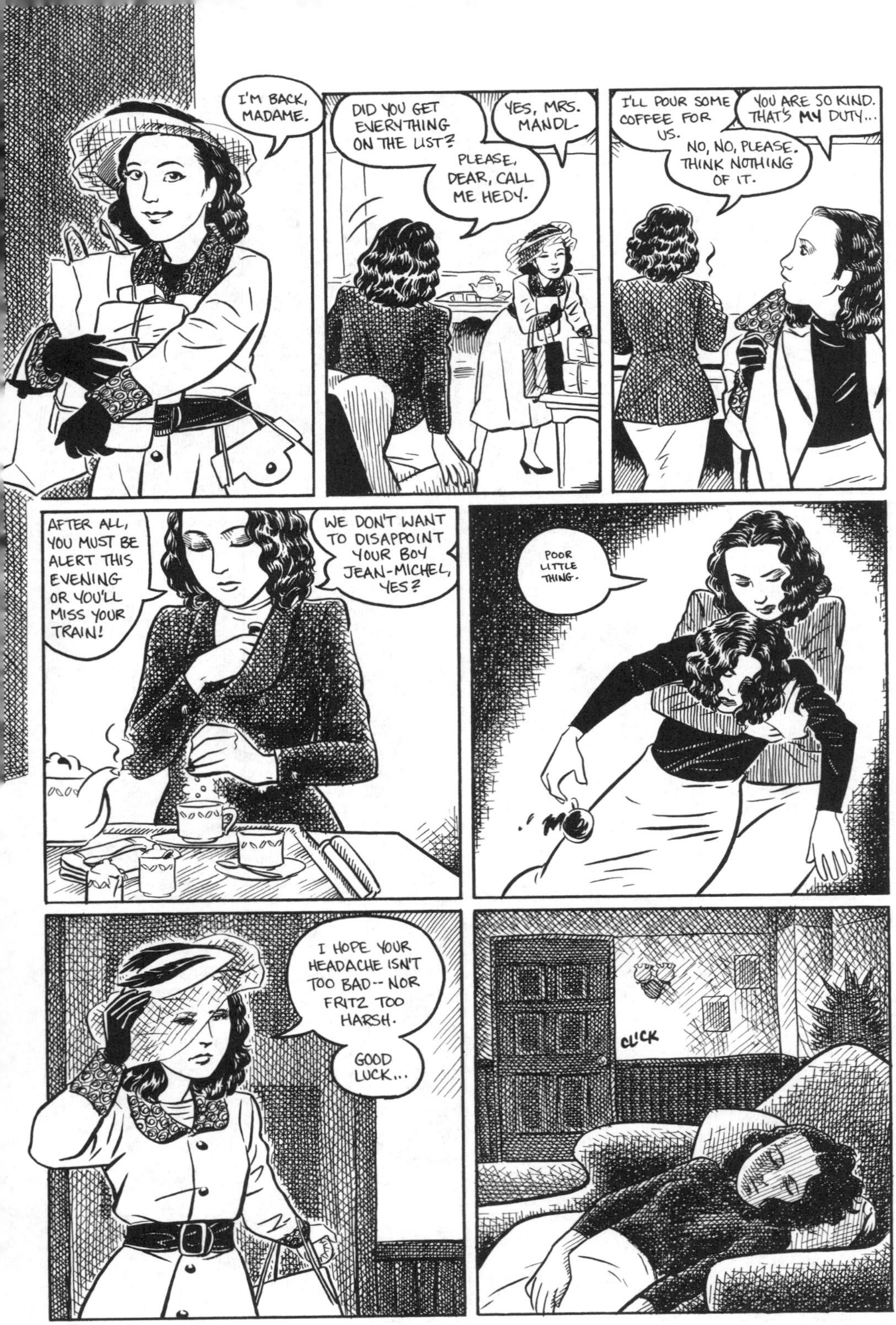

I'M BACK, MADAME.
DID YOU GET EVERYTHING ON THE LIST?
YES, MRS. MANDL.
PLEASE, DEAR, CALL ME HEDY.
I'LL POUR SOME COFFEE FOR US.
YOU ARE SO KIND. THAT'S MY DUTY...
NO, NO, PLEASE. THINK NOTHING OF IT.
AFTER ALL, YOU MUST BE ALERT THIS EVENING OR YOU'LL MISS YOUR TRAIN!
WE DON'T WANT TO DISAPPOINT YOUR BOY JEAN-MICHEL, YES?
POOR LITTLE THING.
I HOPE YOUR HEADACHE ISN'T TOO BAD-- NOR FRITZ TOO HARSH.
GOOD LUCK...
CLICK

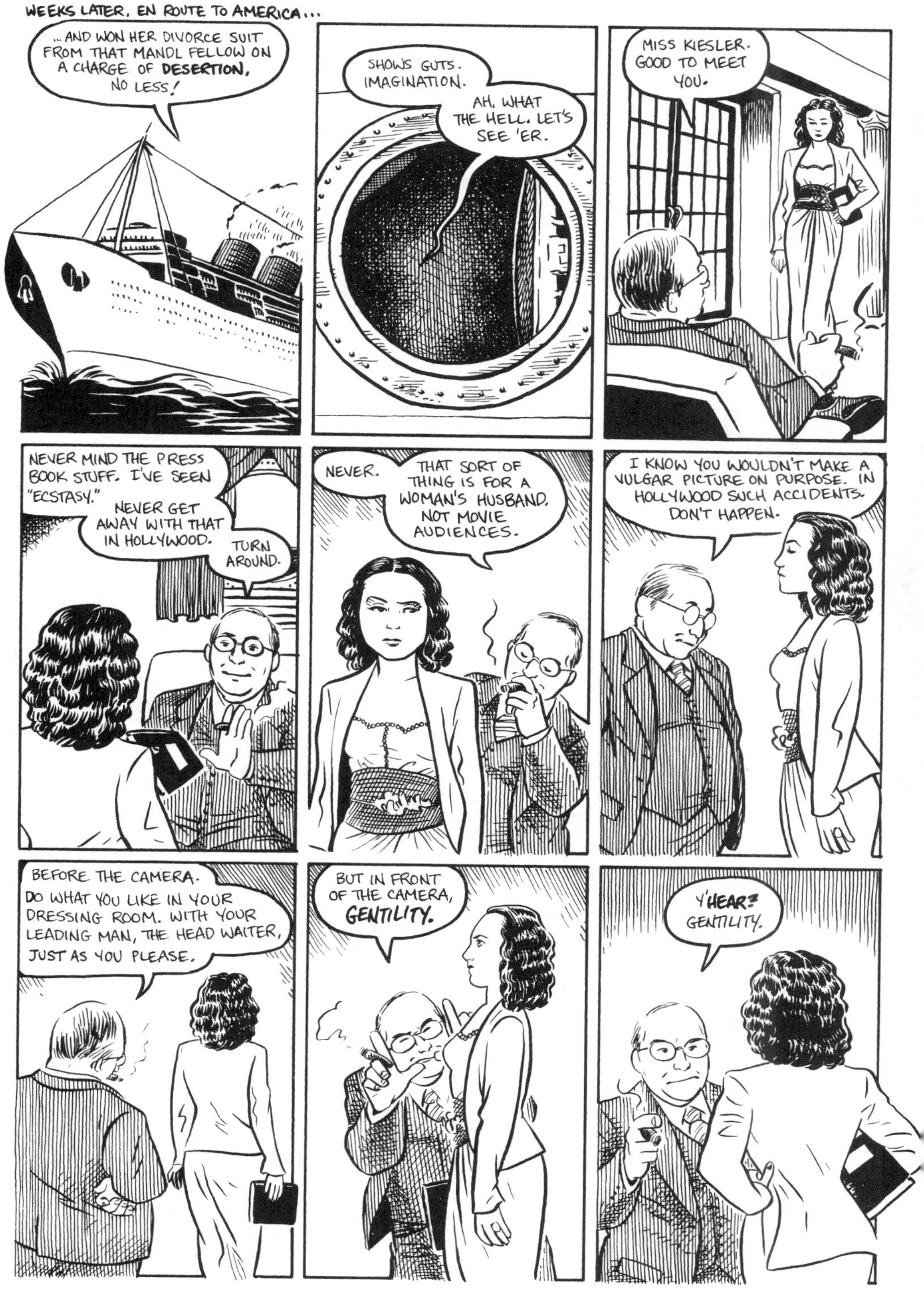
WEEKS LATER. EN ROUTE TO AMERICA...
...AND WON HER DIVORCE SUIT FROM THAT MANDL FELLOW ON A CHARGE OF DESERTION, NO LESS!
SHOWS GUTS. IMAGINATION.
AH, WHAT THE HELL. LET'S SEE 'ER.
MISS KIESLER. GOOD TO MEET YOU.
NEVER MIND THE PRESS BOOK STUFF. I'VE SEEN "ECSTASY."
NEVER GET AWAY WITH THAT IN HOLLYWOOD.
TURN AROUND.
NEVER.
THAT SORT OF THING IS FOR A WOMAN'S HUSBAND, NOT MOVIE AUDIENCES.
I KNOW YOU WOULDN'T MAKE A VULGAR PICTURE ON PURPOSE. IN HOLLYWOOD SUCH ACCIDENTS DON'T HAPPEN.
BEFORE THE CAMERA.
DO WHAT YOU LIKE IN YOUR DRESSING ROOM. WITH YOUR LEADING MAN, THE HEAD WAITER, JUST AS YOU PLEASE.
BUT IN FRONT OF THE CAMERA, GENTILITY.
Y'HEAR? GENTILITY.

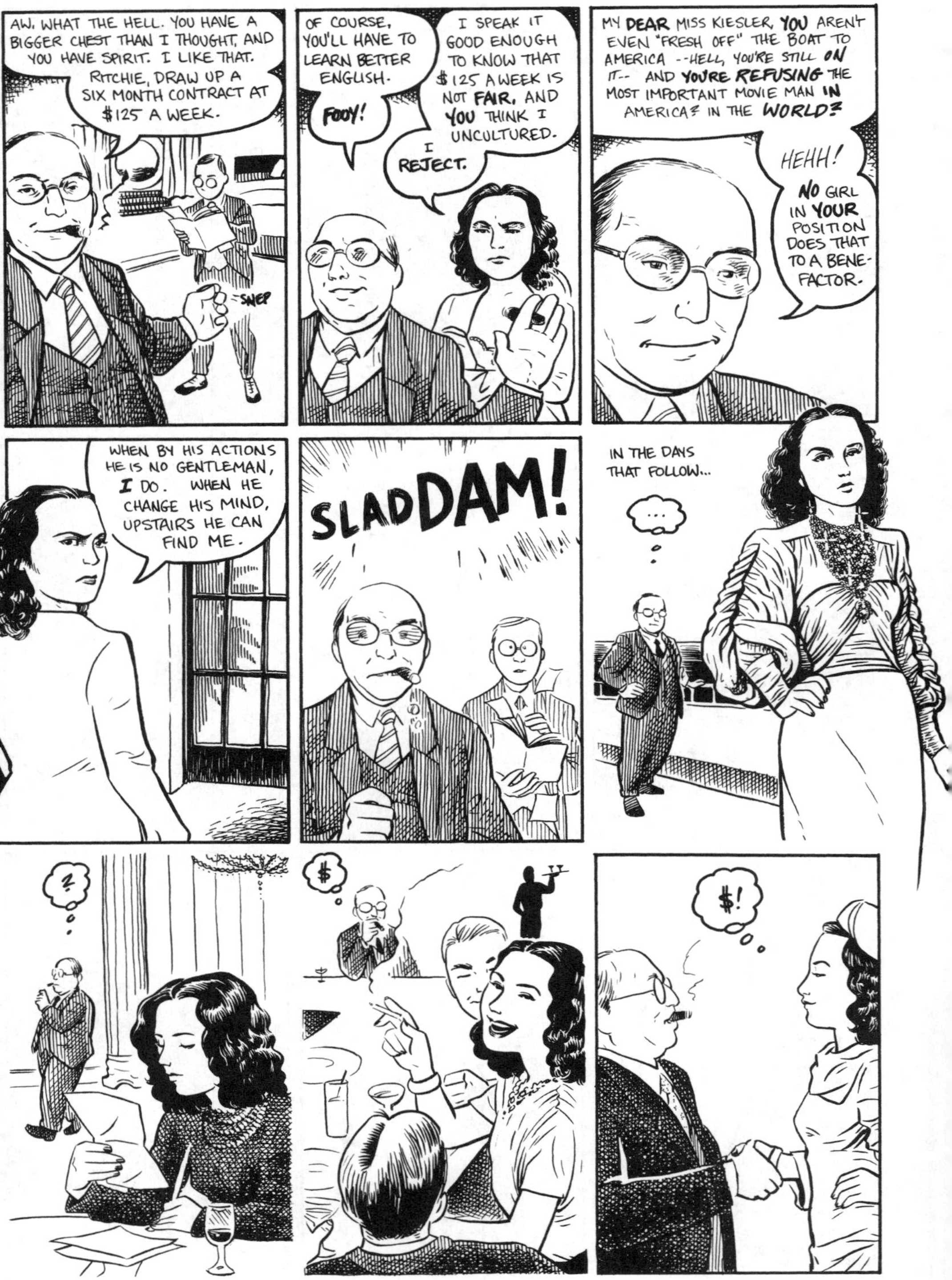
AW, WHAT THE HELL. YOU HAVE A BIGGER CHEST THAN I THOUGHT, AND YOU HAVE SPIRIT. I LIKE THAT.
RITCHIE, DRAW UP A SIX MONTH CONTRACT AT $125 A WEEK.
SNEP
OF COURSE, YOU'LL HAVE TO LEARN BETTER ENGLISH.
FOOY!
I SPEAK IT GOOD ENOUGH TO KNOW THAT $125 A WEEK IS NOT FAIR, AND YOU THINK I UNCULTURED.
I REJECT.
MY DEAR MISS KIESLER, YOU AREN'T EVEN "FRESH OFF" THE BOAT TO AMERICA --HELL, YOU'RE STILL ON IT-- AND YOU'RE REFUSING THE MOST IMPORTANT MOVIE MAN IN AMERICA? IN THE WORLD?
HEHH!
NO GIRL IN YOUR POSITION DOES THAT TO A BENEFACTOR.
WHEN BY HIS ACTIONS HE IS NO GENTLEMAN, I DO. WHEN HE CHANGE HIS MIND, UPSTAIRS HE CAN FIND ME.
SLADDAM!
IN THE DAYS THAT FOLLOW...
...
?
$
$!

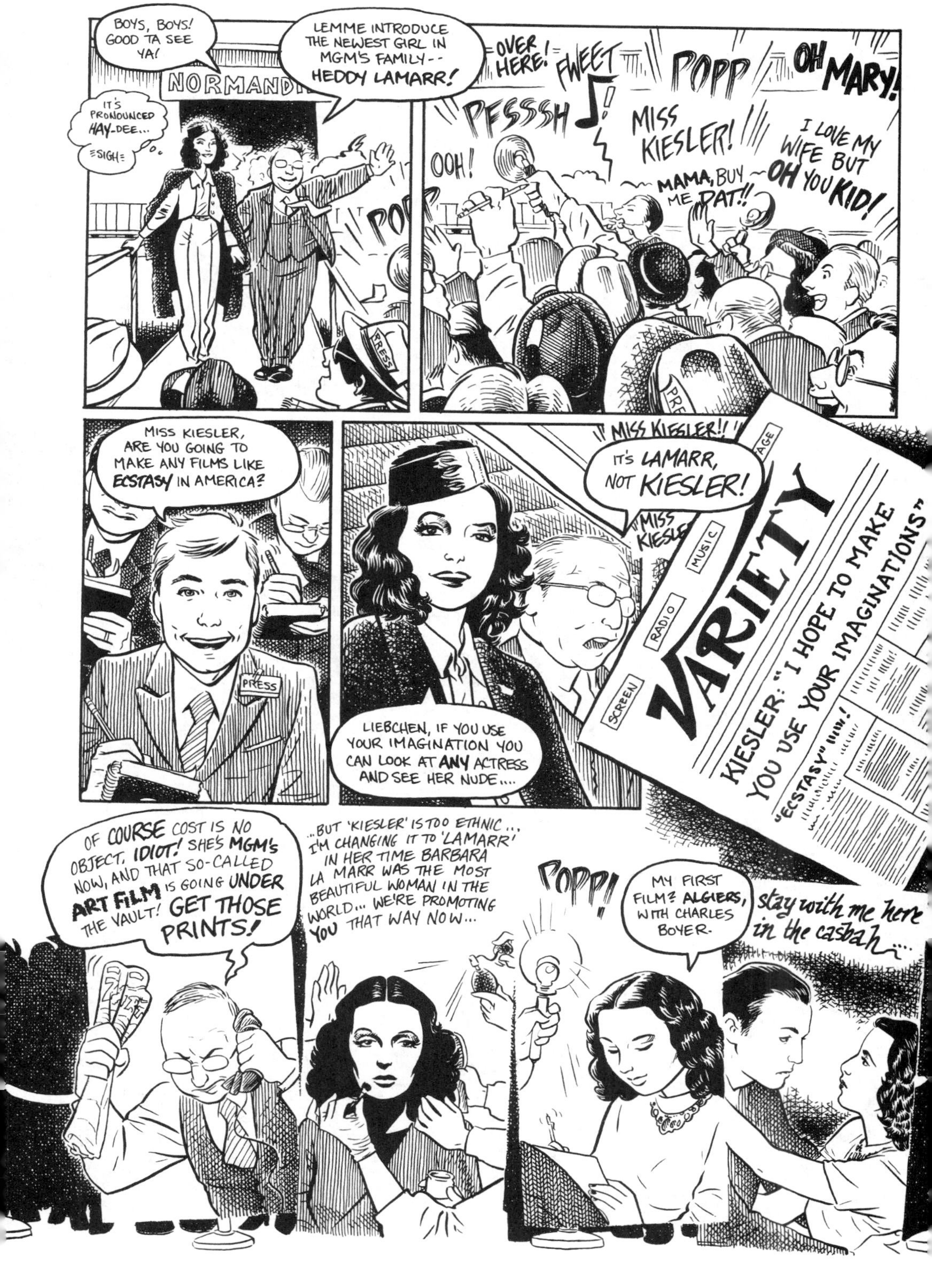
BOYS, BOYS! GOOD TA SEE YA!
LEMME INTRODUCE THE NEWEST GIRL IN MGM'S FAMILY-- HEDDY LAMARR!
NORMANDIE
IT'S PRONOUNCED HAY-DEE... ≡SIGH≡
POPP
OVER HERE!
FWEET
POPP
OH MARY!
PFSSSH
OOH!
MISS KIESLER!
I LOVE MY WIFE BUT OH YOU KID!
MAMA, BUY ME DAT!!
PRESS
MISS KIESLER, ARE YOU GOING TO MAKE ANY FILMS LIKE ECSTASY IN AMERICA?
PRESS
MISS KIESLER!!
IT'S LAMARR, NOT KIESLER!
MISS KIESLER
LIEBCHEN, IF YOU USE YOUR IMAGINATION YOU CAN LOOK AT ANY ACTRESS AND SEE HER NUDE....
VARIETY
SCREEN
RADIO
MUSIC
STAGE
KIESLER: "I HOPE TO MAKE YOU USE YOUR IMAGINATIONS"
"ECSTASY"
OF COURSE COST IS NO OBJECT, IDIOT! SHE'S MGM'S NOW, AND THAT SO-CALLED ART FILM IS GOING UNDER THE VAULT! GET THOSE PRINTS!
...BUT 'KIESLER' IS TOO ETHNIC... I'M CHANGING IT TO 'LAMARR' IN HER TIME BARBARA LA MARR WAS THE MOST BEAUTIFUL WOMAN IN THE WORLD... WE'RE PROMOTING YOU THAT WAY NOW...
POPP!
MY FIRST FILM? ALGIERS, WITH CHARLES BOYER.
stay with me here in the casbah...

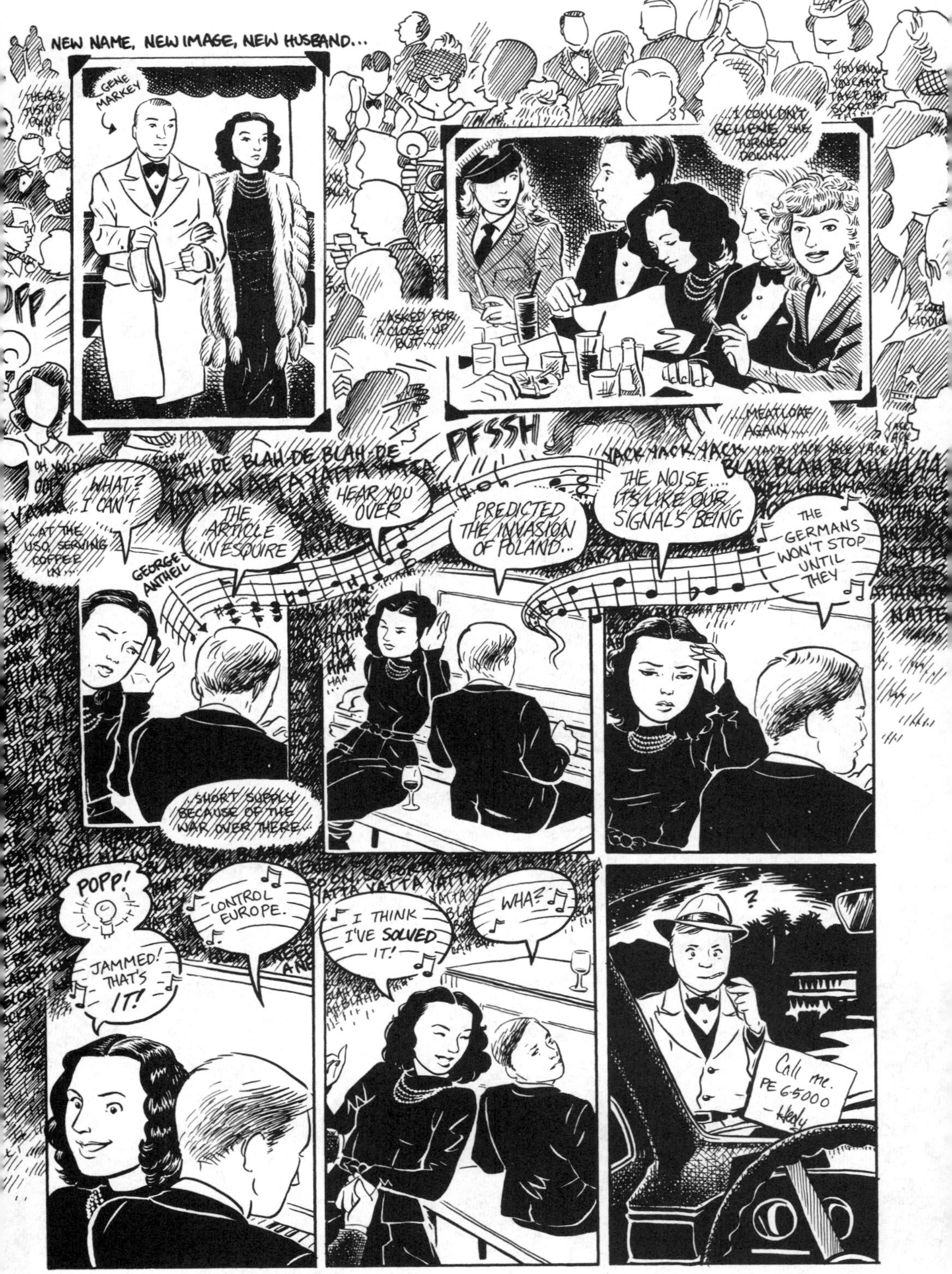
NEW NAME, NEW IMAGE, NEW HUSBAND...
GENE MARKEY
THERE'S JUST NO POINT IN
...I COULDN'T BELIEVE SHE TURNED DOWN...
YOU KNOW YOU CAN'T TAKE THAT SORT OF
ASKED FOR A CLOSE-UP BUT
...MEATLOAF AGAIN...
PFSSH
BLAH-DE BLAH-DE BLAH-DE
YATTA YATTA YATTA YATTA
YACK YACK YACK
BLAH BLAH BLAH
WHAT? I CAN'T
...AT THE USO SERVING COFFEE IN...
GEORGE ANTHEIL
THE ARTICLE IN ESQUIRE
HEAR YOU OVER
PREDICTED THE INVASION OF POLAND...
THE NOISE... IT'S LIKE OUR SIGNALS BEING
THE GERMANS WON'T STOP UNTIL THEY
...SHORT SUPPLY BECAUSE OF THE WAR OVER THERE...
POPP!
CONTROL EUROPE.
JAMMED! THAT'S IT!
I THINK I'VE SOLVED IT!
WHA?
?
Call me. PE 6-5000 —Hedy

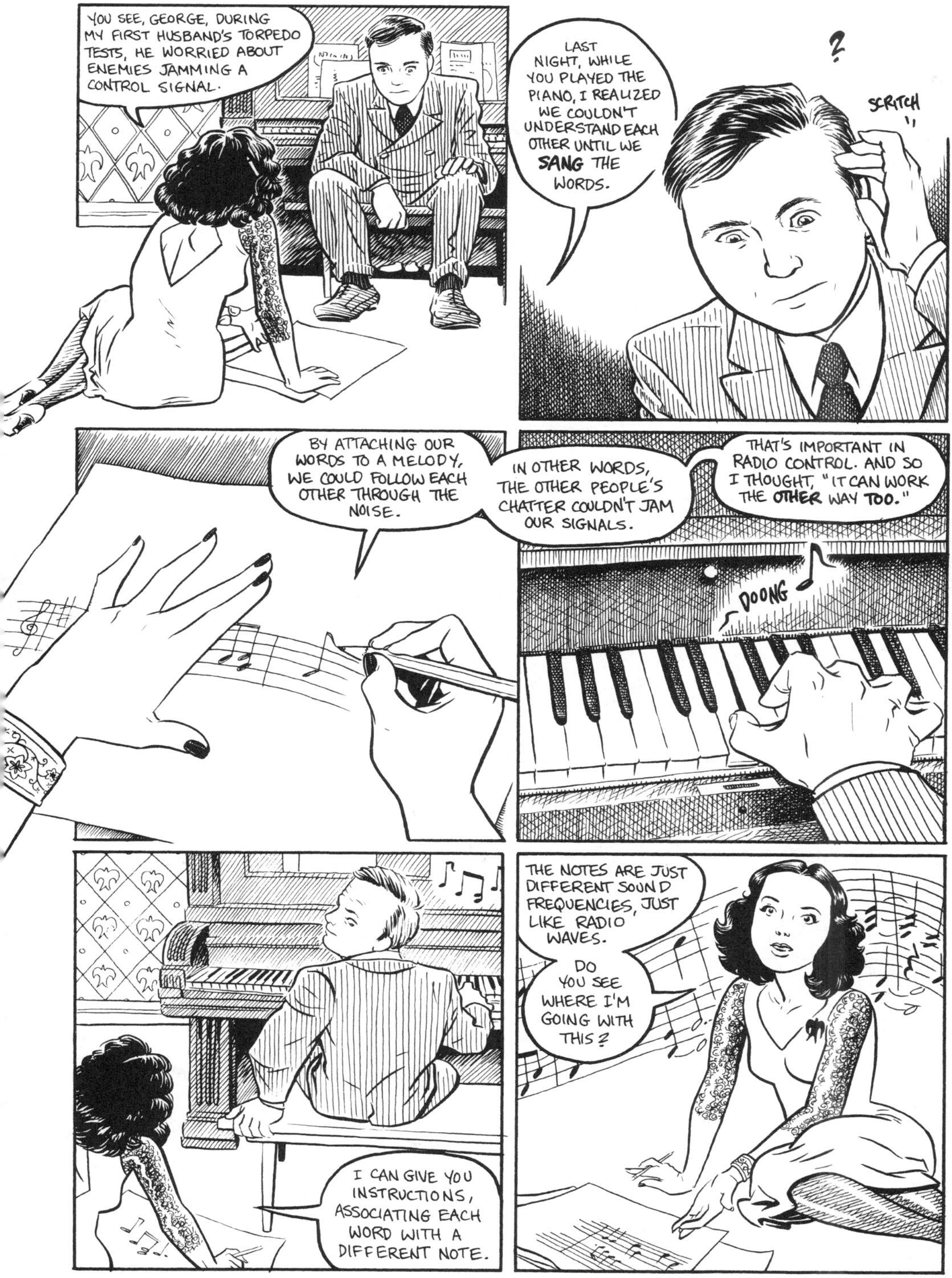
YOU SEE, GEORGE, DURING MY FIRST HUSBAND'S TORPEDO TESTS, HE WORRIED ABOUT ENEMIES JAMMING A CONTROL SIGNAL.
LAST NIGHT, WHILE YOU PLAYED THE PIANO, I REALIZED WE COULDN'T UNDERSTAND EACH OTHER UNTIL WE SANG THE WORDS.
?
SCRITCH
BY ATTACHING OUR WORDS TO A MELODY, WE COULD FOLLOW EACH OTHER THROUGH THE NOISE.
IN OTHER WORDS, THE OTHER PEOPLE'S CHATTER COULDN'T JAM OUR SIGNALS.
THAT'S IMPORTANT IN RADIO CONTROL. AND SO I THOUGHT, "IT CAN WORK THE OTHER WAY TOO."
DOONG
I CAN GIVE YOU INSTRUCTIONS, ASSOCIATING EACH WORD WITH A DIFFERENT NOTE.
THE NOTES ARE JUST DIFFERENT SOUND FREQUENCIES, JUST LIKE RADIO WAVES.
DO YOU SEE WHERE I'M GOING WITH THIS?

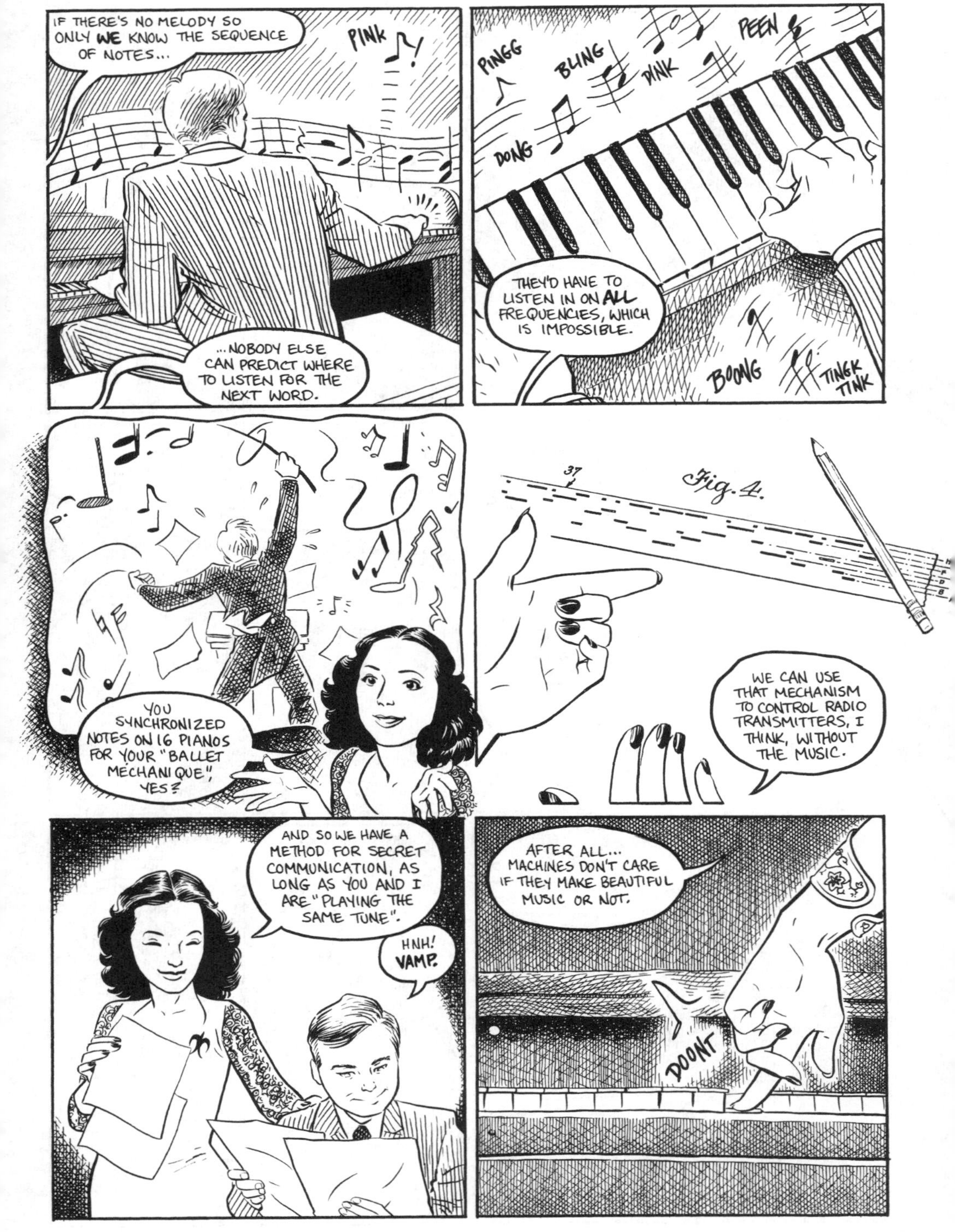
IF THERE'S NO MELODY SO ONLY WE KNOW THE SEQUENCE OF NOTES...
PINK
...NOBODY ELSE CAN PREDICT WHERE TO LISTEN FOR THE NEXT WORD.
PINGG
BLING
DINK
PEEN
DONG
THEY'D HAVE TO LISTEN IN ON ALL FREQUENCIES, WHICH IS IMPOSSIBLE.
BOONG
TINGK
TINK
YOU SYNCHRONIZED NOTES ON 16 PIANOS FOR YOUR "BALLET MECHANIQUE", YES?
37
Fig. 4.
WE CAN USE THAT MECHANISM TO CONTROL RADIO TRANSMITTERS, I THINK, WITHOUT THE MUSIC.
AND SO WE HAVE A METHOD FOR SECRET COMMUNICATION, AS LONG AS YOU AND I ARE "PLAYING THE SAME TUNE".
HNH! VAMP.
AFTER ALL... MACHINES DON'T CARE IF THEY MAKE BEAUTIFUL MUSIC OR NOT.
DOONT

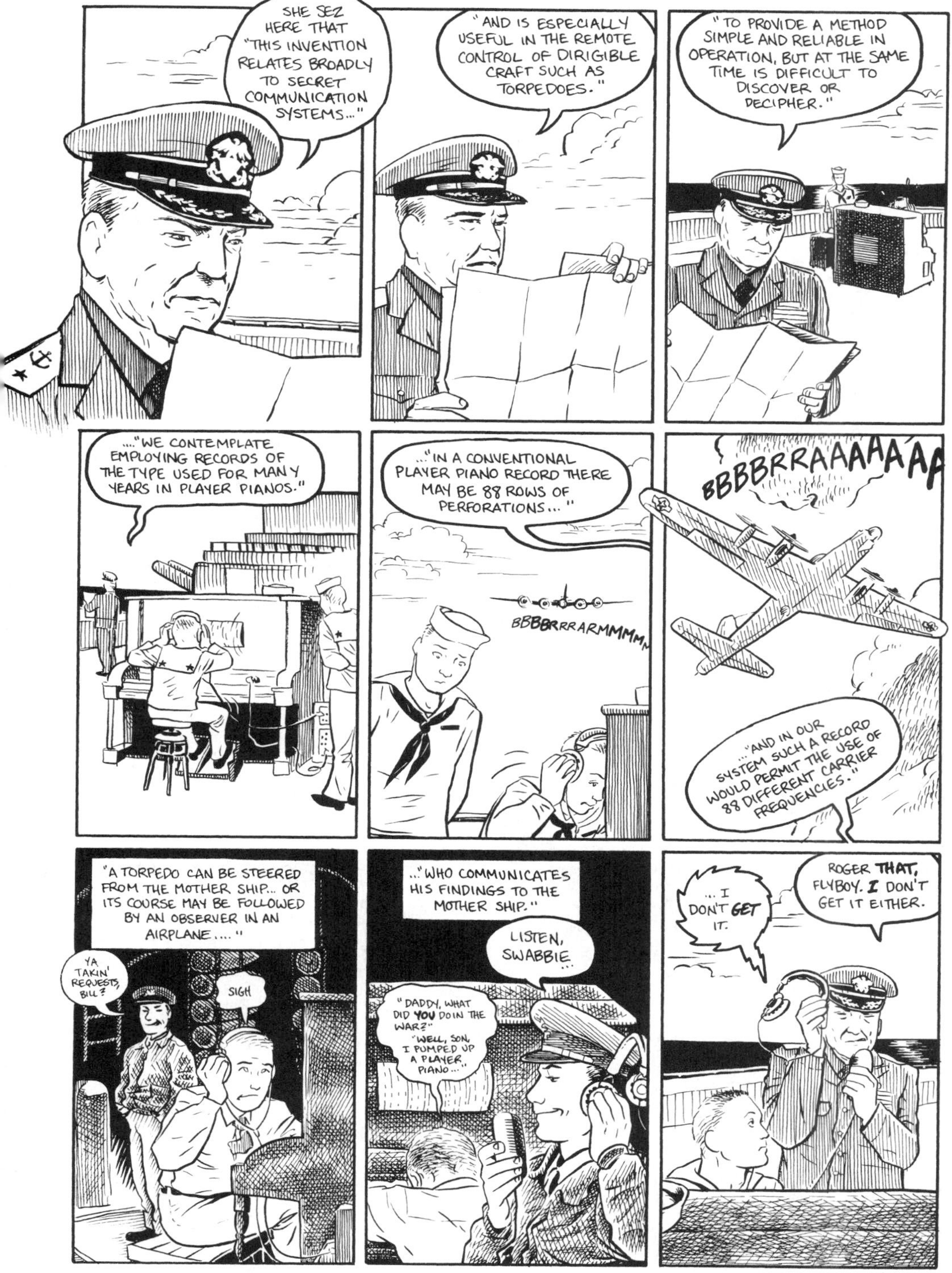
SHE SEZ HERE THAT "THIS INVENTION RELATES BROADLY TO SECRET COMMUNICATION SYSTEMS..."
"AND IS ESPECIALLY USEFUL IN THE REMOTE CONTROL OF DIRIGIBLE CRAFT SUCH AS TORPEDOES."
"TO PROVIDE A METHOD SIMPLE AND RELIABLE IN OPERATION, BUT AT THE SAME TIME IS DIFFICULT TO DISCOVER OR DECIPHER."
..."WE CONTEMPLATE EMPLOYING RECORDS OF THE TYPE USED FOR MANY YEARS IN PLAYER PIANOS."
..."IN A CONVENTIONAL PLAYER PIANO RECORD THERE MAY BE 88 ROWS OF PERFORATIONS..."
BBBBRRRARMMMM
BBBBRRAAAAAAA
..."AND IN OUR SYSTEM SUCH A RECORD WOULD PERMIT THE USE OF 88 DIFFERENT CARRIER FREQUENCIES."
"A TORPEDO CAN BE STEERED FROM THE MOTHER SHIP... OR ITS COURSE MAY BE FOLLOWED BY AN OBSERVER IN AN AIRPLANE...."
YA TAKIN' REQUESTS, BILL?
SIGH
..."WHO COMMUNICATES HIS FINDINGS TO THE MOTHER SHIP."
LISTEN, SWABBIE...
"DADDY, WHAT DID YOU DO IN THE WAR?"
"WELL, SON, I PUMPED UP A PLAYER PIANO..."
...I DON'T GET IT.
ROGER THAT, FLYBOY. I DON'T GET IT EITHER.

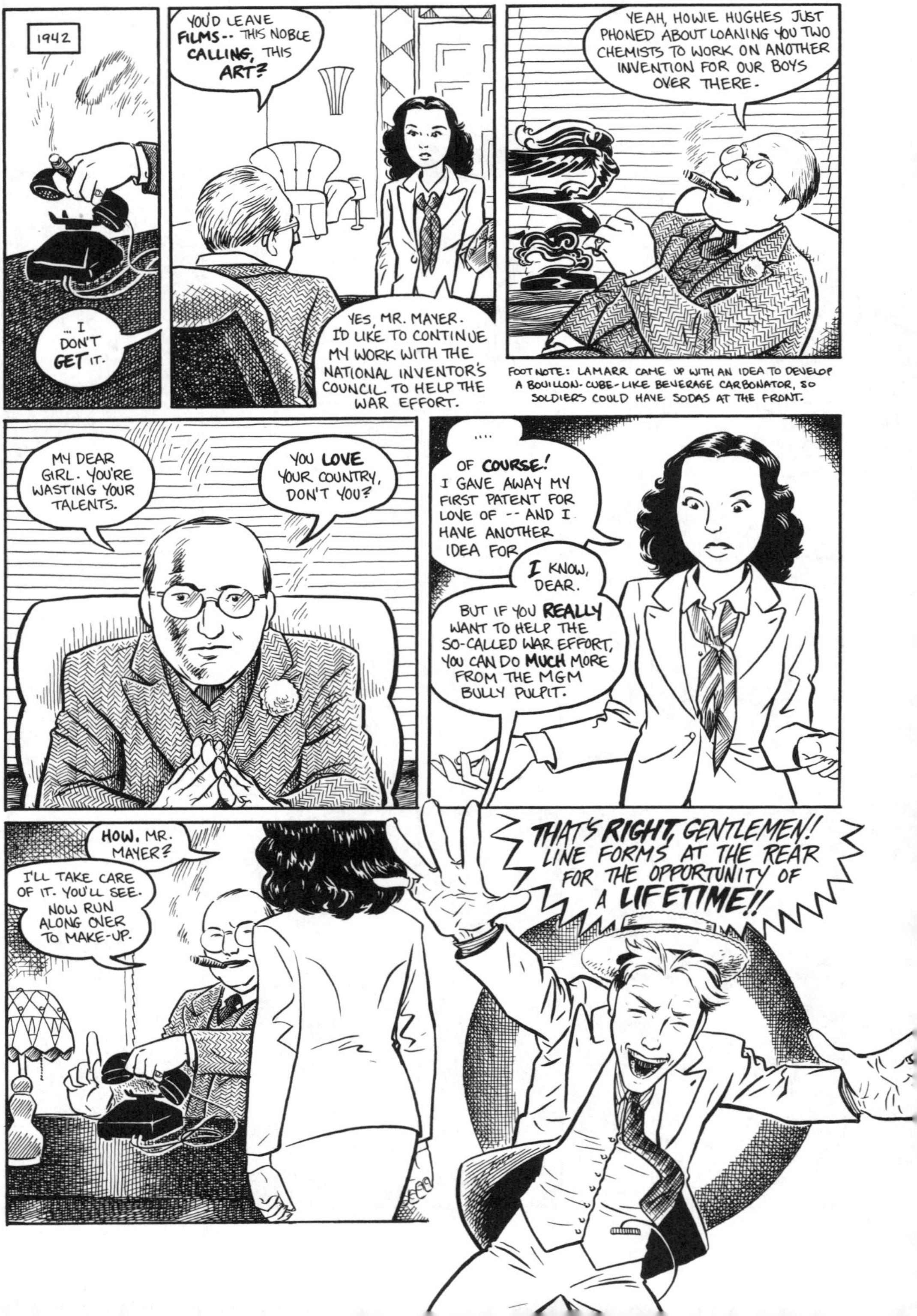
1942
... I DON'T GET IT.
YOU'D LEAVE FILMS-- THIS NOBLE CALLING, THIS ART?
YES, MR. MAYER. I'D LIKE TO CONTINUE MY WORK WITH THE NATIONAL INVENTOR'S COUNCIL TO HELP THE WAR EFFORT.
YEAH, HOWIE HUGHES JUST PHONED ABOUT LOANING YOU TWO CHEMISTS TO WORK ON ANOTHER INVENTION FOR OUR BOYS OVER THERE.
FOOTNOTE: LAMARR CAME UP WITH AN IDEA TO DEVELOP A BOUILLON-CUBE-LIKE BEVERAGE CARBONATOR, SO SOLDIERS COULD HAVE SODAS AT THE FRONT.
MY DEAR GIRL. YOU'RE WASTING YOUR TALENTS.
YOU LOVE YOUR COUNTRY, DON'T YOU?
....
OF COURSE! I GAVE AWAY MY FIRST PATENT FOR LOVE OF -- AND I HAVE ANOTHER IDEA FOR
I KNOW, DEAR.
BUT IF YOU REALLY WANT TO HELP THE SO-CALLED WAR EFFORT, YOU CAN DO MUCH MORE FROM THE MGM BULLY PULPIT.
HOW, MR. MAYER?
I'LL TAKE CARE OF IT. YOU'LL SEE. NOW RUN ALONG OVER TO MAKE-UP.
THAT'S RIGHT, GENTLEMEN! LINE FORMS AT THE REAR FOR THE OPPORTUNITY OF A LIFETIME!!

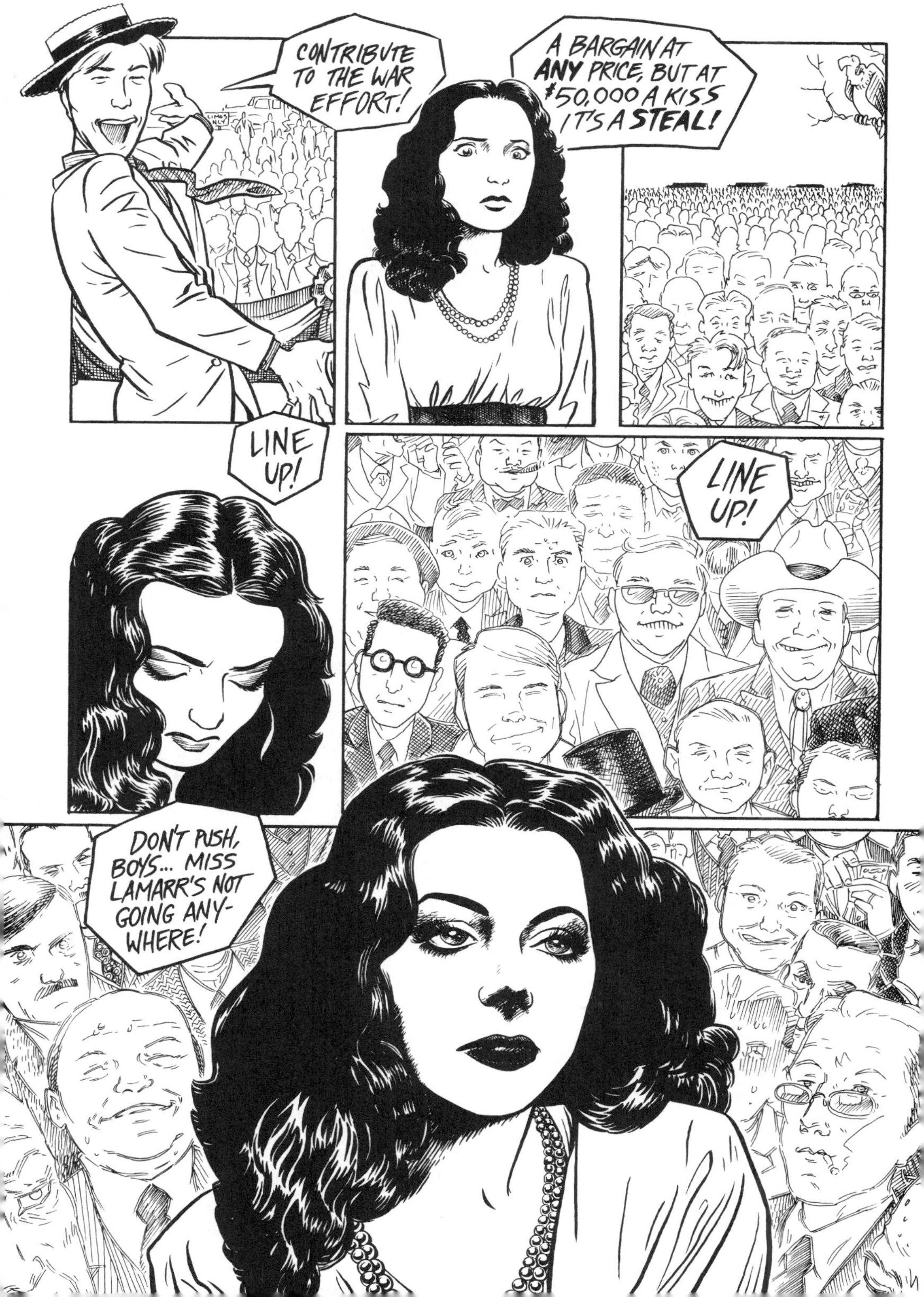
CONTRIBUTE TO THE WAR EFFORT!
A BARGAIN AT ANY PRICE, BUT AT $50,000 A KISS IT'S A STEAL!
LINE UP!
LINE UP!
DON'T PUSH, BOYS... MISS LAMARR'S NOT GOING ANY- WHERE!

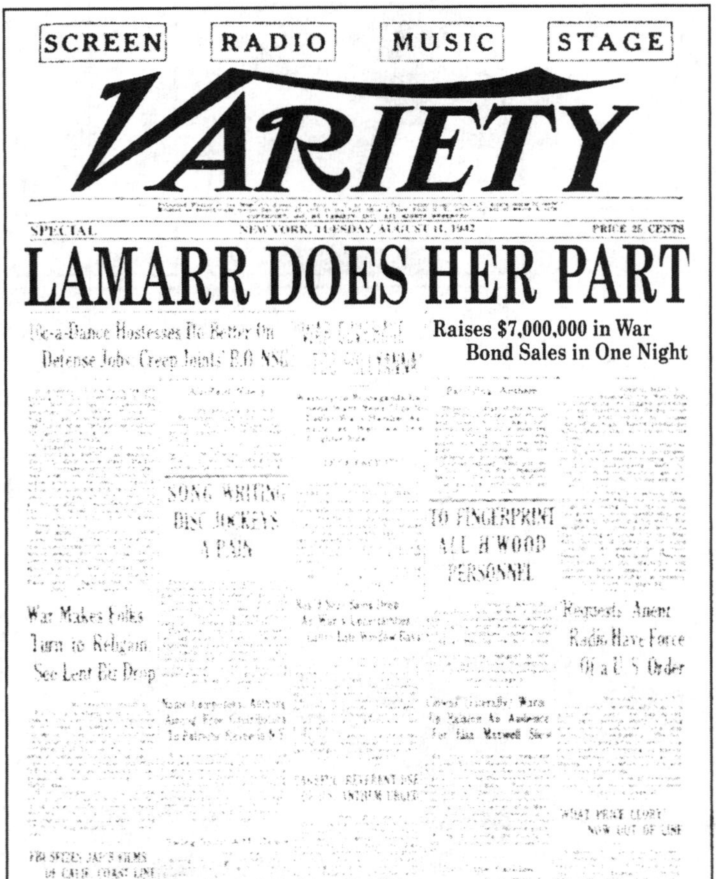
SCREEN RADIO MUSIC STAGE

VARIETY

SPECIAL NEW YORK, TUESDAY, AUGUST 11, 1942 PRICE 25 CENTS

LAMARR DOES HER PART

Raises $7,000,000 in War Bond Sales in One Night

TO FINGERPRINT ALL H'WOOD PERSONNEL

War Makes Folks Turn to Religion

LISE MEITNER

BERLIN, 1920
WE HAVE TO FIND A WAY TO GET DR. BOHR ALONE!
IF WE'RE TO GAIN ANYTHING AT ALL OUT OF HIS VISIT, WE'LL NEED TO DISCUSS THEORY OUTSIDE OF A FORMAL LECTURE.
BUT LISE, THE *BONZE** ARE SWARMING! HOW CAN WE PULL HIM AWAY?
HE LOVES THE OUTDOORS. A PICNIC IN THE COUNTRY WOULD BE IDEAL.
HABER HAS A COUNTRY HOUSE. THAT MIGHT WORK.
I COULD NEVER ASK HIM THAT! I DON'T HAVE THE NERVE.
BESIDES, HOW WOULD WE FEED HIM? INFLATION EATS UP OUR MONEY FASTER THAN WE CAN HAUL IT TO THE GROCER.

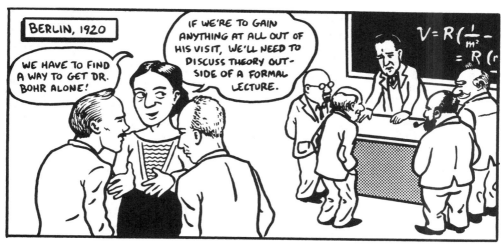

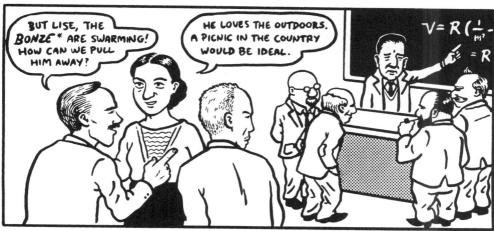

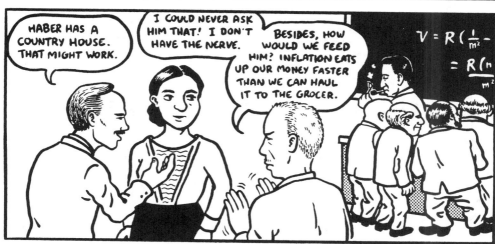

* BONZE = "BIGWIG"

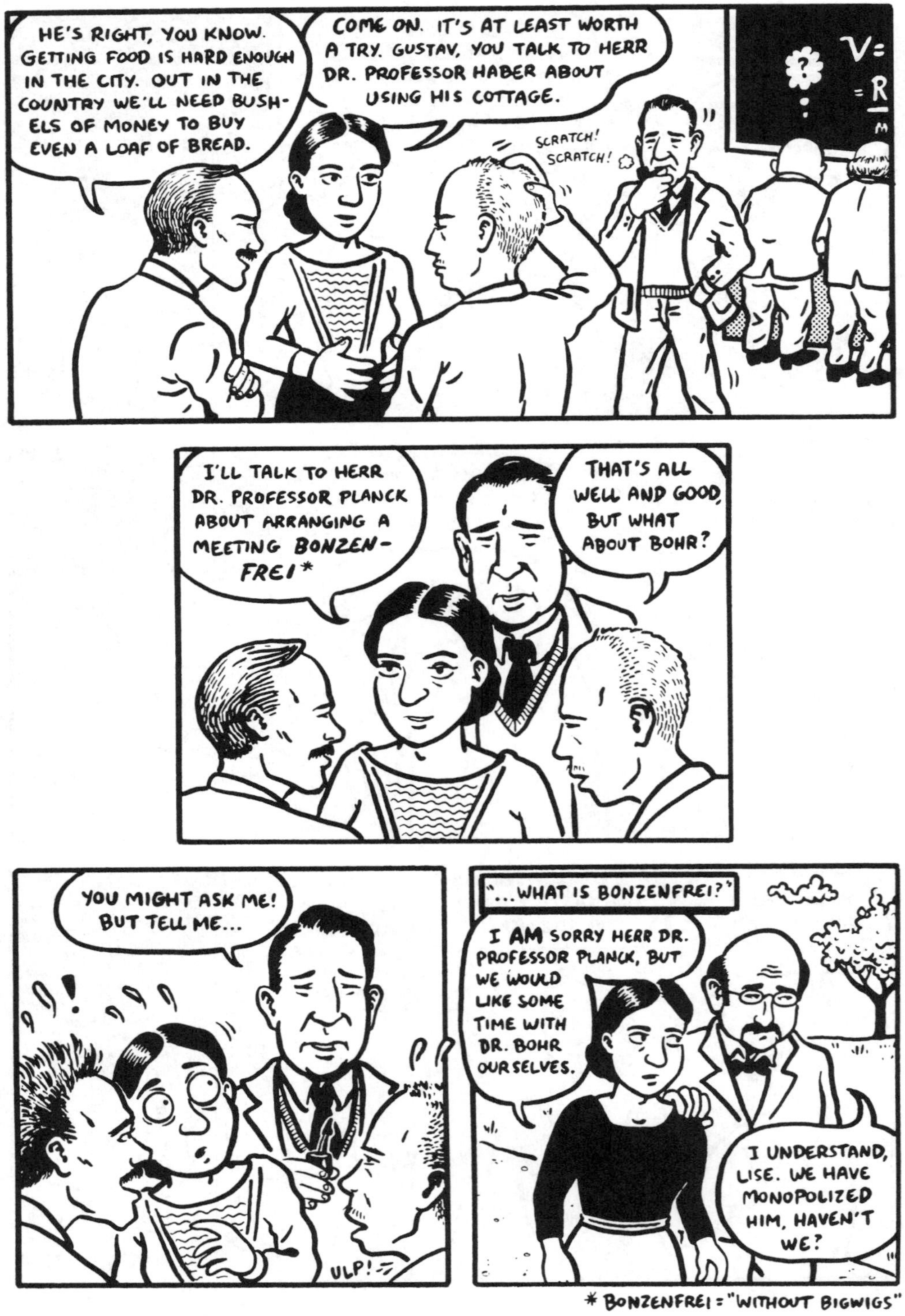
HE'S RIGHT, YOU KNOW. GETTING FOOD IS HARD ENOUGH IN THE CITY. OUT IN THE COUNTRY WE'LL NEED BUSH-ELS OF MONEY TO BUY EVEN A LOAF OF BREAD.
COME ON. IT'S AT LEAST WORTH A TRY. GUSTAV, YOU TALK TO HERR DR. PROFESSOR HABER ABOUT USING HIS COTTAGE.
SCRATCH! SCRATCH!
I'LL TALK TO HERR DR. PROFESSOR PLANCK ABOUT ARRANGING A MEETING BONZEN-FREI*
THAT'S ALL WELL AND GOOD, BUT WHAT ABOUT BOHR?
YOU MIGHT ASK ME! BUT TELL ME...
!
ULP!
"...WHAT IS BONZENFREI?"
I AM SORRY HERR DR. PROFESSOR PLANCK, BUT WE WOULD LIKE SOME TIME WITH DR. BOHR OURSELVES.
I UNDERSTAND, LISE. WE HAVE MONOPOLIZED HIM, HAVEN'T WE?

* BONZENFREI = "WITHOUT BIGWIGS"

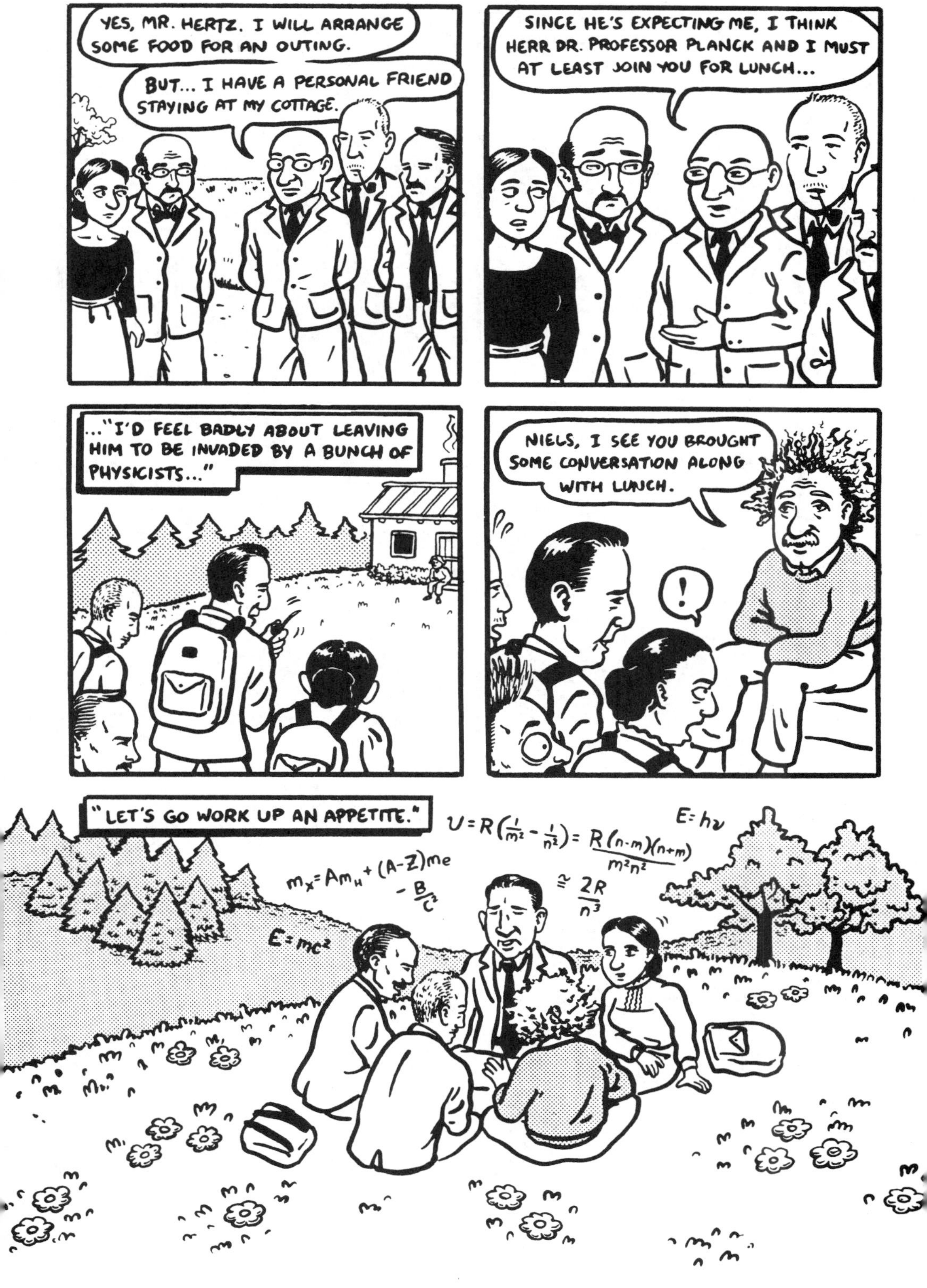
YES, MR. HERTZ. I WILL ARRANGE SOME FOOD FOR AN OUTING.
BUT... I HAVE A PERSONAL FRIEND STAYING AT MY COTTAGE.
SINCE HE'S EXPECTING ME, I THINK HERR DR. PROFESSOR PLANCK AND I MUST AT LEAST JOIN YOU FOR LUNCH...
..."I'D FEEL BADLY ABOUT LEAVING HIM TO BE INVADED BY A BUNCH OF PHYSICISTS..."
NIELS, I SEE YOU BROUGHT SOME CONVERSATION ALONG WITH LUNCH.
!
"LET'S GO WORK UP AN APPETITE."
$\nu = R\left(\frac{1}{m^2} - \frac{1}{n^2}\right) = \frac{R(n-m)(n+m)}{m^2 n^2} \cong \frac{2R}{n^3}$
$E = h\nu$
$m_x = Am_H + (A-Z)m_e - \frac{B}{c^2}$
$E = mc^2$

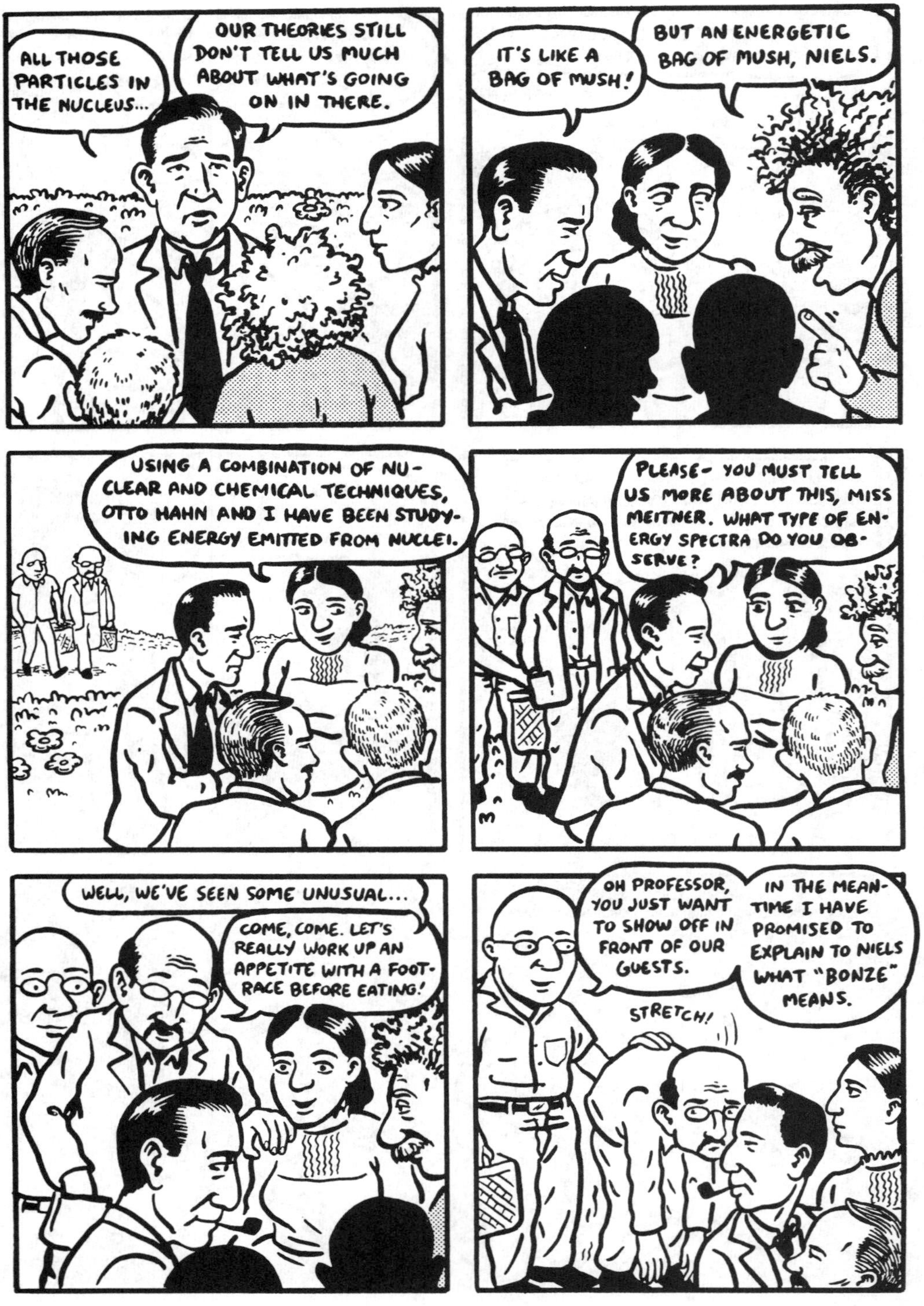
ALL THOSE PARTICLES IN THE NUCLEUS...
OUR THEORIES STILL DON'T TELL US MUCH ABOUT WHAT'S GOING ON IN THERE.
IT'S LIKE A BAG OF MUSH!
BUT AN ENERGETIC BAG OF MUSH, NIELS.
USING A COMBINATION OF NU-CLEAR AND CHEMICAL TECHNIQUES, OTTO HAHN AND I HAVE BEEN STUDY-ING ENERGY EMITTED FROM NUCLEI.
PLEASE- YOU MUST TELL US MORE ABOUT THIS, MISS MEITNER. WHAT TYPE OF EN-ERGY SPECTRA DO YOU OB-SERVE?
WELL, WE'VE SEEN SOME UNUSUAL...
COME, COME. LET'S REALLY WORK UP AN APPETITE WITH A FOOT-RACE BEFORE EATING!
OH PROFESSOR, YOU JUST WANT TO SHOW OFF IN FRONT OF OUR GUESTS.
IN THE MEAN-TIME I HAVE PROMISED TO EXPLAIN TO NIELS WHAT "BONZE" MEANS.
STRETCH!

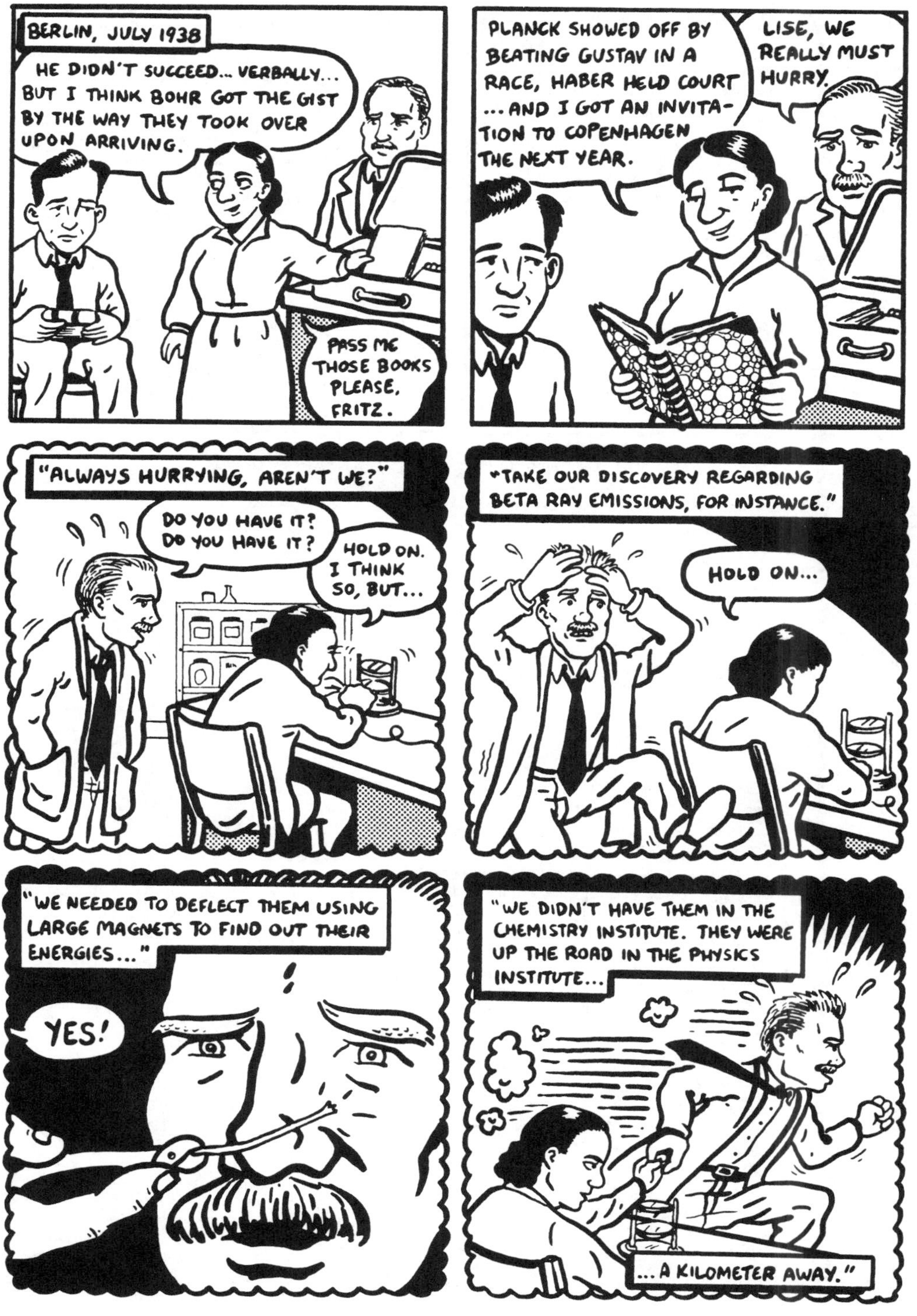
BERLIN, JULY 1938
HE DIDN'T SUCCEED... VERBALLY... BUT I THINK BOHR GOT THE GIST BY THE WAY THEY TOOK OVER UPON ARRIVING.
PASS ME THOSE BOOKS PLEASE, FRITZ.
PLANCK SHOWED OFF BY BEATING GUSTAV IN A RACE, HABER HELD COURT ...AND I GOT AN INVITATION TO COPENHAGEN THE NEXT YEAR.
LISE, WE REALLY MUST HURRY.
"ALWAYS HURRYING, AREN'T WE?"
DO YOU HAVE IT? DO YOU HAVE IT?
HOLD ON. I THINK SO, BUT...
"TAKE OUR DISCOVERY REGARDING BETA RAY EMISSIONS, FOR INSTANCE."
HOLD ON...
"WE NEEDED TO DEFLECT THEM USING LARGE MAGNETS TO FIND OUT THEIR ENERGIES..."
YES!
"WE DIDN'T HAVE THEM IN THE CHEMISTRY INSTITUTE. THEY WERE UP THE ROAD IN THE PHYSICS INSTITUTE...
...A KILOMETER AWAY."

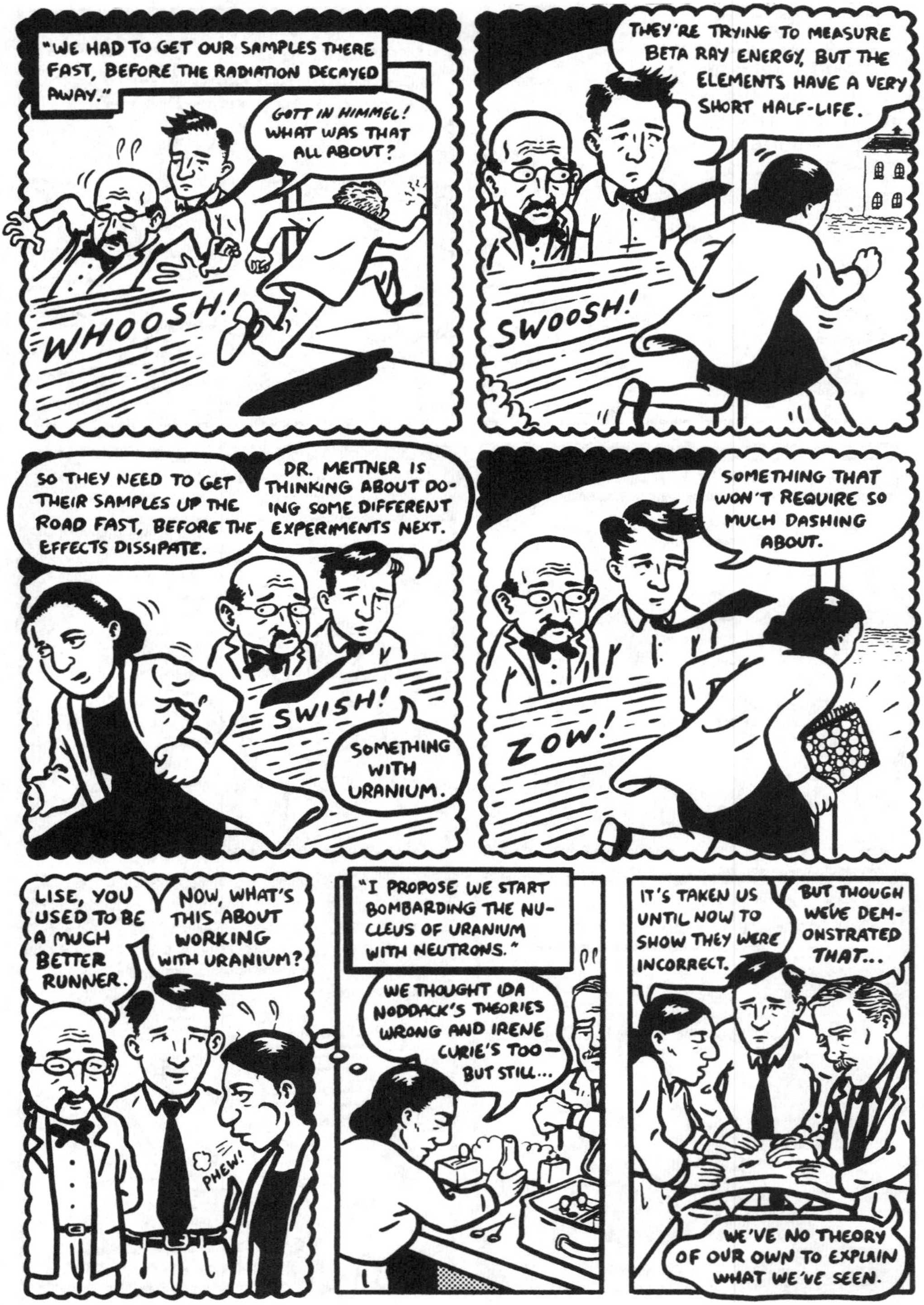
"WE HAD TO GET OUR SAMPLES THERE FAST, BEFORE THE RADIATION DECAYED AWAY."
GOTT IN HIMMEL! WHAT WAS THAT ALL ABOUT?
WHOOSH!
THEY'RE TRYING TO MEASURE BETA RAY ENERGY, BUT THE ELEMENTS HAVE A VERY SHORT HALF-LIFE.
SWOOSH!
SO THEY NEED TO GET THEIR SAMPLES UP THE ROAD FAST, BEFORE THE EFFECTS DISSIPATE.
DR. MEITNER IS THINKING ABOUT DOING SOME DIFFERENT EXPERIMENTS NEXT.
SWISH!
SOMETHING WITH URANIUM.
SOMETHING THAT WON'T REQUIRE SO MUCH DASHING ABOUT.
ZOW!
LISE, YOU USED TO BE A MUCH BETTER RUNNER.
NOW, WHAT'S THIS ABOUT WORKING WITH URANIUM?
PHEW!
"I PROPOSE WE START BOMBARDING THE NUCLEUS OF URANIUM WITH NEUTRONS."
WE THOUGHT IDA NODDACK'S THEORIES WRONG AND IRENE CURIE'S TOO— BUT STILL...
IT'S TAKEN US UNTIL NOW TO SHOW THEY WERE INCORRECT.
BUT THOUGH WE'VE DEMONSTRATED THAT...
WE'VE NO THEORY OF OUR OWN TO EXPLAIN WHAT WE'VE SEEN.

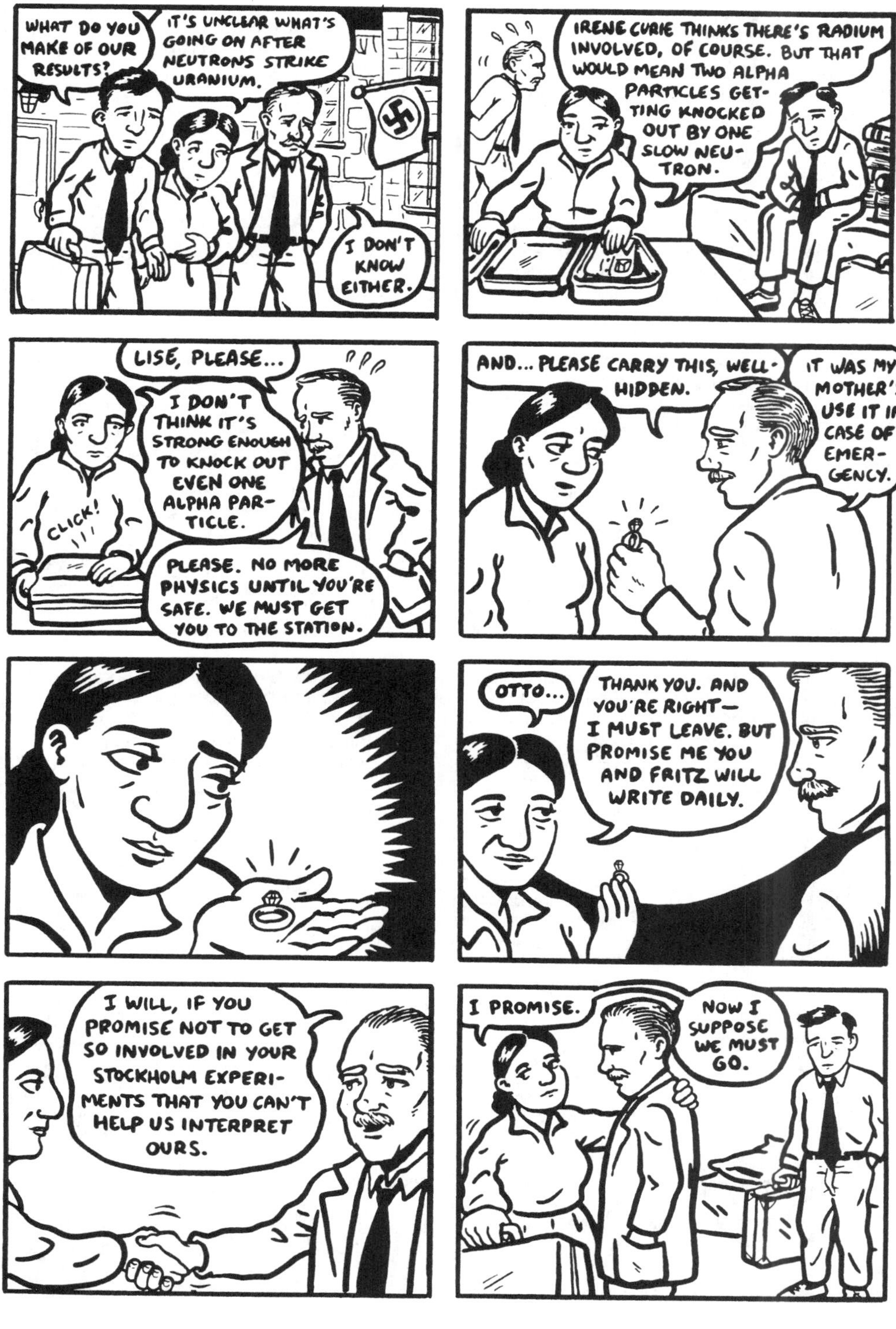
WHAT DO YOU MAKE OF OUR RESULTS?
IT'S UNCLEAR WHAT'S GOING ON AFTER NEUTRONS STRIKE URANIUM.
I DON'T KNOW EITHER.
IRENE CURIE THINKS THERE'S RADIUM INVOLVED, OF COURSE. BUT THAT WOULD MEAN TWO ALPHA PARTICLES GETTING KNOCKED OUT BY ONE SLOW NEUTRON.
LISE, PLEASE...
I DON'T THINK IT'S STRONG ENOUGH TO KNOCK OUT EVEN ONE ALPHA PARTICLE.
CLICK!
PLEASE. NO MORE PHYSICS UNTIL YOU'RE SAFE. WE MUST GET YOU TO THE STATION.
AND... PLEASE CARRY THIS, WELL-HIDDEN.
IT WAS MY MOTHER'S. USE IT IN CASE OF EMERGENCY.
OTTO...
THANK YOU. AND YOU'RE RIGHT— I MUST LEAVE. BUT PROMISE ME YOU AND FRITZ WILL WRITE DAILY.
I WILL, IF YOU PROMISE NOT TO GET SO INVOLVED IN YOUR STOCKHOLM EXPERIMENTS THAT YOU CAN'T HELP US INTERPRET OURS.
I PROMISE.
NOW I SUPPOSE WE MUST GO.

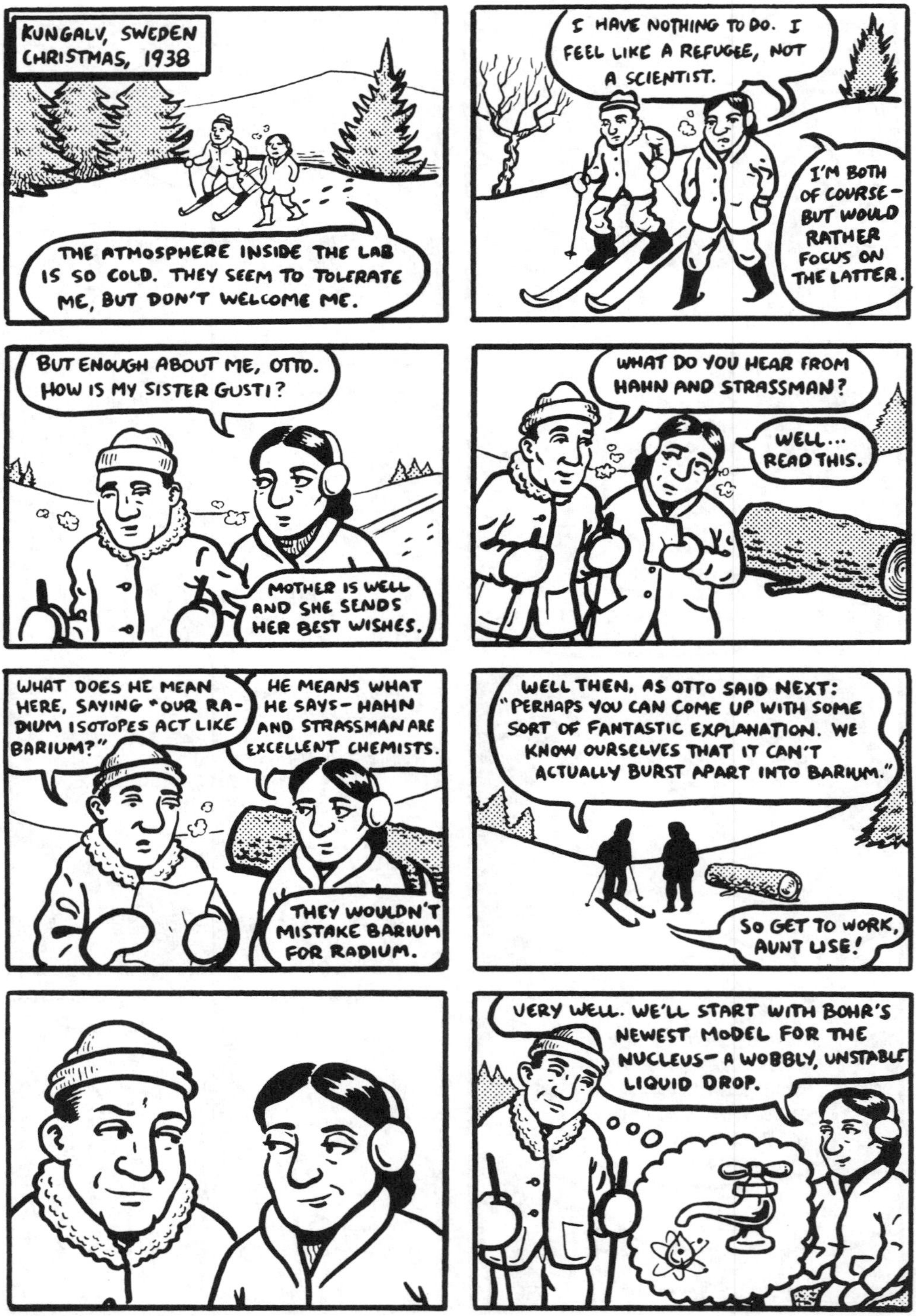
KUNGALV, SWEDEN
CHRISTMAS, 1938
THE ATMOSPHERE INSIDE THE LAB IS SO COLD. THEY SEEM TO TOLERATE ME, BUT DON'T WELCOME ME.
I HAVE NOTHING TO DO. I FEEL LIKE A REFUGEE, NOT A SCIENTIST.
I'M BOTH OF COURSE- BUT WOULD RATHER FOCUS ON THE LATTER.
BUT ENOUGH ABOUT ME, OTTO. HOW IS MY SISTER GUSTI?
MOTHER IS WELL AND SHE SENDS HER BEST WISHES.
WHAT DO YOU HEAR FROM HAHN AND STRASSMAN?
WELL... READ THIS.
WHAT DOES HE MEAN HERE, SAYING "OUR RADIUM ISOTOPES ACT LIKE BARIUM?"
HE MEANS WHAT HE SAYS- HAHN AND STRASSMAN ARE EXCELLENT CHEMISTS.
THEY WOULDN'T MISTAKE BARIUM FOR RADIUM.
WELL THEN, AS OTTO SAID NEXT: "PERHAPS YOU CAN COME UP WITH SOME SORT OF FANTASTIC EXPLANATION. WE KNOW OURSELVES THAT IT CAN'T ACTUALLY BURST APART INTO BARIUM."
SO GET TO WORK, AUNT LISE!
VERY WELL. WE'LL START WITH BOHR'S NEWEST MODEL FOR THE NUCLEUS- A WOBBLY, UNSTABLE LIQUID DROP.

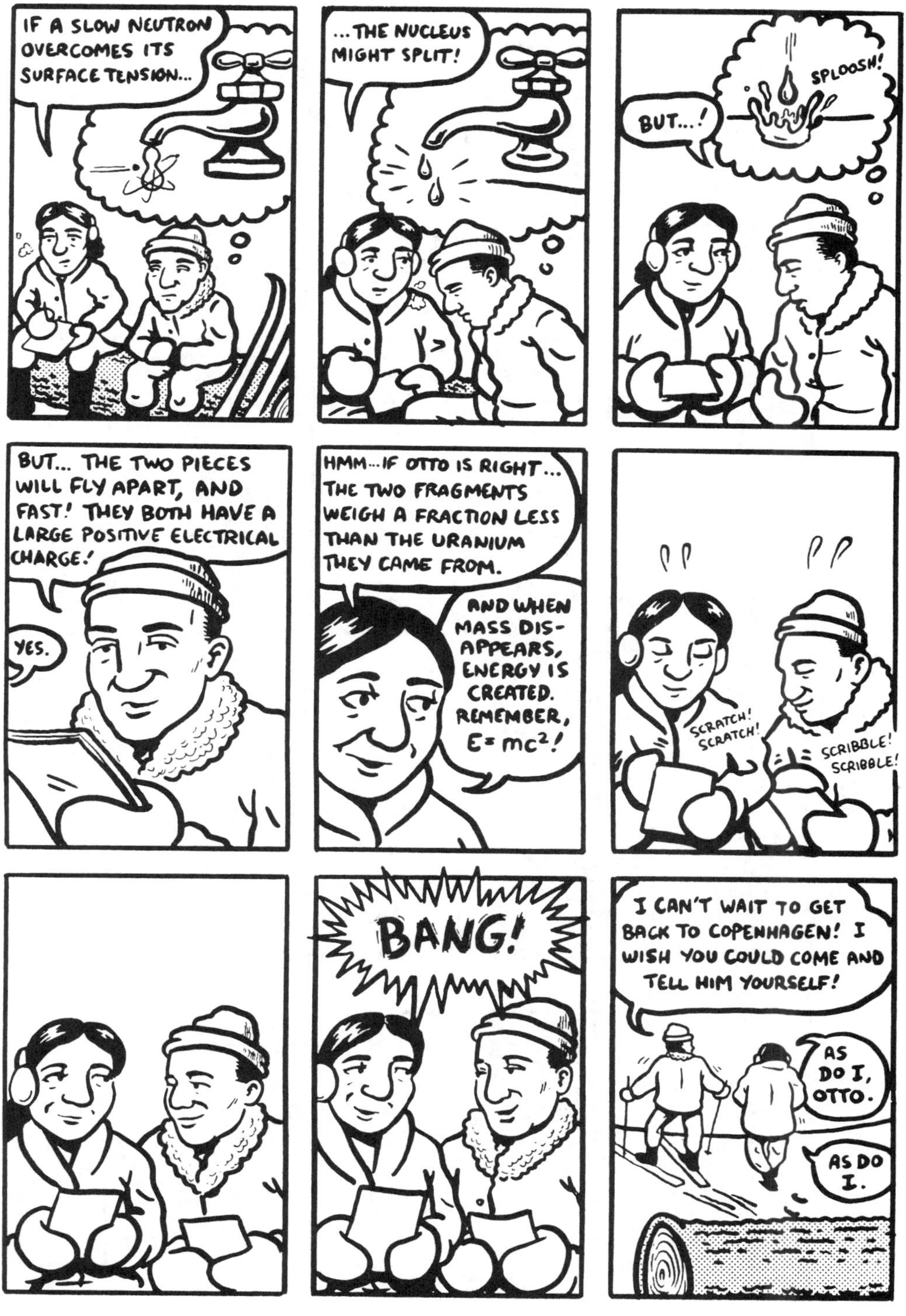
IF A SLOW NEUTRON OVERCOMES ITS SURFACE TENSION...
...THE NUCLEUS MIGHT SPLIT!
BUT...!
SPLOOSH!
BUT... THE TWO PIECES WILL FLY APART, AND FAST! THEY BOTH HAVE A LARGE POSITIVE ELECTRICAL CHARGE!
YES.
HMM...IF OTTO IS RIGHT... THE TWO FRAGMENTS WEIGH A FRACTION LESS THAN THE URANIUM THEY CAME FROM.
AND WHEN MASS DISAPPEARS, ENERGY IS CREATED. REMEMBER, E=mc²!
SCRATCH! SCRATCH!
SCRIBBLE! SCRIBBLE!
BANG!
I CAN'T WAIT TO GET BACK TO COPENHAGEN! I WISH YOU COULD COME AND TELL HIM YOURSELF!
AS DO I, OTTO.
AS DO I.

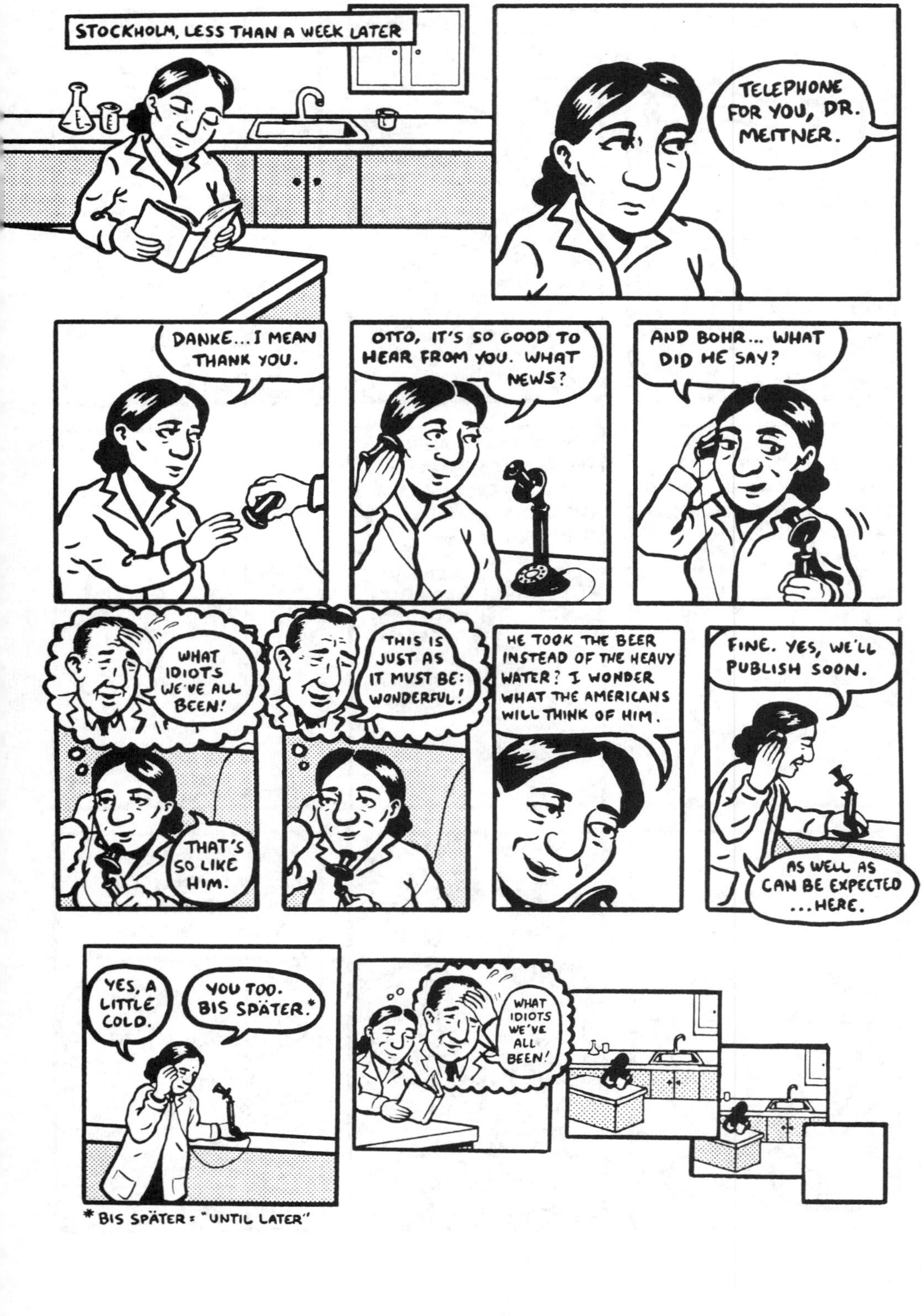
STOCKHOLM, LESS THAN A WEEK LATER
TELEPHONE FOR YOU, DR. MEITNER.
DANKE... I MEAN THANK YOU.
OTTO, IT'S SO GOOD TO HEAR FROM YOU. WHAT NEWS?
AND BOHR... WHAT DID HE SAY?
WHAT IDIOTS WE'VE ALL BEEN!
THAT'S SO LIKE HIM.
THIS IS JUST AS IT MUST BE: WONDERFUL!
HE TOOK THE BEER INSTEAD OF THE HEAVY WATER? I WONDER WHAT THE AMERICANS WILL THINK OF HIM.
FINE. YES, WE'LL PUBLISH SOON.
AS WELL AS CAN BE EXPECTED ...HERE.
YES, A LITTLE COLD.
YOU TOO. BIS SPÄTER.*
WHAT IDIOTS WE'VE ALL BEEN!

* BIS SPÄTER = "UNTIL LATER"

ROSALIND FRANKLIN

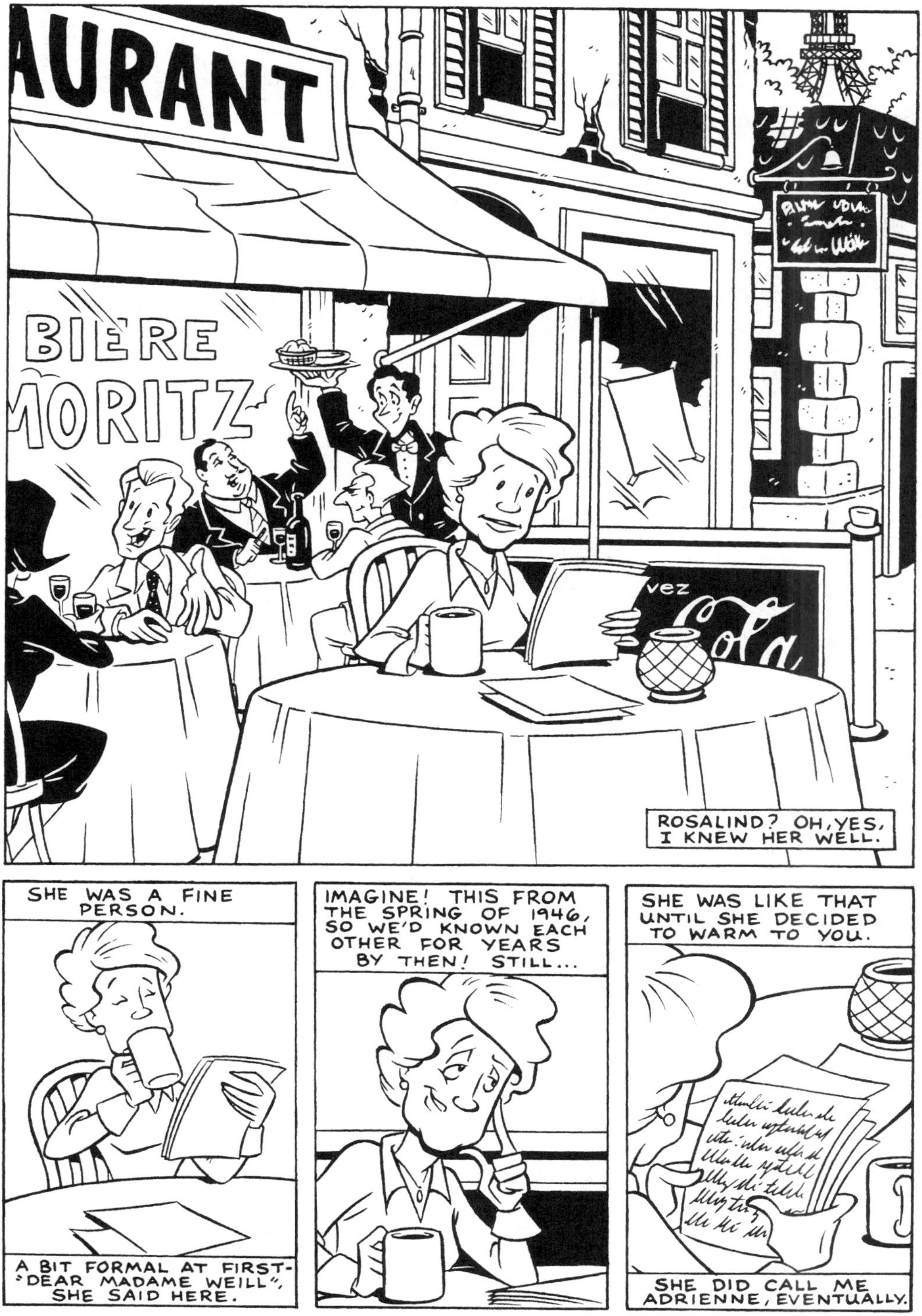
AURANT
BIERE MORITZ
vez Cola
ROSALIND? OH, YES, I KNEW HER WELL.
SHE WAS A FINE PERSON.
A BIT FORMAL AT FIRST- "DEAR MADAME WEILL", SHE SAID HERE.
IMAGINE! THIS FROM THE SPRING OF 1946, SO WE'D KNOWN EACH OTHER FOR YEARS BY THEN! STILL...
SHE WAS LIKE THAT UNTIL SHE DECIDED TO WARM TO YOU.
SHE DID CALL ME ADRIENNE, EVENTUALLY.

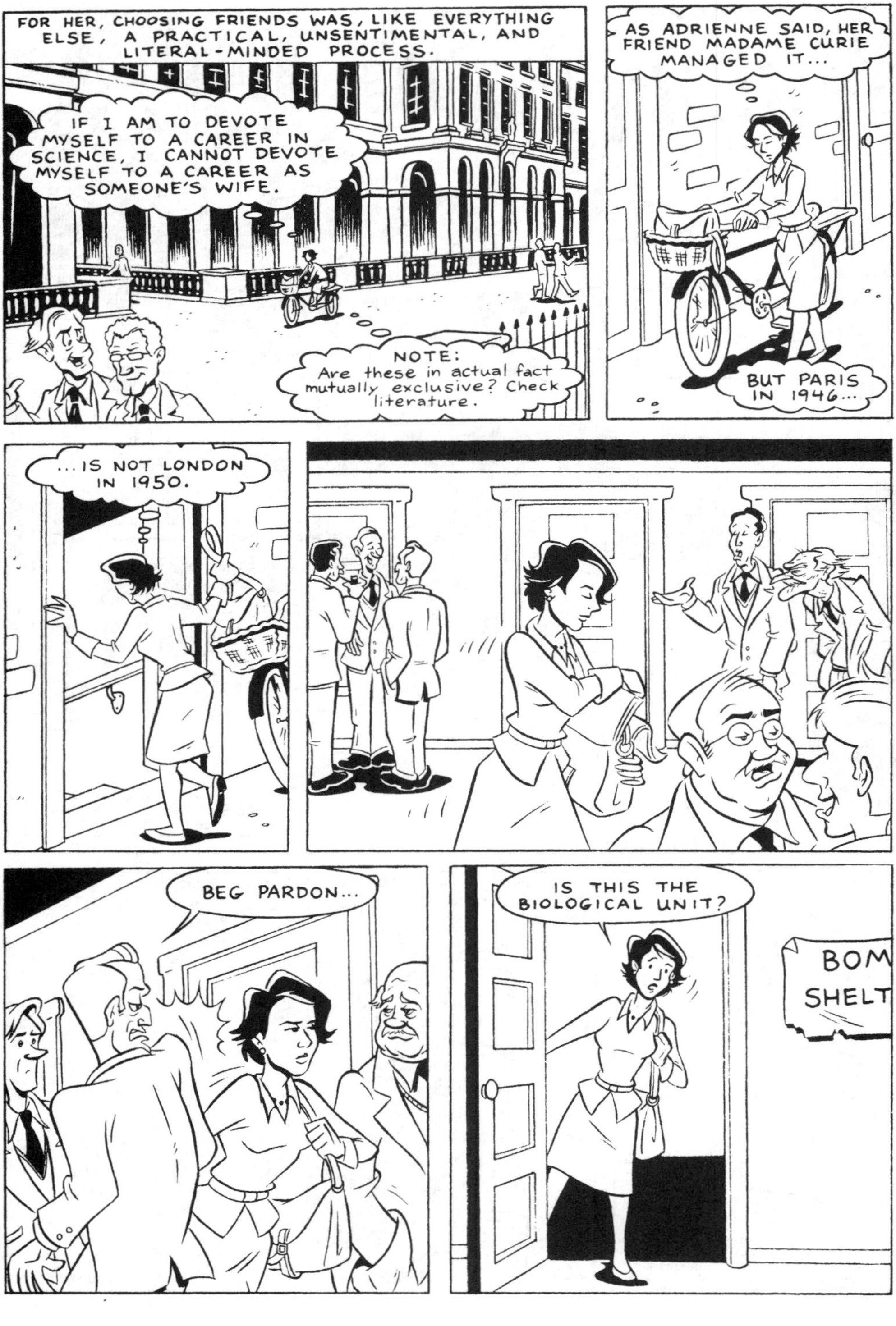
FOR HER, CHOOSING FRIENDS WAS, LIKE EVERYTHING ELSE, A PRACTICAL, UNSENTIMENTAL, AND LITERAL-MINDED PROCESS.
IF I AM TO DEVOTE MYSELF TO A CAREER IN SCIENCE, I CANNOT DEVOTE MYSELF TO A CAREER AS SOMEONE'S WIFE.
NOTE: Are these in actual fact mutually exclusive? Check literature.
AS ADRIENNE SAID, HER FRIEND MADAME CURIE MANAGED IT...
BUT PARIS IN 1946...
...IS NOT LONDON IN 1950.
BEG PARDON...
IS THIS THE BIOLOGICAL UNIT?
BOM
SHELT

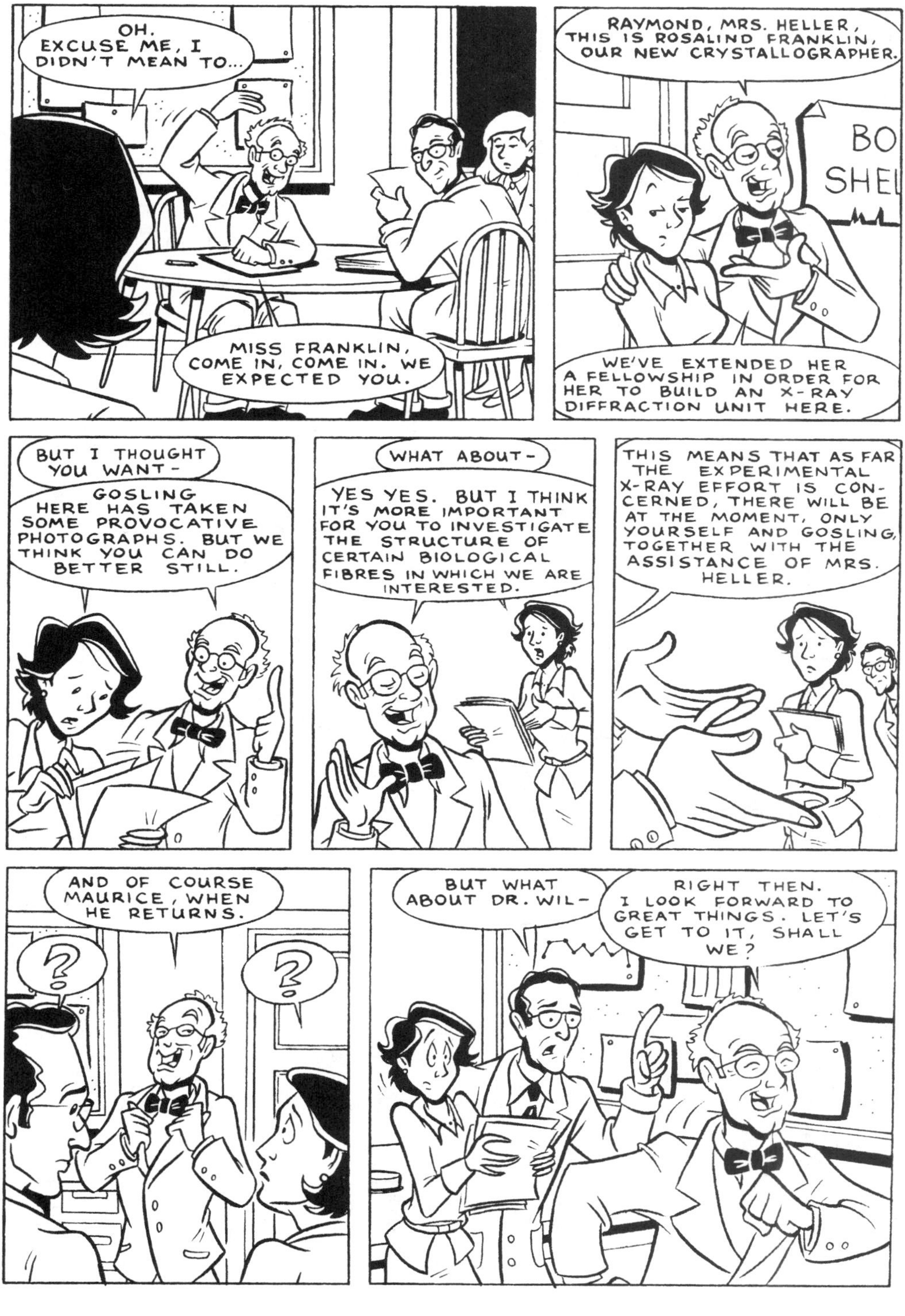
OH. EXCUSE ME, I DIDN'T MEAN TO...
MISS FRANKLIN, COME IN, COME IN. WE EXPECTED YOU.
RAYMOND, MRS. HELLER, THIS IS ROSALIND FRANKLIN, OUR NEW CRYSTALLOGRAPHER.
WE'VE EXTENDED HER A FELLOWSHIP IN ORDER FOR HER TO BUILD AN X-RAY DIFFRACTION UNIT HERE.
BUT I THOUGHT YOU WANT-
GOSLING HERE HAS TAKEN SOME PROVOCATIVE PHOTOGRAPHS. BUT WE THINK YOU CAN DO BETTER STILL.
WHAT ABOUT-
YES YES. BUT I THINK IT'S MORE IMPORTANT FOR YOU TO INVESTIGATE THE STRUCTURE OF CERTAIN BIOLOGICAL FIBRES IN WHICH WE ARE INTERESTED.
THIS MEANS THAT AS FAR THE EXPERIMENTAL X-RAY EFFORT IS CONCERNED, THERE WILL BE AT THE MOMENT, ONLY YOURSELF AND GOSLING, TOGETHER WITH THE ASSISTANCE OF MRS. HELLER.
AND OF COURSE MAURICE, WHEN HE RETURNS.
?
?
BUT WHAT ABOUT DR. WIL-
RIGHT THEN. I LOOK FORWARD TO GREAT THINGS. LET'S GET TO IT, SHALL WE?

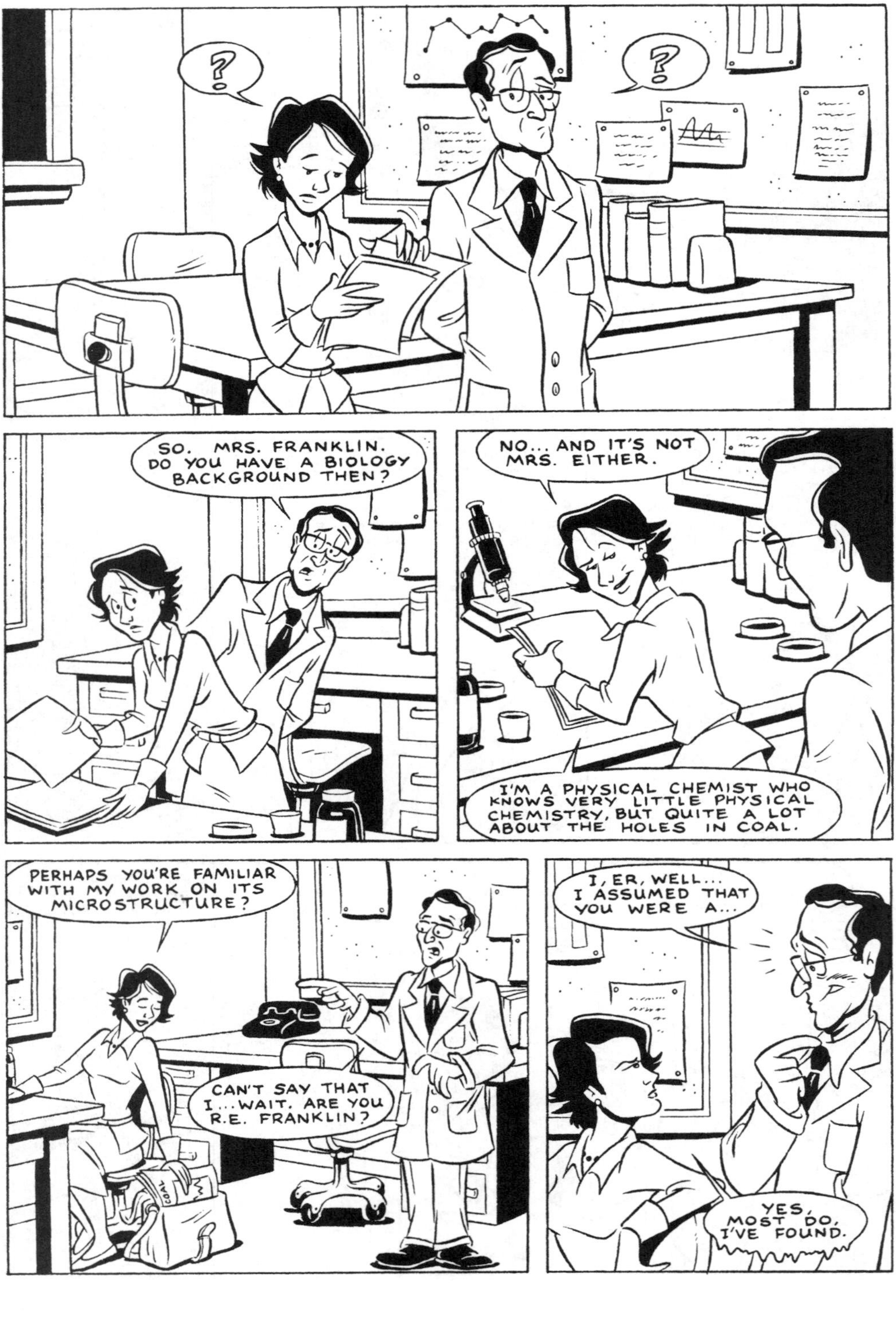
?
?
SO. MRS. FRANKLIN. DO YOU HAVE A BIOLOGY BACKGROUND THEN?
NO... AND IT'S NOT MRS. EITHER.
I'M A PHYSICAL CHEMIST WHO KNOWS VERY LITTLE PHYSICAL CHEMISTRY, BUT QUITE A LOT ABOUT THE HOLES IN COAL.
PERHAPS YOU'RE FAMILIAR WITH MY WORK ON ITS MICROSTRUCTURE?
CAN'T SAY THAT I... WAIT. ARE YOU R.E. FRANKLIN?
COAL
I, ER, WELL... I ASSUMED THAT YOU WERE A...
YES, MOST DO, I'VE FOUND.

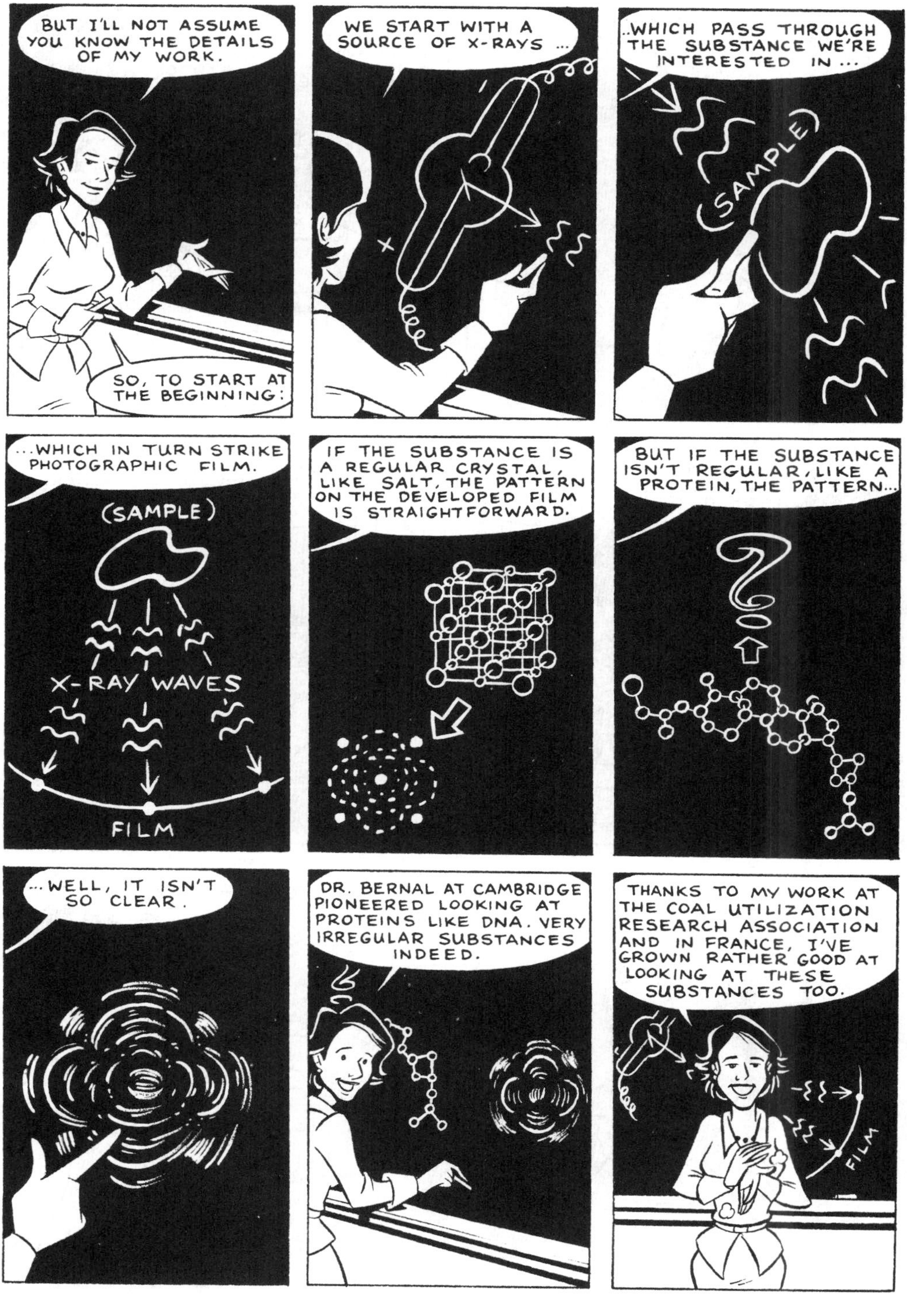
BUT I'LL NOT ASSUME YOU KNOW THE DETAILS OF MY WORK.
SO, TO START AT THE BEGINNING:
WE START WITH A SOURCE OF X-RAYS ...
..WHICH PASS THROUGH THE SUBSTANCE WE'RE INTERESTED IN ...
(SAMPLE)
...WHICH IN TURN STRIKE PHOTOGRAPHIC FILM.
(SAMPLE)
X-RAY WAVES
FILM
IF THE SUBSTANCE IS A REGULAR CRYSTAL, LIKE SALT, THE PATTERN ON THE DEVELOPED FILM IS STRAIGHTFORWARD.
BUT IF THE SUBSTANCE ISN'T REGULAR, LIKE A PROTEIN, THE PATTERN...
...WELL, IT ISN'T SO CLEAR.
DR. BERNAL AT CAMBRIDGE PIONEERED LOOKING AT PROTEINS LIKE DNA. VERY IRREGULAR SUBSTANCES INDEED.
THANKS TO MY WORK AT THE COAL UTILIZATION RESEARCH ASSOCIATION AND IN FRANCE, I'VE GROWN RATHER GOOD AT LOOKING AT THESE SUBSTANCES TOO.
FILM

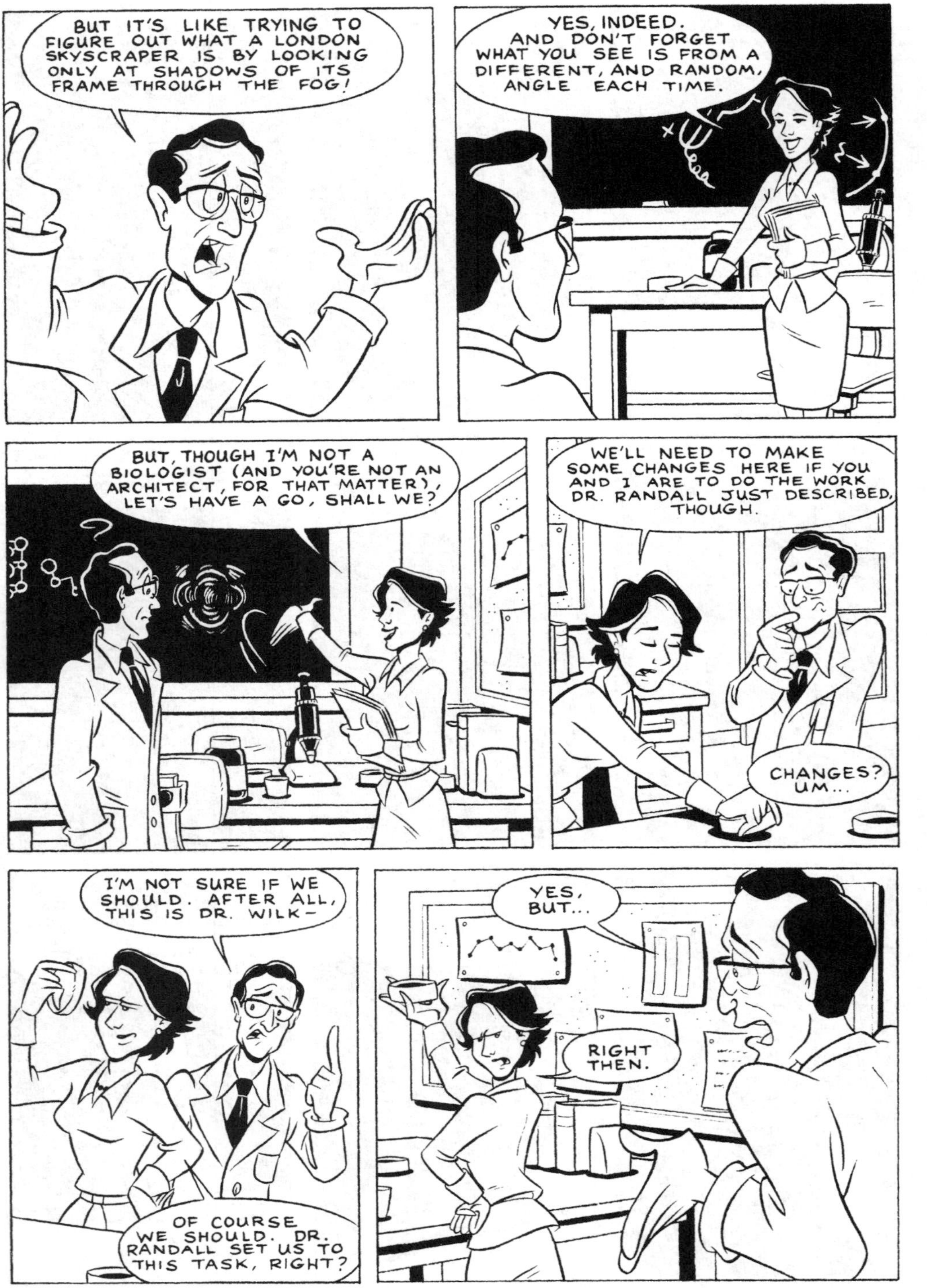
BUT IT'S LIKE TRYING TO FIGURE OUT WHAT A LONDON SKYSCRAPER IS BY LOOKING ONLY AT SHADOWS OF ITS FRAME THROUGH THE FOG!
YES, INDEED. AND DON'T FORGET WHAT YOU SEE IS FROM A DIFFERENT, AND RANDOM, ANGLE EACH TIME.
BUT, THOUGH I'M NOT A BIOLOGIST (AND YOU'RE NOT AN ARCHITECT, FOR THAT MATTER), LET'S HAVE A GO, SHALL WE?
WE'LL NEED TO MAKE SOME CHANGES HERE IF YOU AND I ARE TO DO THE WORK DR. RANDALL JUST DESCRIBED, THOUGH.
CHANGES? UM...
I'M NOT SURE IF WE SHOULD. AFTER ALL, THIS IS DR. WILK-
OF COURSE WE SHOULD. DR. RANDALL SET US TO THIS TASK, RIGHT?
YES, BUT...
RIGHT THEN.

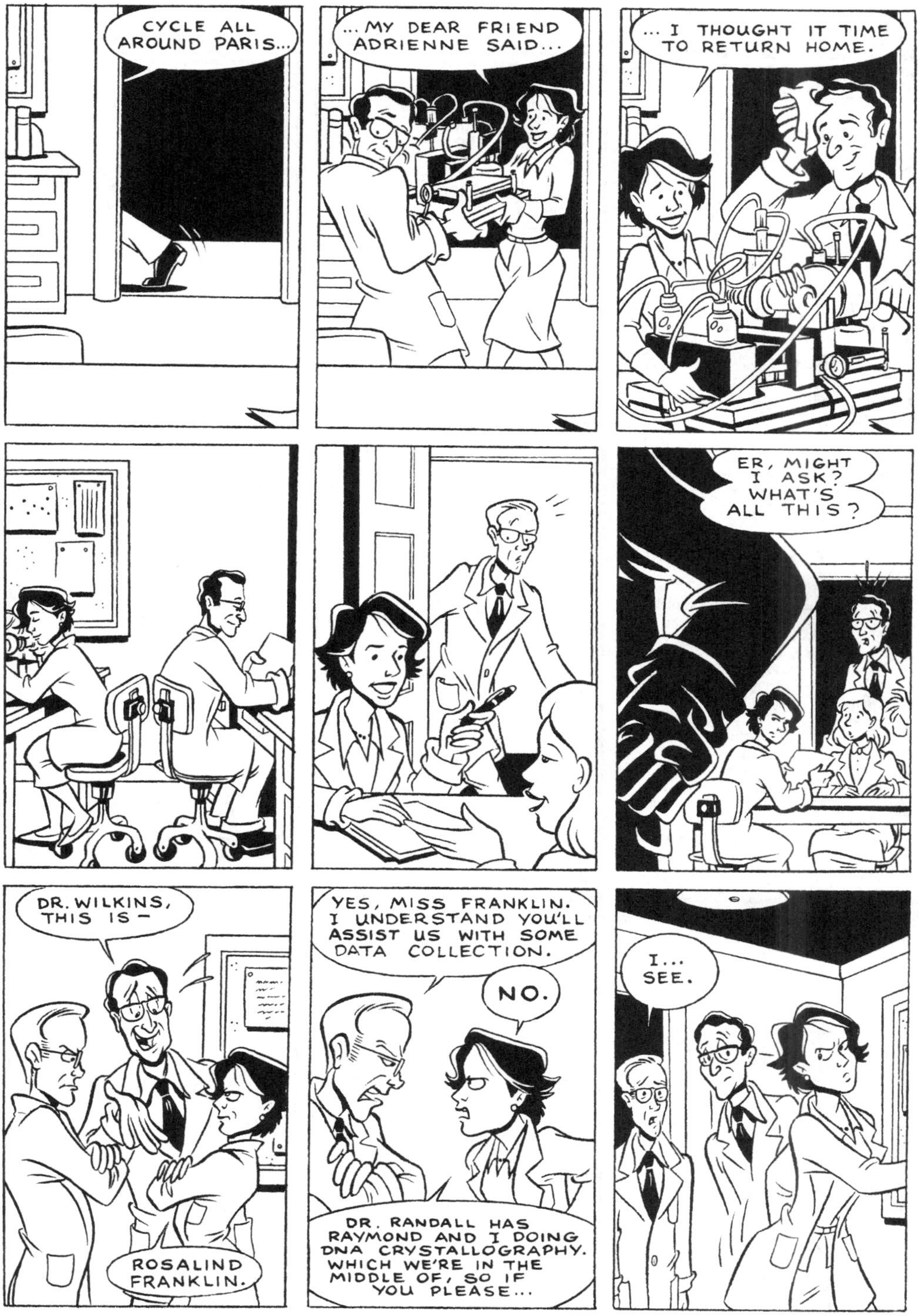
CYCLE ALL AROUND PARIS...
...MY DEAR FRIEND ADRIENNE SAID...
...I THOUGHT IT TIME TO RETURN HOME.
ER, MIGHT I ASK? WHAT'S ALL THIS?
DR. WILKINS, THIS IS—
ROSALIND FRANKLIN.
YES, MISS FRANKLIN. I UNDERSTAND YOU'LL ASSIST US WITH SOME DATA COLLECTION.
NO.
DR. RANDALL HAS RAYMOND AND I DOING DNA CRYSTALLOGRAPHY. WHICH WE'RE IN THE MIDDLE OF, SO IF YOU PLEASE...
I... SEE.

M.F. WILKINS

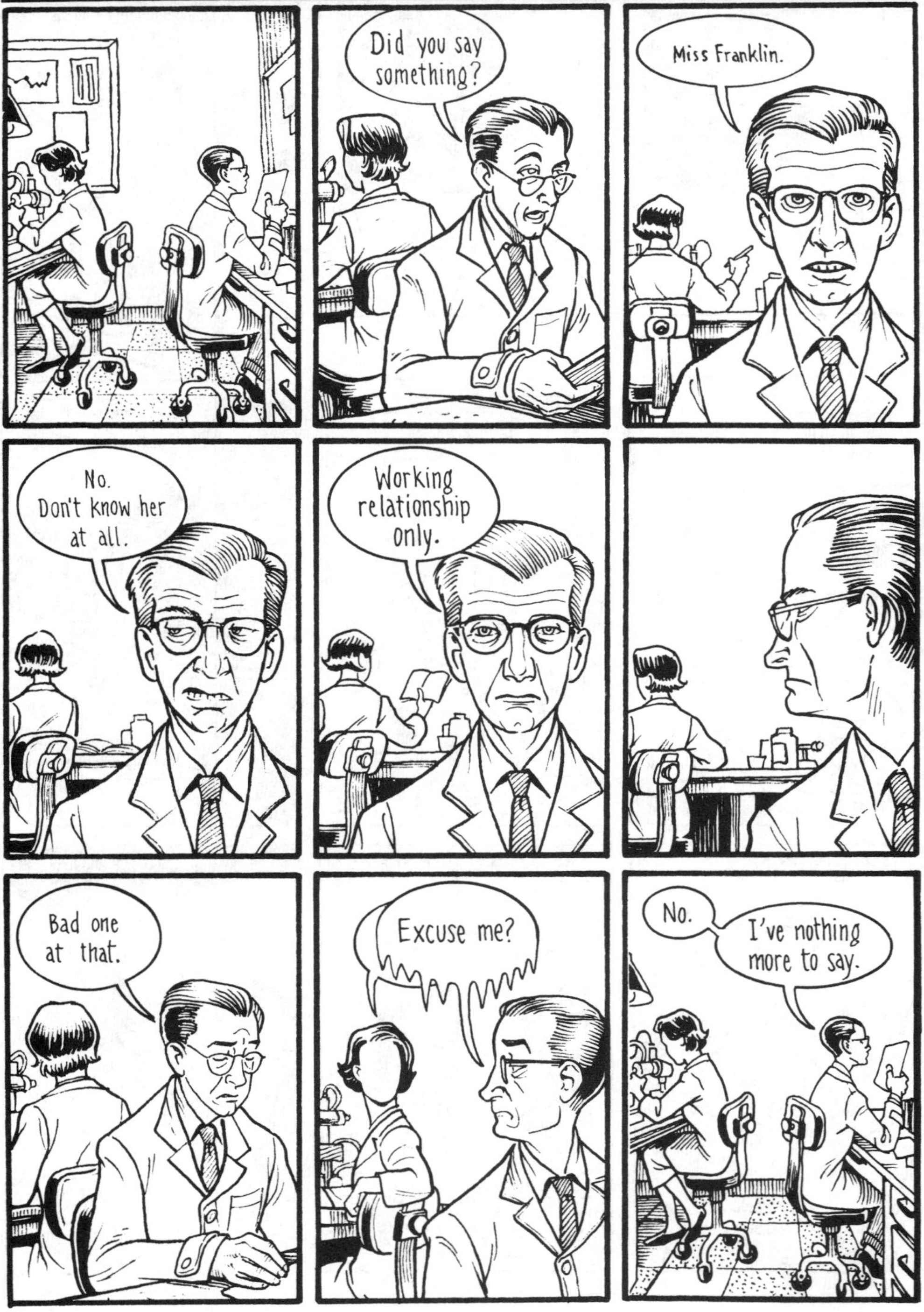
Did you say something?
Miss Franklin.
No. Don't know her at all.
Working relationship only.
Bad one at that.
Excuse me?
No.
I've nothing more to say.

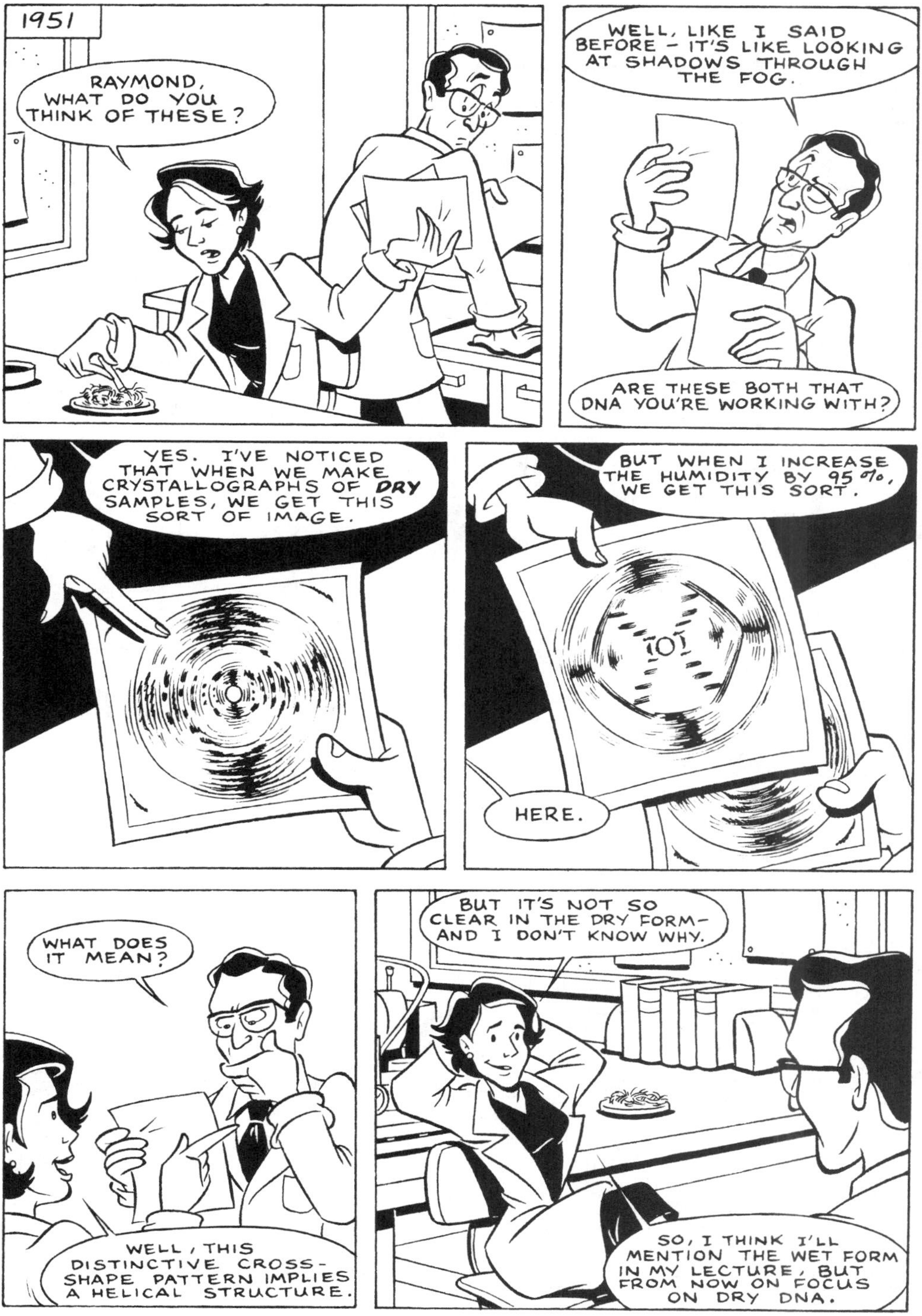
1951
RAYMOND, WHAT DO YOU THINK OF THESE?
WELL, LIKE I SAID BEFORE - IT'S LIKE LOOKING AT SHADOWS THROUGH THE FOG.
ARE THESE BOTH THAT DNA YOU'RE WORKING WITH?
YES. I'VE NOTICED THAT WHEN WE MAKE CRYSTALLOGRAPHS OF DRY SAMPLES, WE GET THIS SORT OF IMAGE.
BUT WHEN I INCREASE THE HUMIDITY BY 95%, WE GET THIS SORT.
HERE.
WHAT DOES IT MEAN?
WELL, THIS DISTINCTIVE CROSS-SHAPE PATTERN IMPLIES A HELICAL STRUCTURE.
BUT IT'S NOT SO CLEAR IN THE DRY FORM- AND I DON'T KNOW WHY.
SO, I THINK I'LL MENTION THE WET FORM IN MY LECTURE, BUT FROM NOW ON FOCUS ON DRY DNA.

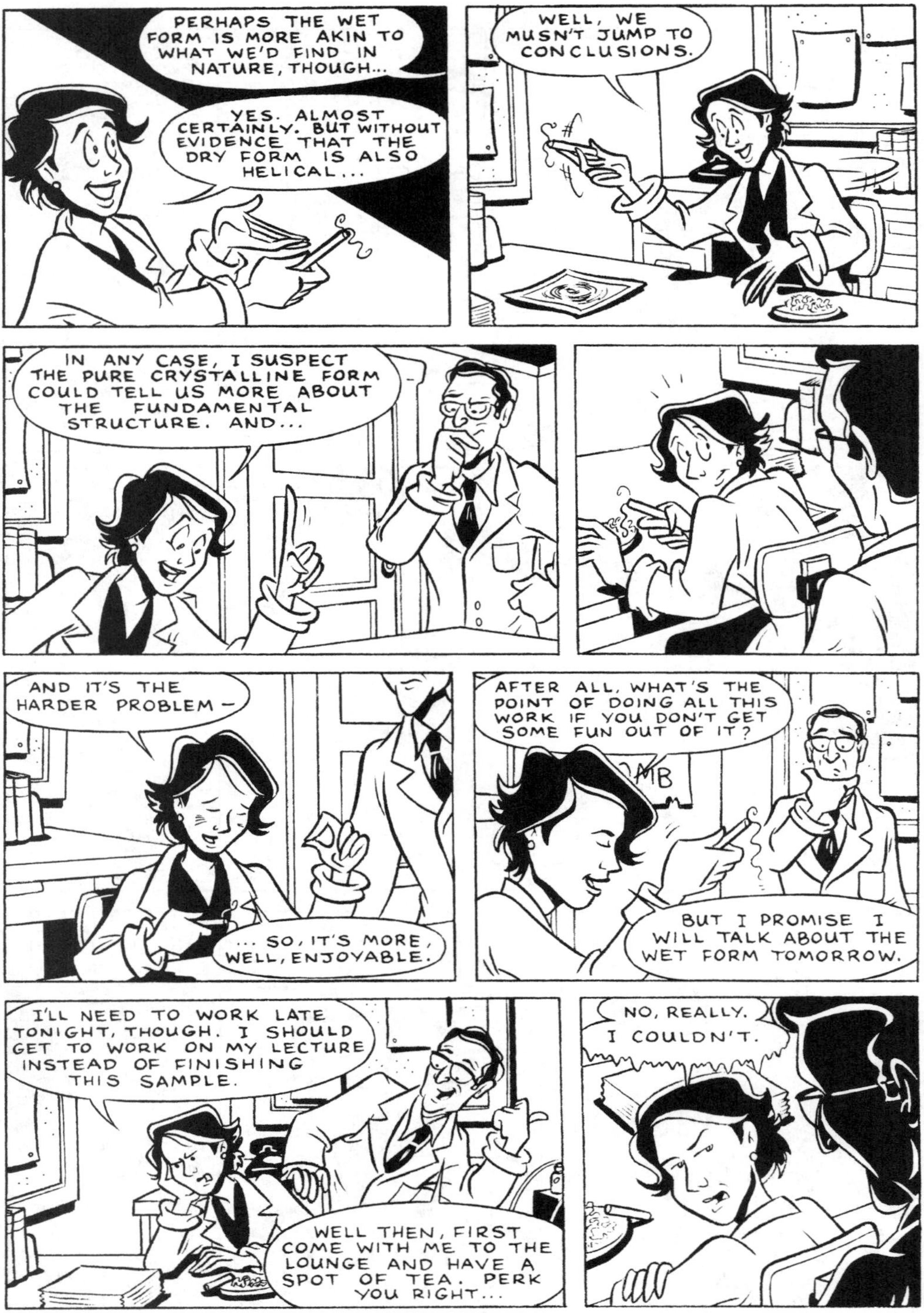
PERHAPS THE WET FORM IS MORE AKIN TO WHAT WE'D FIND IN NATURE, THOUGH...
YES. ALMOST CERTAINLY. BUT WITHOUT EVIDENCE THAT THE DRY FORM IS ALSO HELICAL...
WELL, WE MUSN'T JUMP TO CONCLUSIONS.
IN ANY CASE, I SUSPECT THE PURE CRYSTALLINE FORM COULD TELL US MORE ABOUT THE FUNDAMENTAL STRUCTURE. AND...
AND IT'S THE HARDER PROBLEM —
... SO, IT'S MORE, WELL, ENJOYABLE.
AFTER ALL, WHAT'S THE POINT OF DOING ALL THIS WORK IF YOU DON'T GET SOME FUN OUT OF IT?
BUT I PROMISE I WILL TALK ABOUT THE WET FORM TOMORROW.
I'LL NEED TO WORK LATE TONIGHT, THOUGH. I SHOULD GET TO WORK ON MY LECTURE INSTEAD OF FINISHING THIS SAMPLE.
WELL THEN, FIRST COME WITH ME TO THE LOUNGE AND HAVE A SPOT OF TEA. PERK YOU RIGHT...
NO, REALLY.
I COULDN'T.

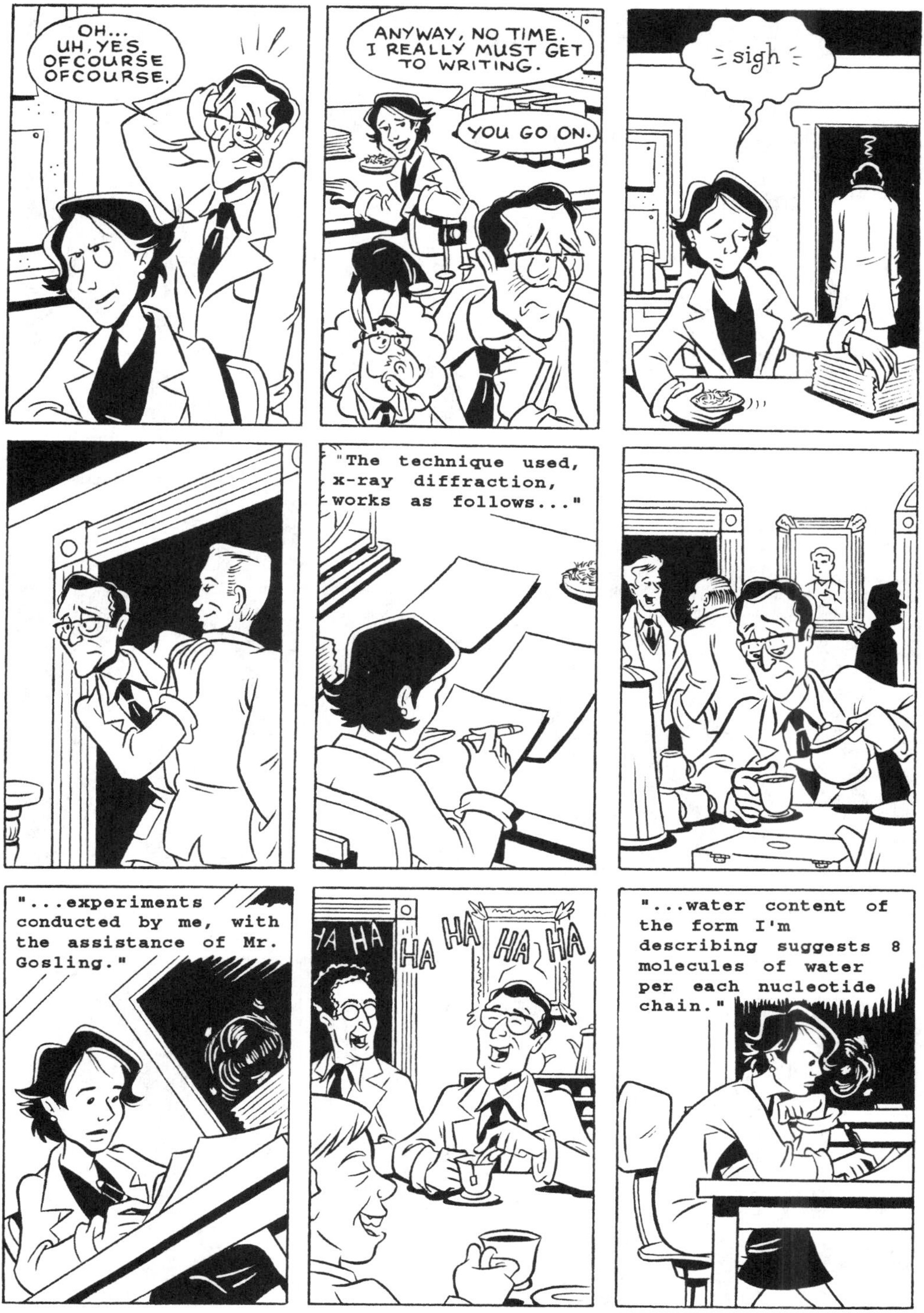
OH... UH, YES. OF COURSE OF COURSE.
ANYWAY, NO TIME. I REALLY MUST GET TO WRITING.
YOU GO ON.
sigh
"The technique used, x-ray diffraction, works as follows..."
"...experiments conducted by me, with the assistance of Mr. Gosling."
HA HA HA HA HA HA
"...water content of the form I'm describing suggests 8 molecules of water per each nucleotide chain."

JIM WATSON

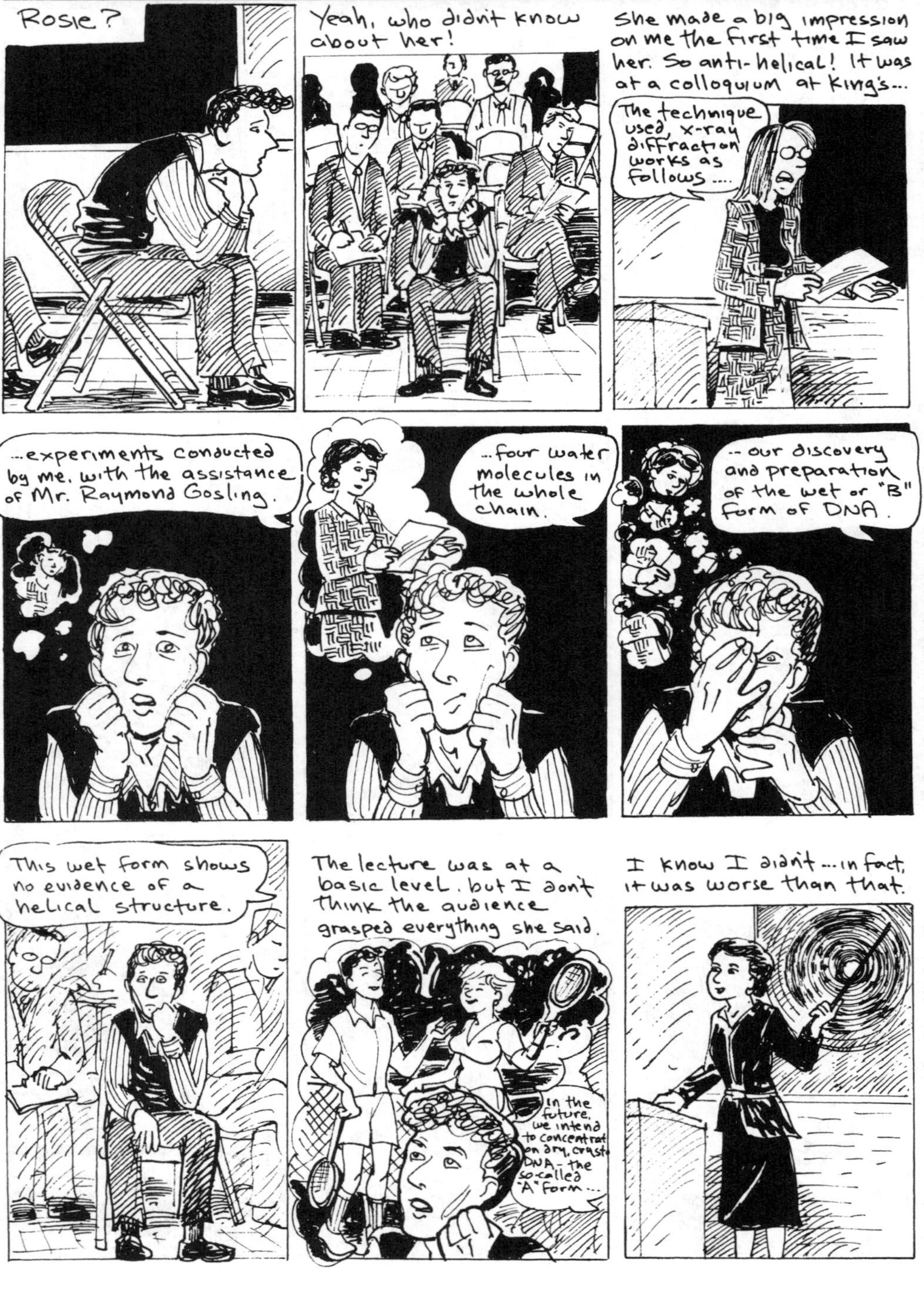
Rosie?
Yeah, who didn't know about her!
She made a big impression on me the first time I saw her. So anti-helical! It was at a colloquium at King's...
The technique used, x-ray diffraction works as follows....
...experiments conducted by me, with the assistance of Mr. Raymond Gosling.
...four water molecules in the whole chain.
-- our discovery and preparation of the wet or "B" form of DNA.
This wet form shows no evidence of a helical structure.
The lecture was at a basic level, but I don't think the audience grasped everything she said.
In the future, we intend to concentrat on dry, crysto DNA - the so-called "A" form...
I know I didn't ... in fact, it was worse than that.

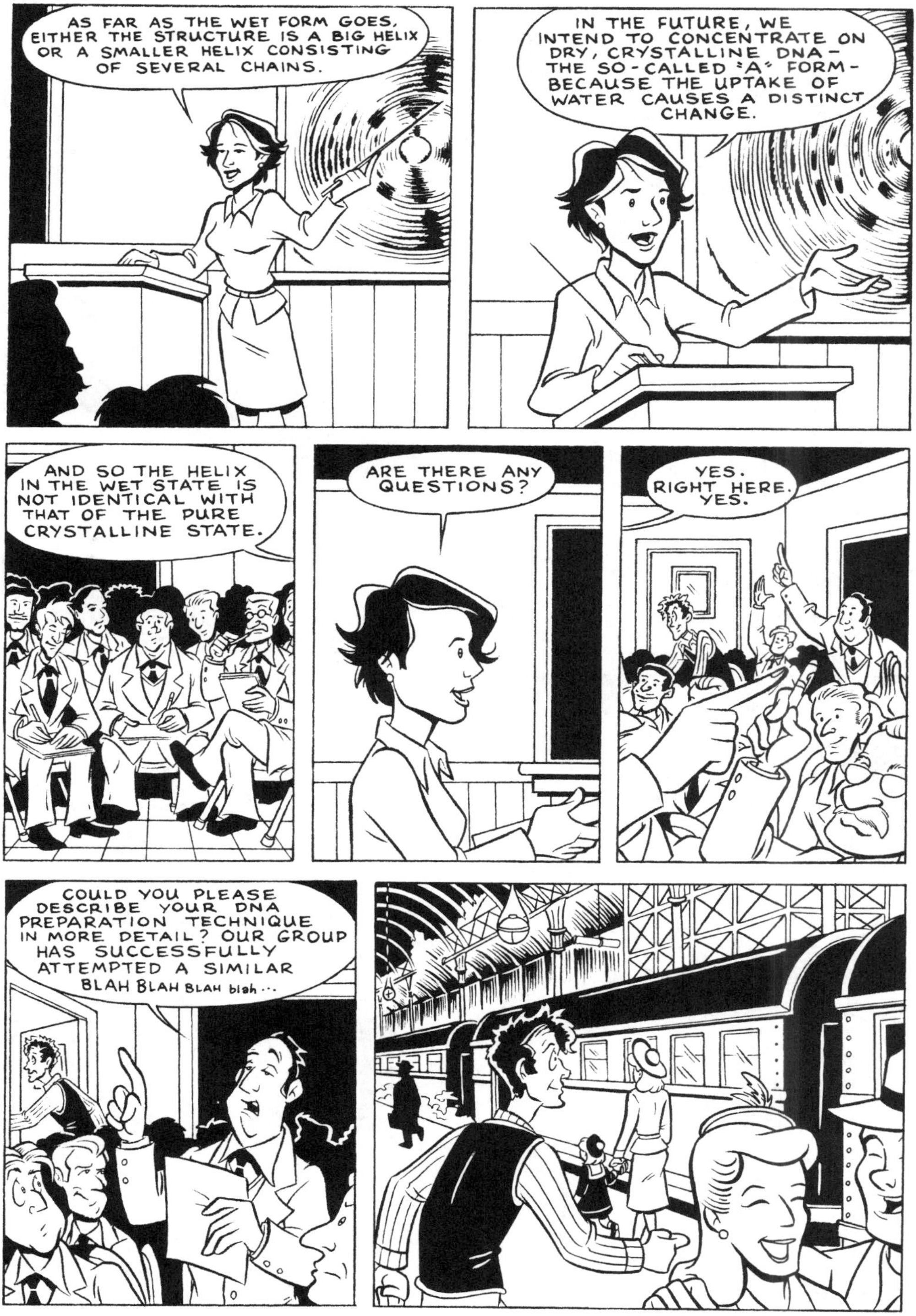
AS FAR AS THE WET FORM GOES, EITHER THE STRUCTURE IS A BIG HELIX OR A SMALLER HELIX CONSISTING OF SEVERAL CHAINS.
IN THE FUTURE, WE INTEND TO CONCENTRATE ON DRY, CRYSTALLINE DNA - THE SO-CALLED "A" FORM - BECAUSE THE UPTAKE OF WATER CAUSES A DISTINCT CHANGE.
AND SO THE HELIX IN THE WET STATE IS NOT IDENTICAL WITH THAT OF THE PURE CRYSTALLINE STATE.
ARE THERE ANY QUESTIONS?
YES. RIGHT HERE. YES.
COULD YOU PLEASE DESCRIBE YOUR DNA PREPARATION TECHNIQUE IN MORE DETAIL? OUR GROUP HAS SUCCESSFULLY ATTEMPTED A SIMILAR BLAH BLAH BLAH blah...

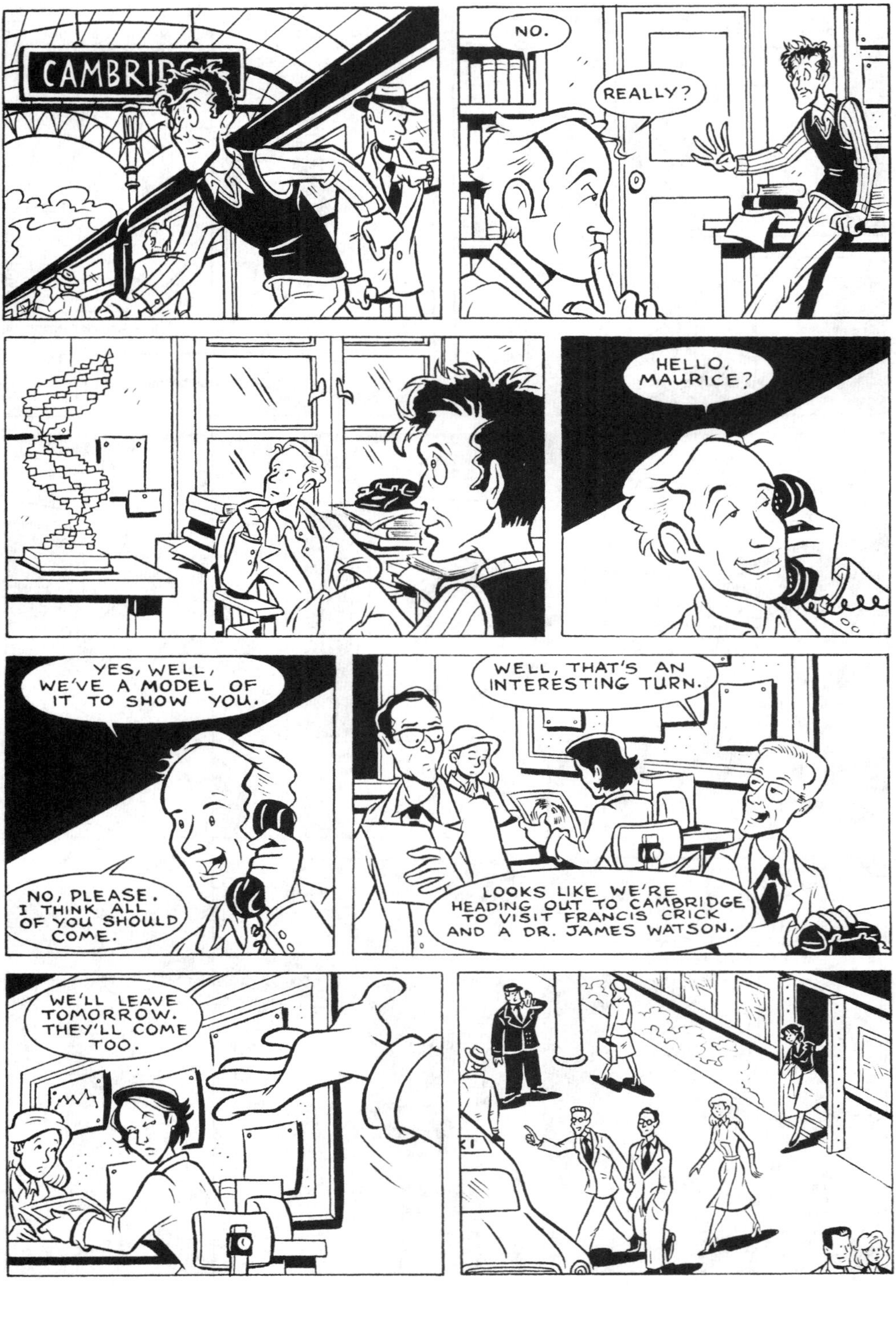
CAMBRIDGE
NO.
REALLY?
HELLO, MAURICE?
YES, WELL, WE'VE A MODEL OF IT TO SHOW YOU.
NO, PLEASE. I THINK ALL OF YOU SHOULD COME.
WELL, THAT'S AN INTERESTING TURN.
LOOKS LIKE WE'RE HEADING OUT TO CAMBRIDGE TO VISIT FRANCIS CRICK AND A DR. JAMES WATSON.
WE'LL LEAVE TOMORROW. THEY'LL COME TOO.

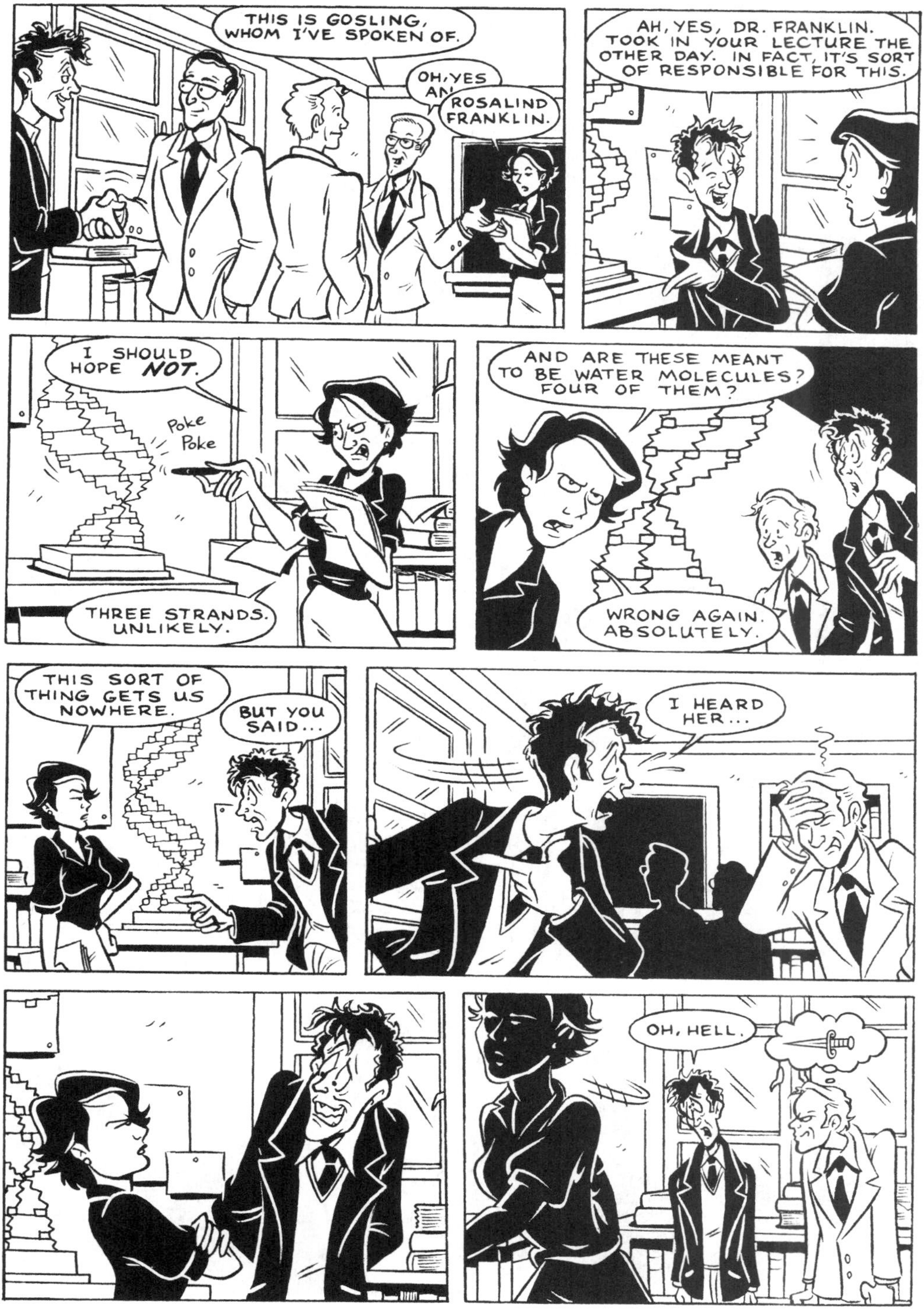
THIS IS GOSLING, WHOM I'VE SPOKEN OF.
OH, YES AN
ROSALIND FRANKLIN.
AH, YES, DR. FRANKLIN. TOOK IN YOUR LECTURE THE OTHER DAY. IN FACT, IT'S SORT OF RESPONSIBLE FOR THIS.
I SHOULD HOPE NOT.
Poke Poke
THREE STRANDS. UNLIKELY.
AND ARE THESE MEANT TO BE WATER MOLECULES? FOUR OF THEM?
WRONG AGAIN. ABSOLUTELY.
THIS SORT OF THING GETS US NOWHERE.
BUT YOU SAID...
I HEARD HER...
OH, HELL.

FRANCIS CRICK

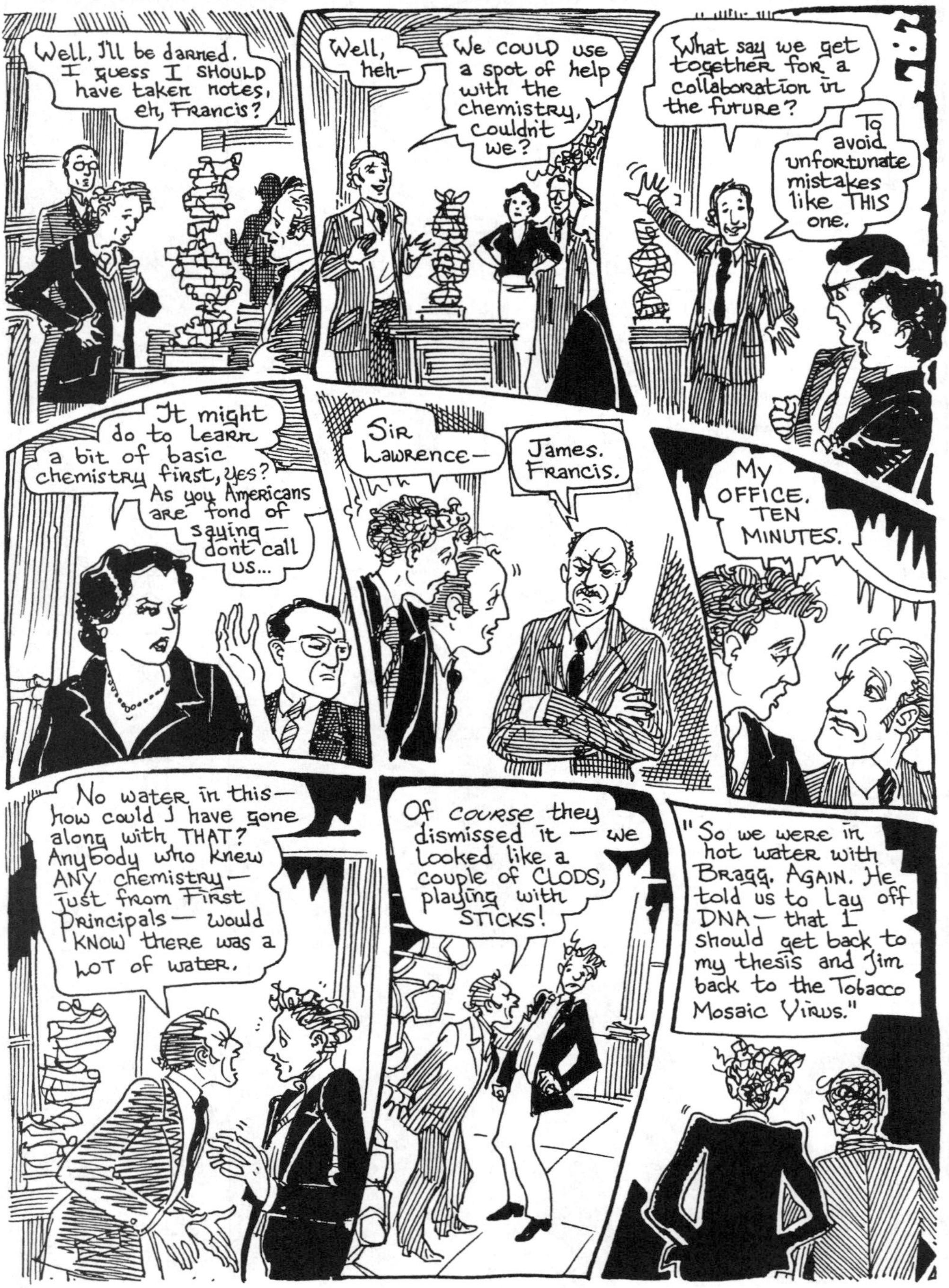
Well, I'll be darned. I guess I SHOULD have taken notes, eh, Francis?
Well, heh—
We COULD use a spot of help with the chemistry, couldn't we?
What say we get together for a collaboration in the future?
To avoid unfortunate mistakes like THIS one.
It might do to learn a bit of basic chemistry first, yes?
As you Americans are fond of saying— don't call us...
Sir Lawrence—
James. Francis.
My OFFICE. TEN MINUTES.
No water in this— how could I have gone along with THAT? Anybody who knew ANY chemistry— just from First Principals— would KNOW there was a LOT of water.
Of course they dismissed it — we looked like a couple of CLODS, playing with STICKS!
"So we were in hot water with Bragg. AGAIN. He told us to lay off DNA— that I should get back to my thesis and Jim back to the Tobacco Mosaic Virus."

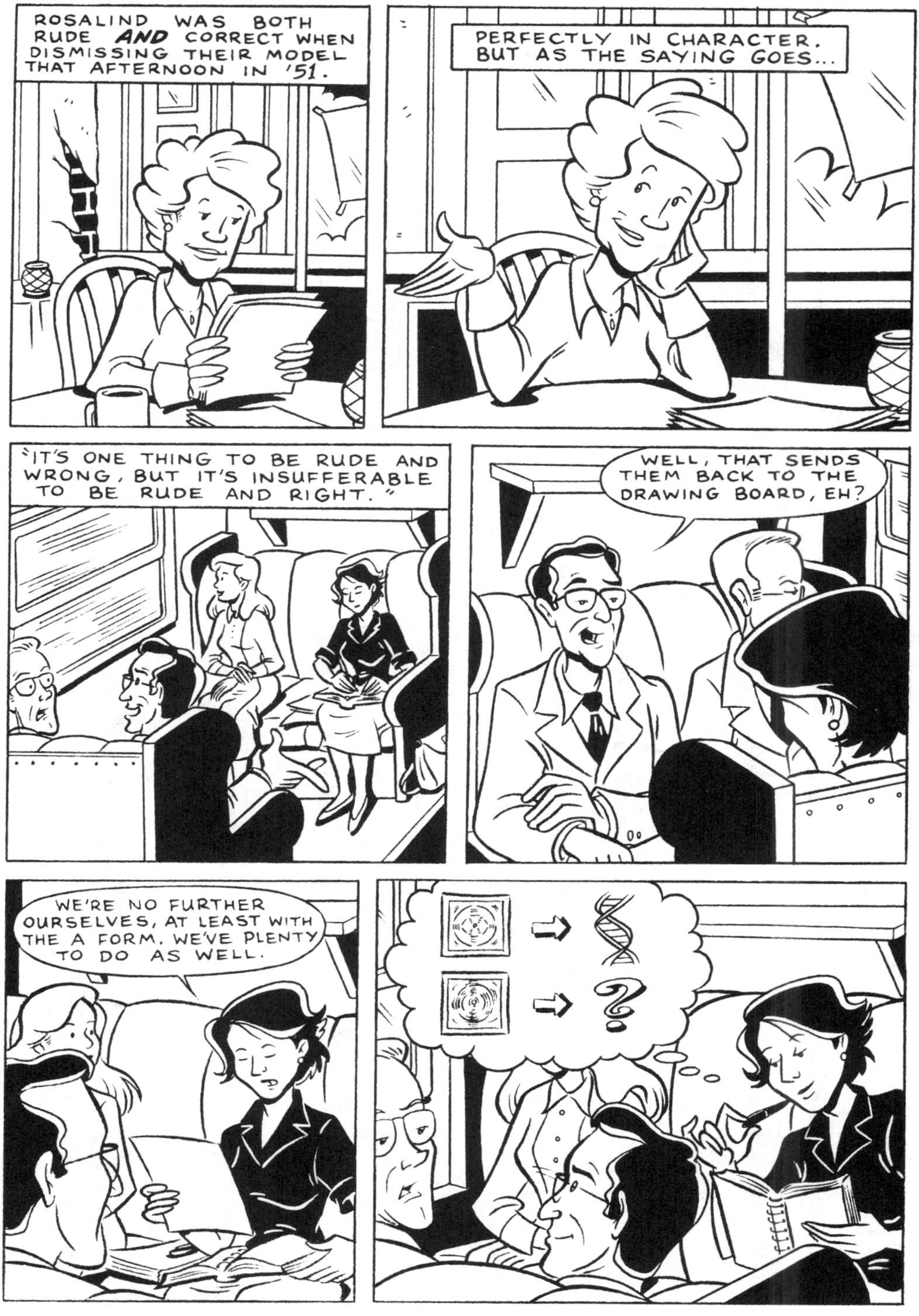
ROSALIND WAS BOTH RUDE AND CORRECT WHEN DISMISSING THEIR MODEL THAT AFTERNOON IN '51.
PERFECTLY IN CHARACTER. BUT AS THE SAYING GOES...
"IT'S ONE THING TO BE RUDE AND WRONG, BUT IT'S INSUFFERABLE TO BE RUDE AND RIGHT."
WELL, THAT SENDS THEM BACK TO THE DRAWING BOARD, EH?
WE'RE NO FURTHER OURSELVES, AT LEAST WITH THE A FORM. WE'VE PLENTY TO DO AS WELL.
?

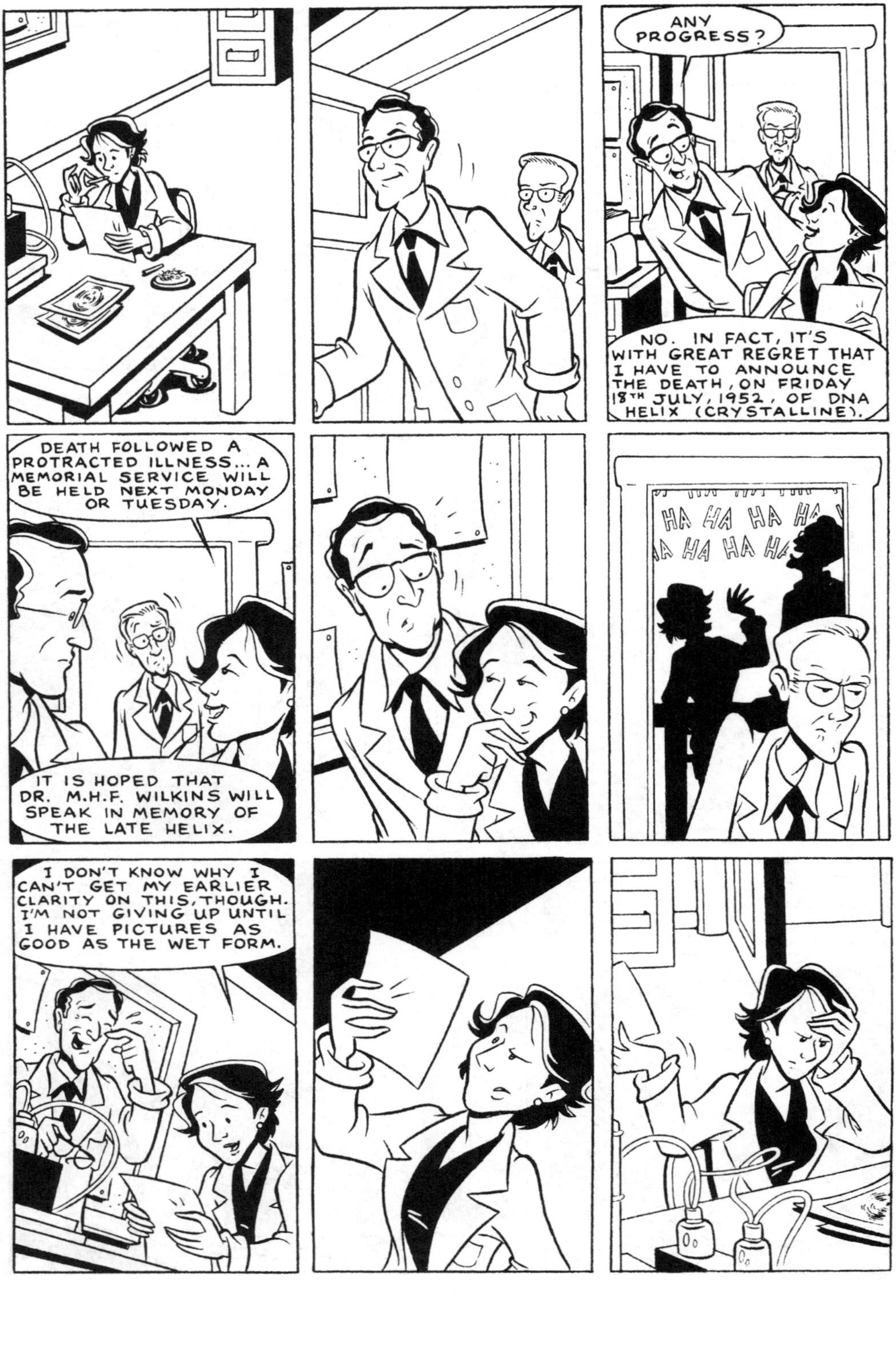
ANY PROGRESS?
NO. IN FACT, IT'S WITH GREAT REGRET THAT I HAVE TO ANNOUNCE THE DEATH, ON FRIDAY 18TH JULY, 1952, OF DNA HELIX (CRYSTALLINE).
DEATH FOLLOWED A PROTRACTED ILLNESS... A MEMORIAL SERVICE WILL BE HELD NEXT MONDAY OR TUESDAY.
IT IS HOPED THAT DR. M.H.F. WILKINS WILL SPEAK IN MEMORY OF THE LATE HELIX.
HA HA HA HA
HA HA HA HA
I DON'T KNOW WHY I CAN'T GET MY EARLIER CLARITY ON THIS, THOUGH. I'M NOT GIVING UP UNTIL I HAVE PICTURES AS GOOD AS THE WET FORM.

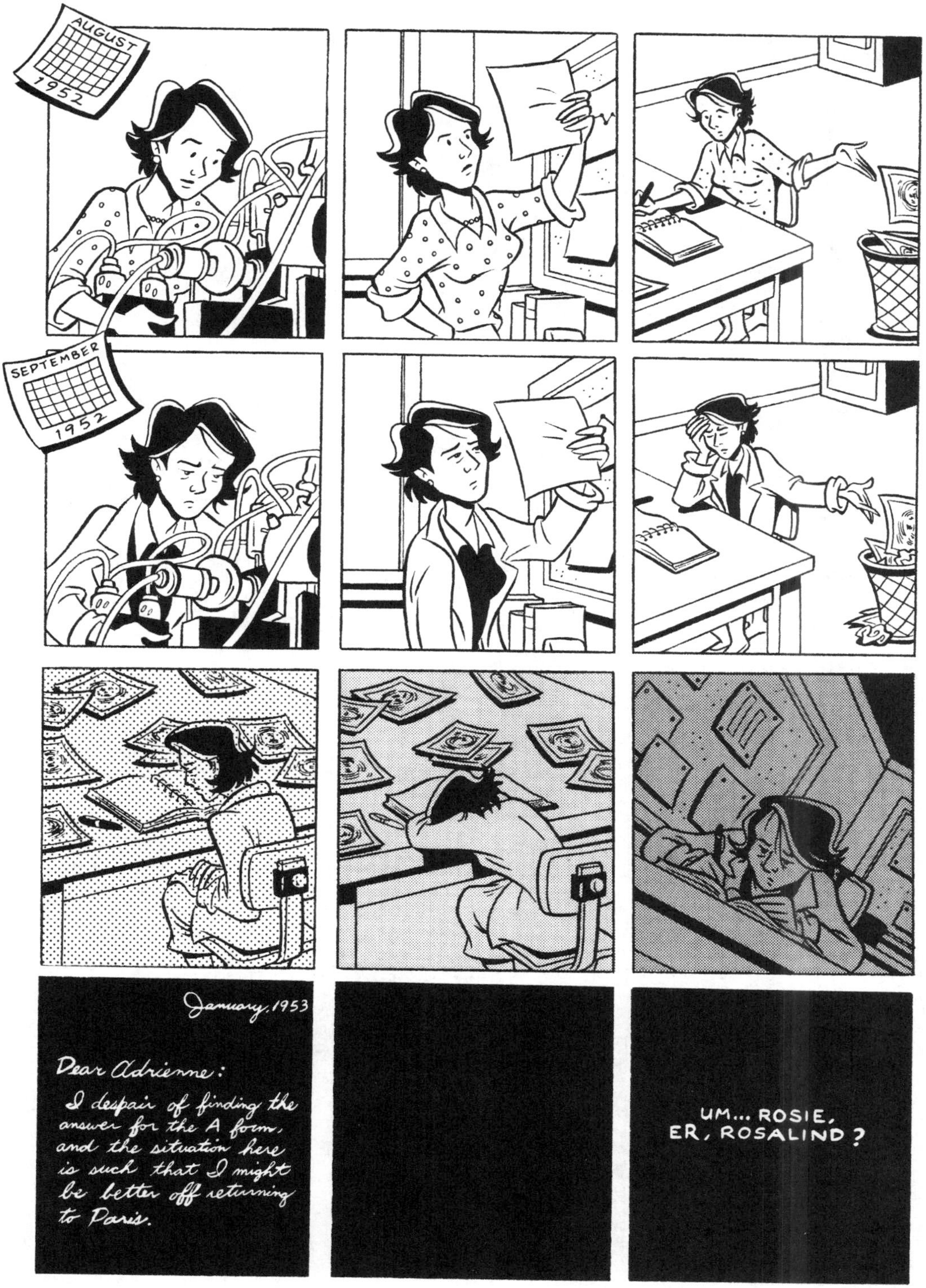
AUGUST
1952
SEPTEMBER
1952
January, 1953
Dear Adrienne:
I despair of finding the answer for the A form, and the situation here is such that I might be better off returning to Paris.
UM... ROSIE, ER, ROSALIND?

JIM WATSON

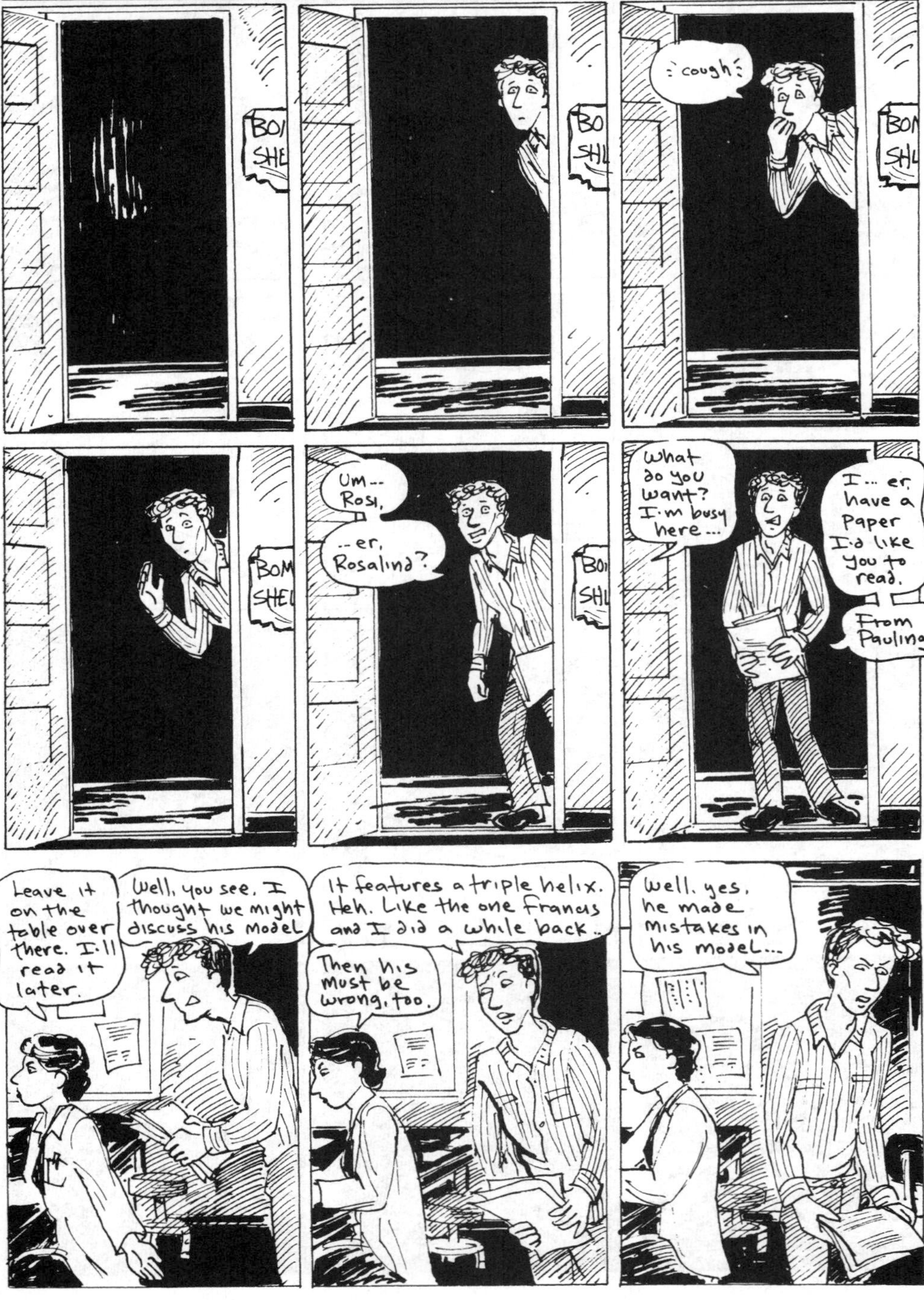
cough
Um-- Rosi,
...er, Rosalind?
What do you want? I'm busy here...
I... er, have a paper I'd like you to read.
From Pauling.
Leave it on the table over there. I'll read it later.
Well, you see, I thought we might discuss his model
It features a triple helix. Heh. Like the one Francis and I did a while back..
Then his must be wrong, too.
Well, yes, he made mistakes in his model...

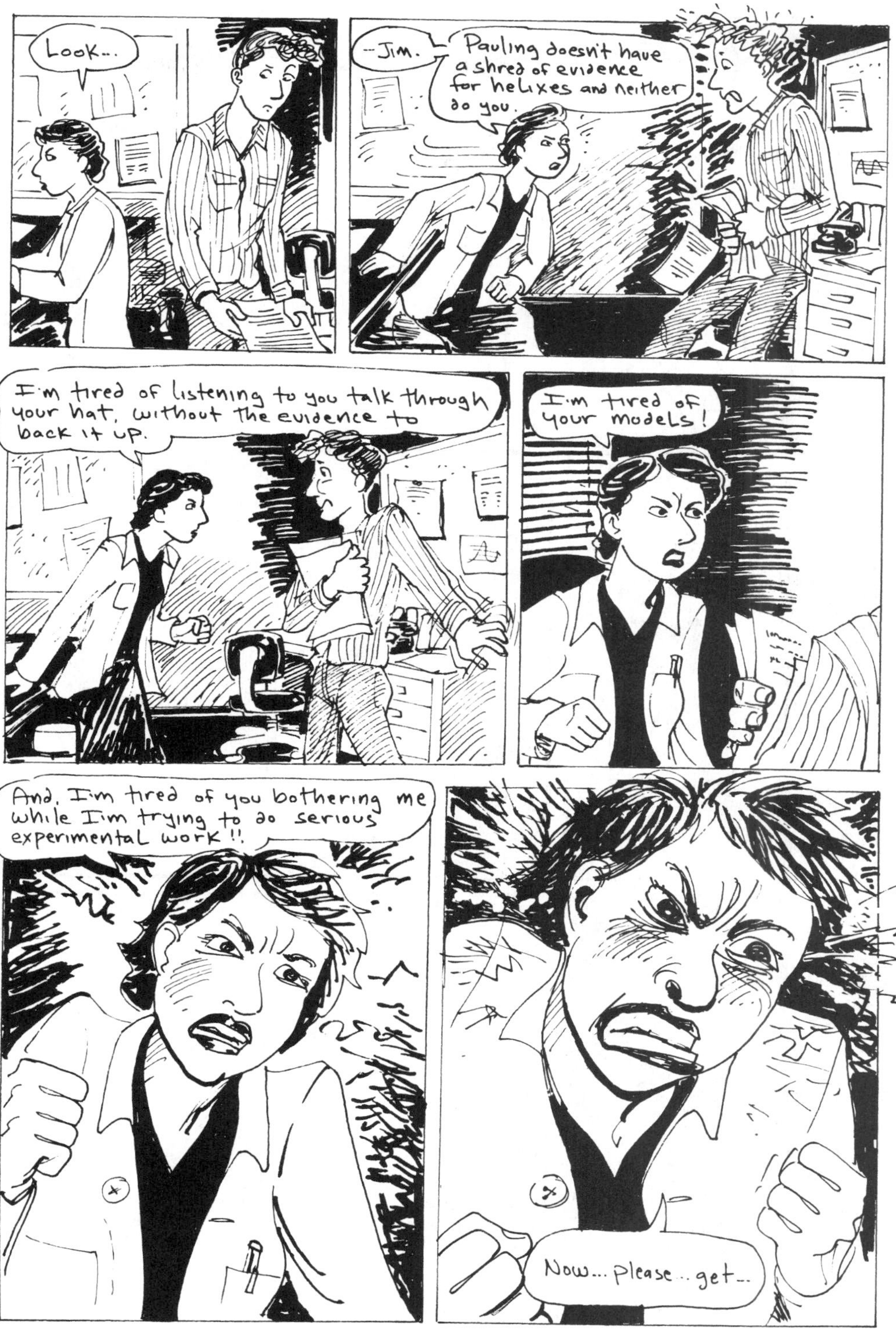
Look...
--Jim.
Pauling doesn't have a shred of evidence for helixes and neither do you.
I'm tired of listening to you talk through your hat, without the evidence to back it up.
I'm tired of your models!
And, I'm tired of you bothering me while I'm trying to do serious experimental work!!
Now... please... get...

M.F. WILKINS

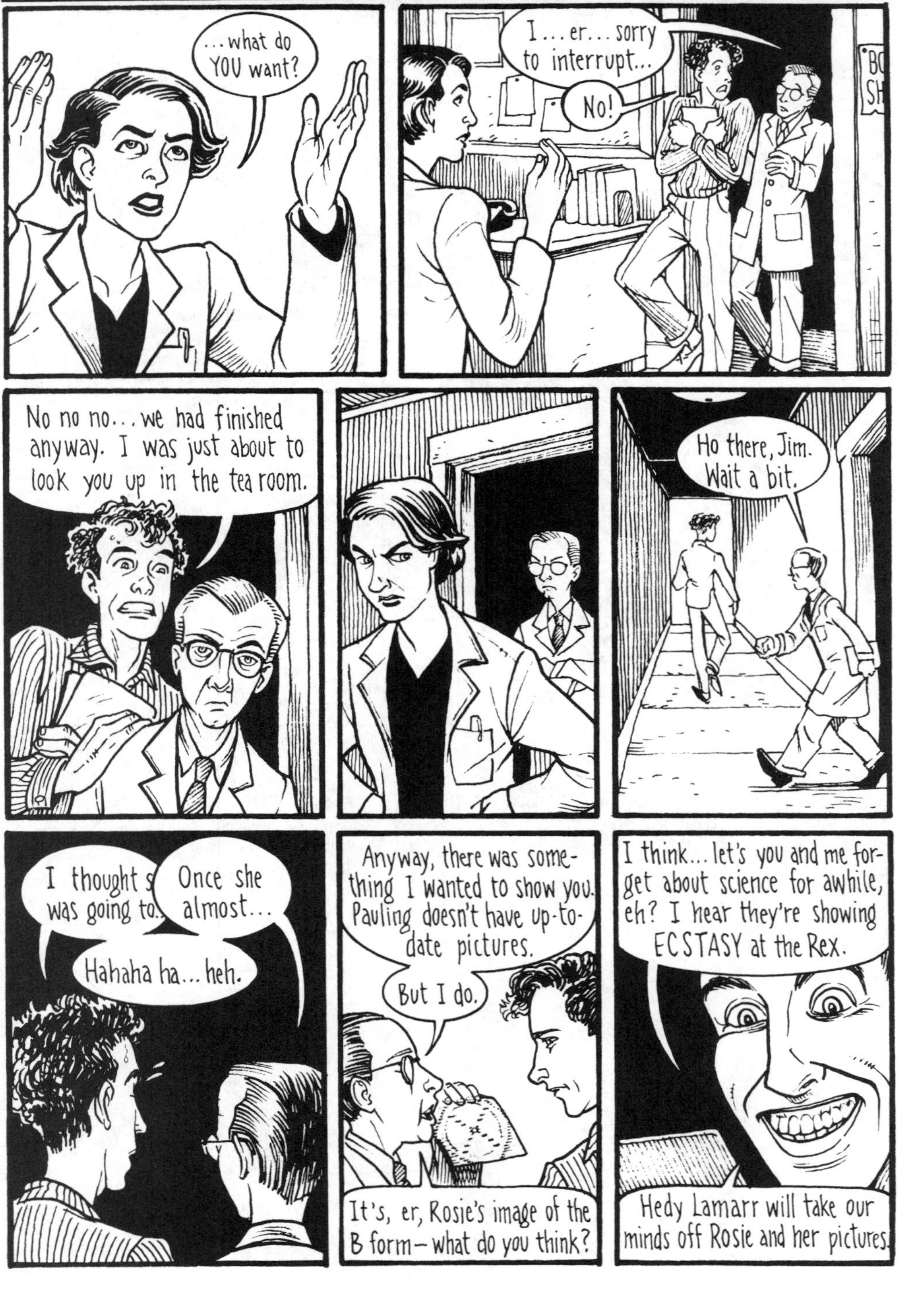
...what do YOU want?
I... er... sorry to interrupt...
No!
No no no... we had finished anyway. I was just about to look you up in the tea room.
Ho there, Jim. Wait a bit.
I thought s
was going to...
Once she almost...
Hahaha ha... heh.
Anyway, there was something I wanted to show you. Pauling doesn't have up-to-date pictures.
But I do.
It's, er, Rosie's image of the B form–what do you think?
I think... let's you and me forget about science for awhile, eh? I hear they're showing ECSTASY at the Rex.
Hedy Lamarr will take our minds off Rosie and her pictures.

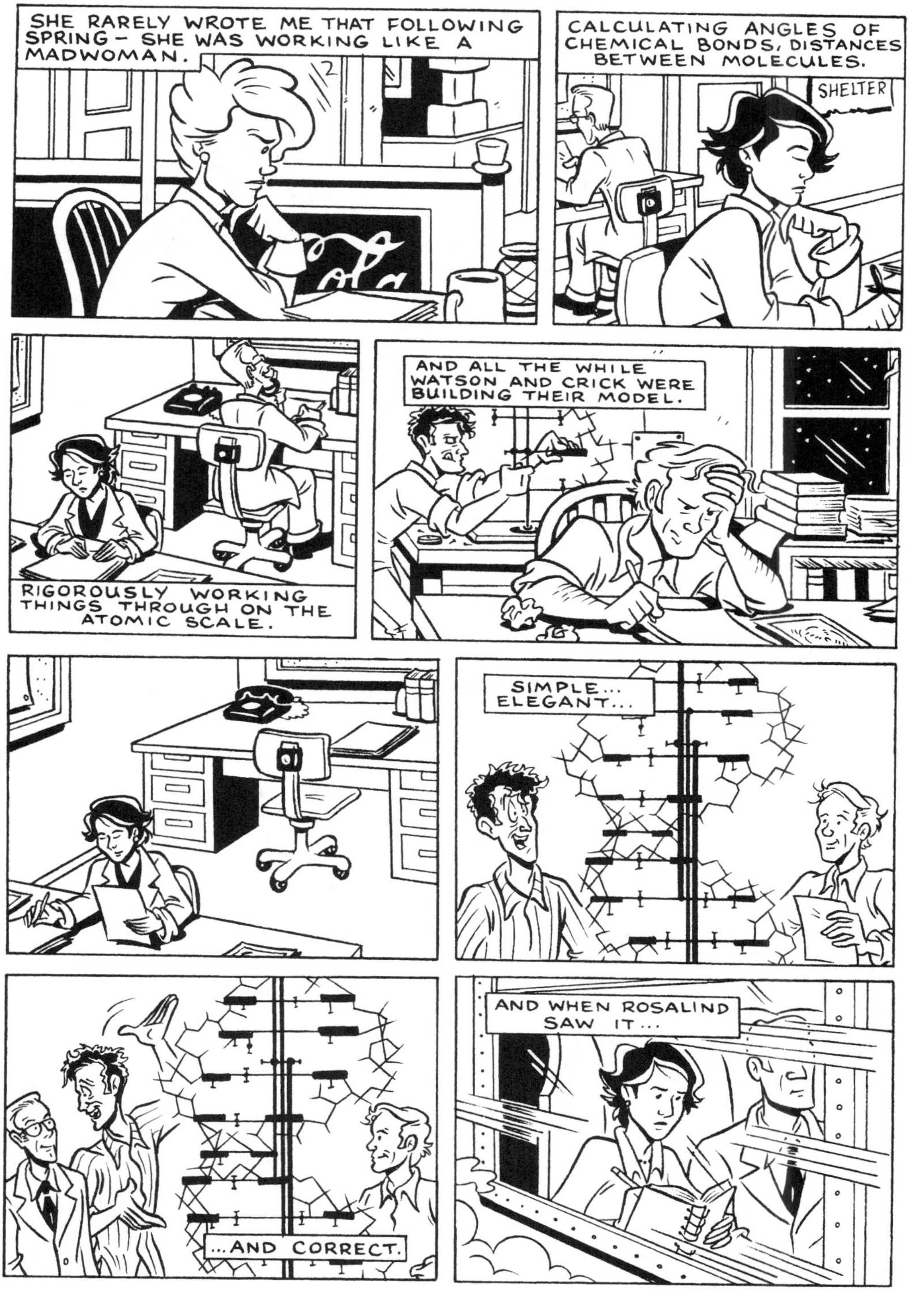
SHE RARELY WROTE ME THAT FOLLOWING SPRING - SHE WAS WORKING LIKE A MADWOMAN.
CALCULATING ANGLES OF CHEMICAL BONDS, DISTANCES BETWEEN MOLECULES.
SHELTER
RIGOROUSLY WORKING THINGS THROUGH ON THE ATOMIC SCALE.
AND ALL THE WHILE WATSON AND CRICK WERE BUILDING THEIR MODEL.
SIMPLE... ELEGANT...
...AND CORRECT.
AND WHEN ROSALIND SAW IT...

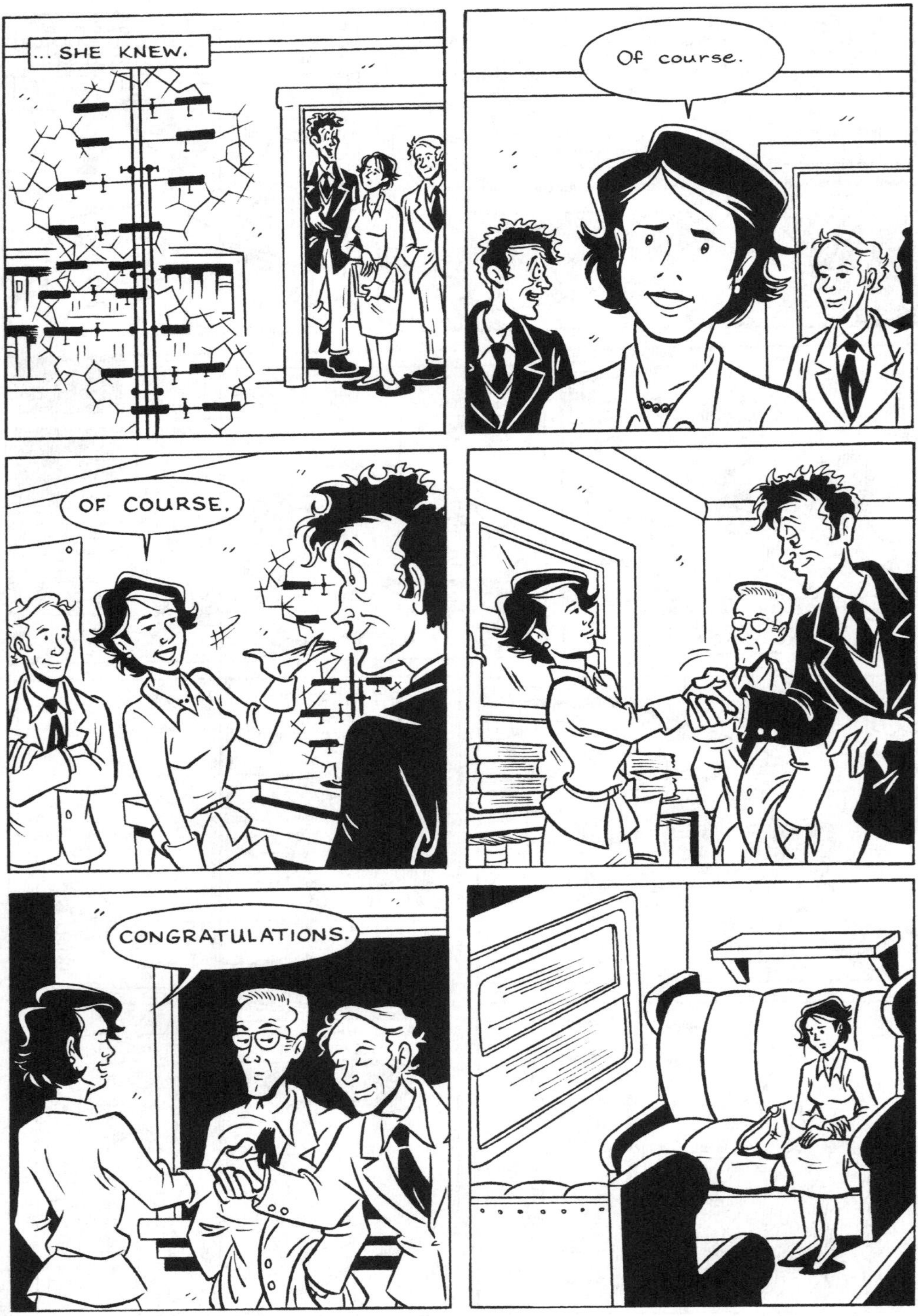
... SHE KNEW.
Of course.
OF COURSE.
CONGRATULATIONS.

FRANCIS CRICK

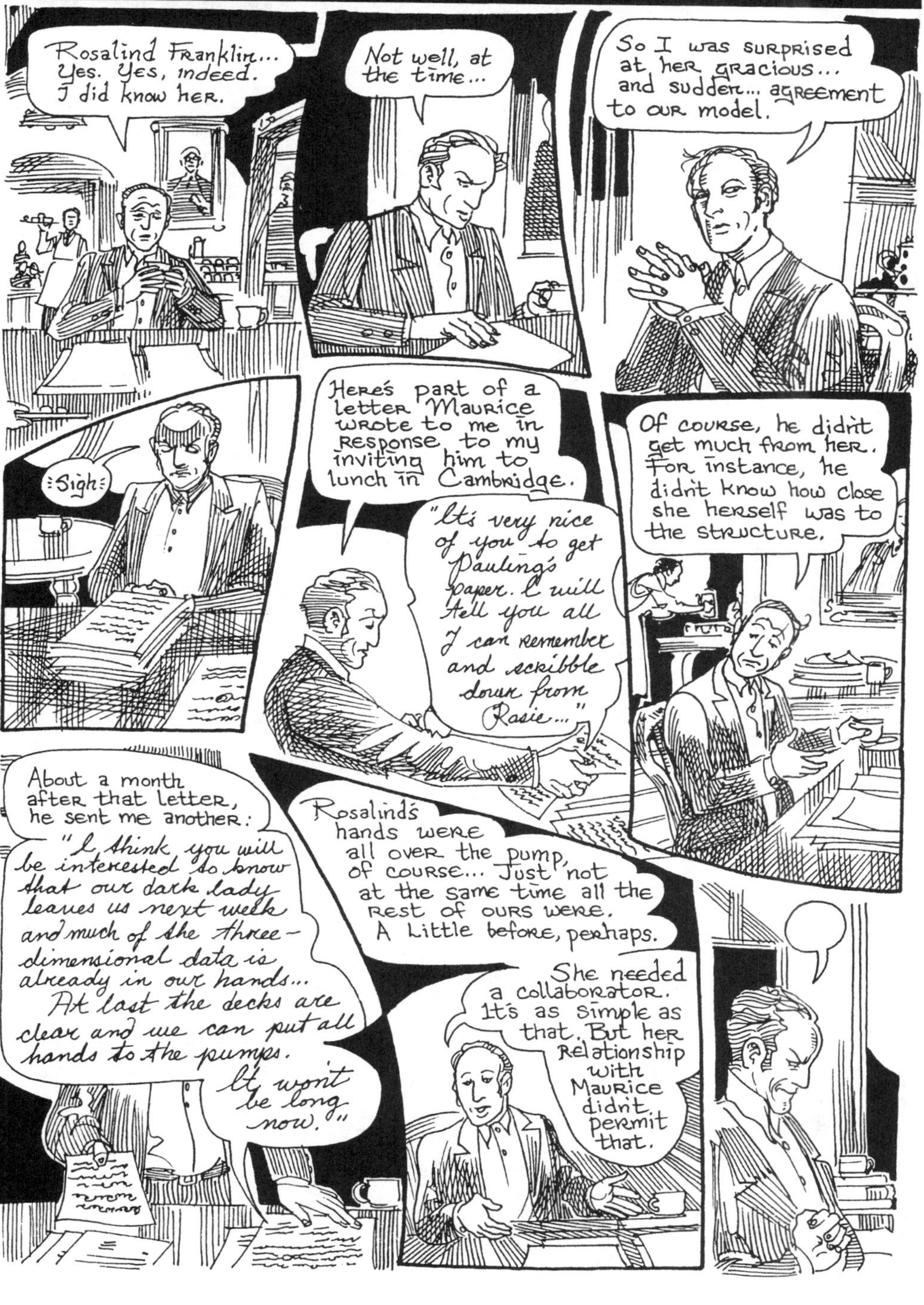

Rosalind Franklin... Yes. Yes, indeed. I did know her.
Not well, at the time...
So I was surprised at her gracious... and sudden... agreement to our model.
Sigh
Here's part of a letter Maurice wrote to me in response to my inviting him to lunch in Cambridge.
"It's very nice of you to get Pauling's paper. I will tell you all I can remember and scribble down from Rosie..."
Of course, he didn't get much from her. For instance, he didn't know how close she herself was to the structure.
About a month after that letter, he sent me another:
"I think you will be interested to know that our dark lady leaves us next week and much of the three-dimensional data is already in our hands... At last the decks are clear and we can put all hands to the pumps.
It won't be long now."
Rosalind's hands were all over the pump, of course... Just not at the same time all the rest of ours were. A little before, perhaps.
She needed a collaborator. It's as simple as that. But her relationship with Maurice didn't permit that.

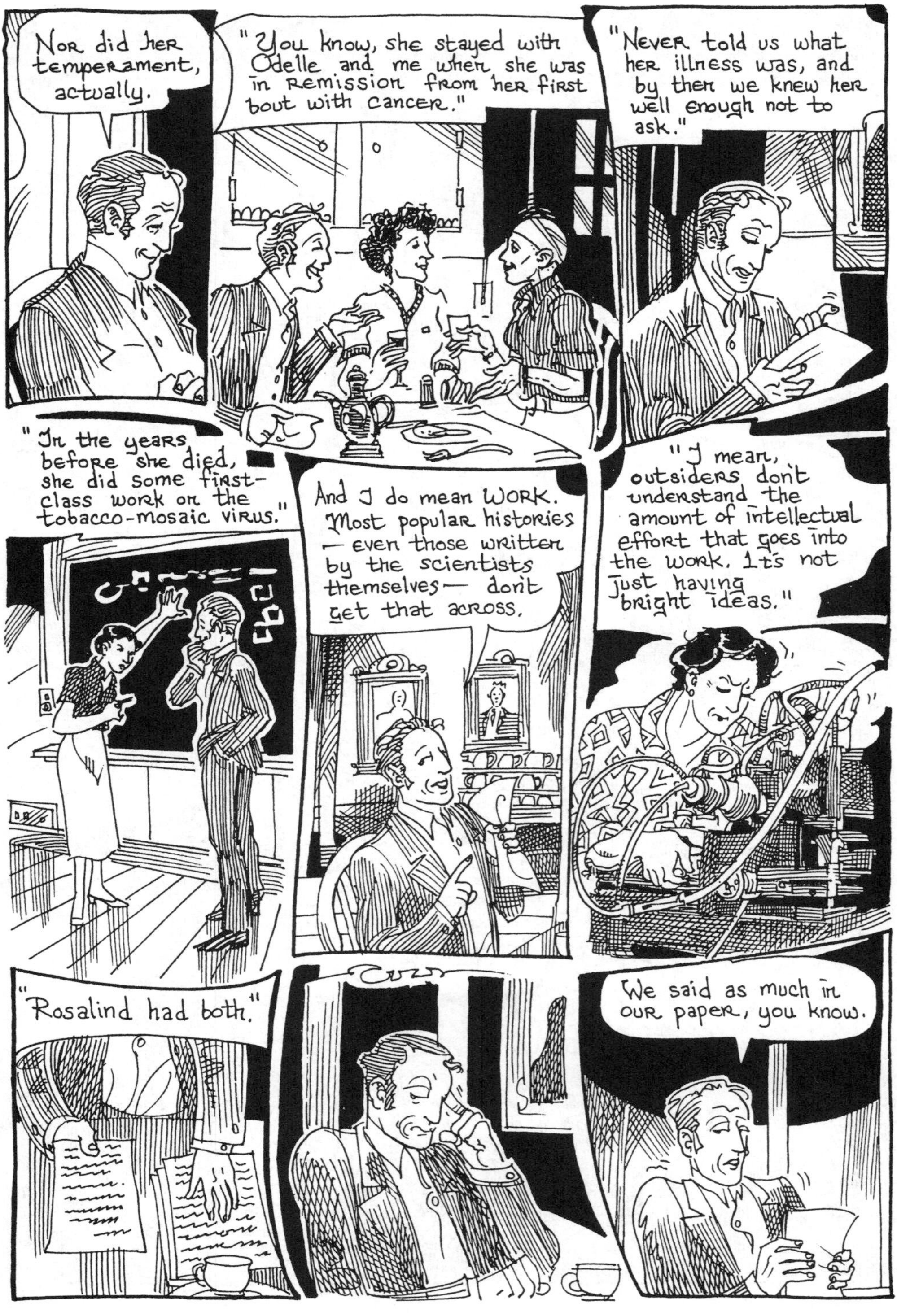
Nor did her temperament, actually.
"You know, she stayed with Odelle and me when she was in remission from her first bout with cancer."
"Never told us what her illness was, and by then we knew her well enough not to ask."
"In the years before she died, she did some first-class work on the tobacco-mosaic virus."
And I do mean WORK. Most popular histories — even those written by the scientists themselves — don't get that across.
"I mean, outsiders don't understand the amount of intellectual effort that goes into the work. It's not just having bright ideas."
"Rosalind had both."
We said as much in our paper, you know.

HERE'S HOW THAT FAMOUS PAPER BY WATSON & CRICK ENDED:

tap tap

"It has not escaped our notice that the specific pairing we have postulated immediately suggests a possible copying mechanism for the genetic material."

THOUGH THEY WEREN'T CONFIDANT ENOUGH TO STATE IT OUTRIGHT, THEY WANTED TO ESTABLISH THEIR CLAIM TO THE IDEA THAT DNA IS THE KEY TO GENETIC CODING.

AS OTHERS HAVE SAID, A REMARKABLY COY BIT OF WRITING.

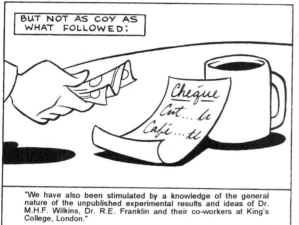

BUT NOT AS COY AS WHAT FOLLOWED:

Chèque
Cut ... la
Café ... te

"We have also been stimulated by a knowledge of the general nature of the unpublished experimental results and ideas of Dr. M.H.F. Wilkins, Dr. R.E. Franklin and their co-workers at King's College, London."

'STIMULATED'? 'UNPUBLISHED'?

INDEED.

WHEN IT CAME TIME TO AWARD THE NOBEL PRIZE FOR THE DISCOVERY, SIR LAWRENCE BRAGG INSISTED KING'S COLLEGE SHOULD SHARE IT.

SO WILKINS GOT THE HONORS.

AND FOR ALL THEIR ENMITY FOR EACH OTHER, HE WAS THE ONLY ONE TO MENTION, MUCH LESS PRAISE, ROSALIND IN HIS NOBEL LECTURE.

WHY WILKINS? WELL, ROSALIND DIED YOUNG.

BIÈRE MORITZ

CAFE · RESTAURANT

AND THEY DON'T AWARD THE NOBEL PRIZE POSTHUMOUSLY.

I DON'T KNOW WHETHER THAT'S WHY ROSALIND WASN'T HONORED.

BIÈRE MORITZ

CAFE · RESTAURANT

BUT...

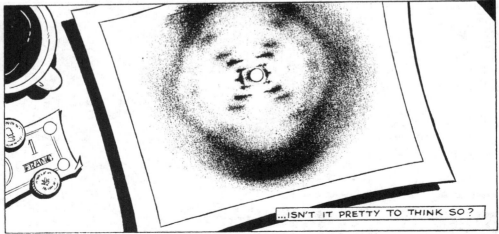

...ISN'T IT PRETTY TO THINK SO?

BARBARA McCLINTOCK

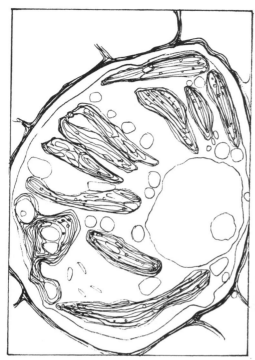

COLD SPRING HARBOR, 1985

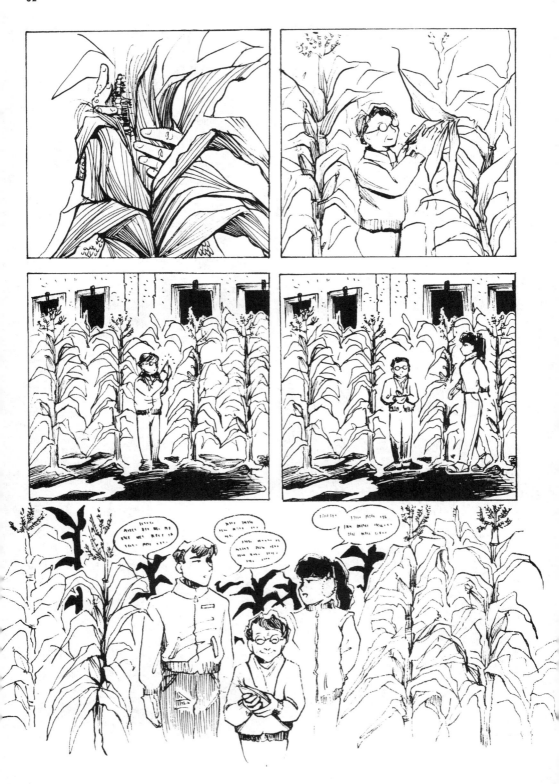

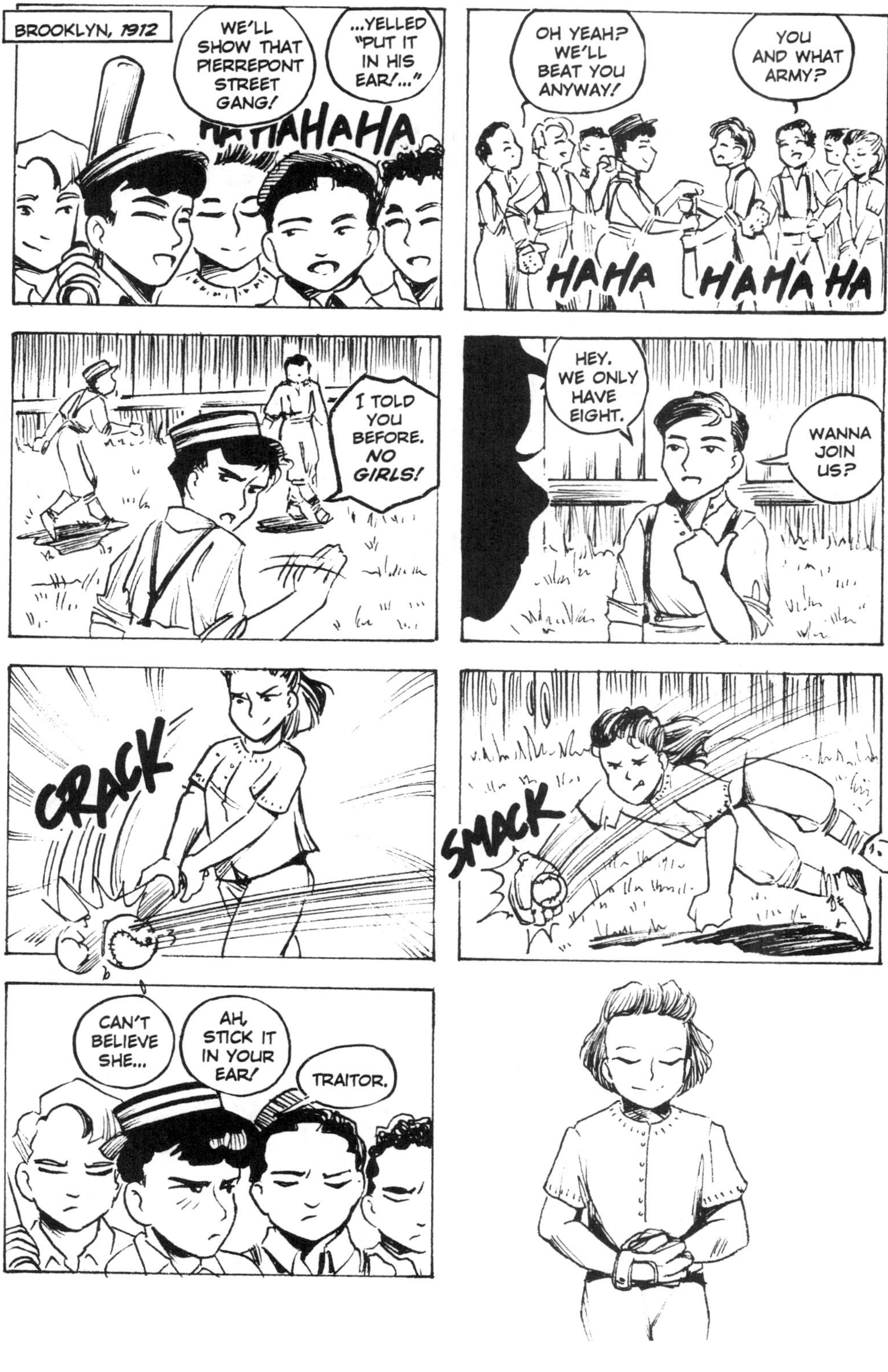
BROOKLYN, 1912
WE'LL SHOW THAT PIERREPONT STREET GANG!
...YELLED "PUT IT IN HIS EAR!..."
HAHAHAHA
OH YEAH? WE'LL BEAT YOU ANYWAY!
YOU AND WHAT ARMY?
HAHA HAHAHA
I TOLD YOU BEFORE. NO GIRLS!
HEY. WE ONLY HAVE EIGHT.
WANNA JOIN US?
CRACK
SMACK
CAN'T BELIEVE SHE...
AH, STICK IT IN YOUR EAR!
TRAITOR.

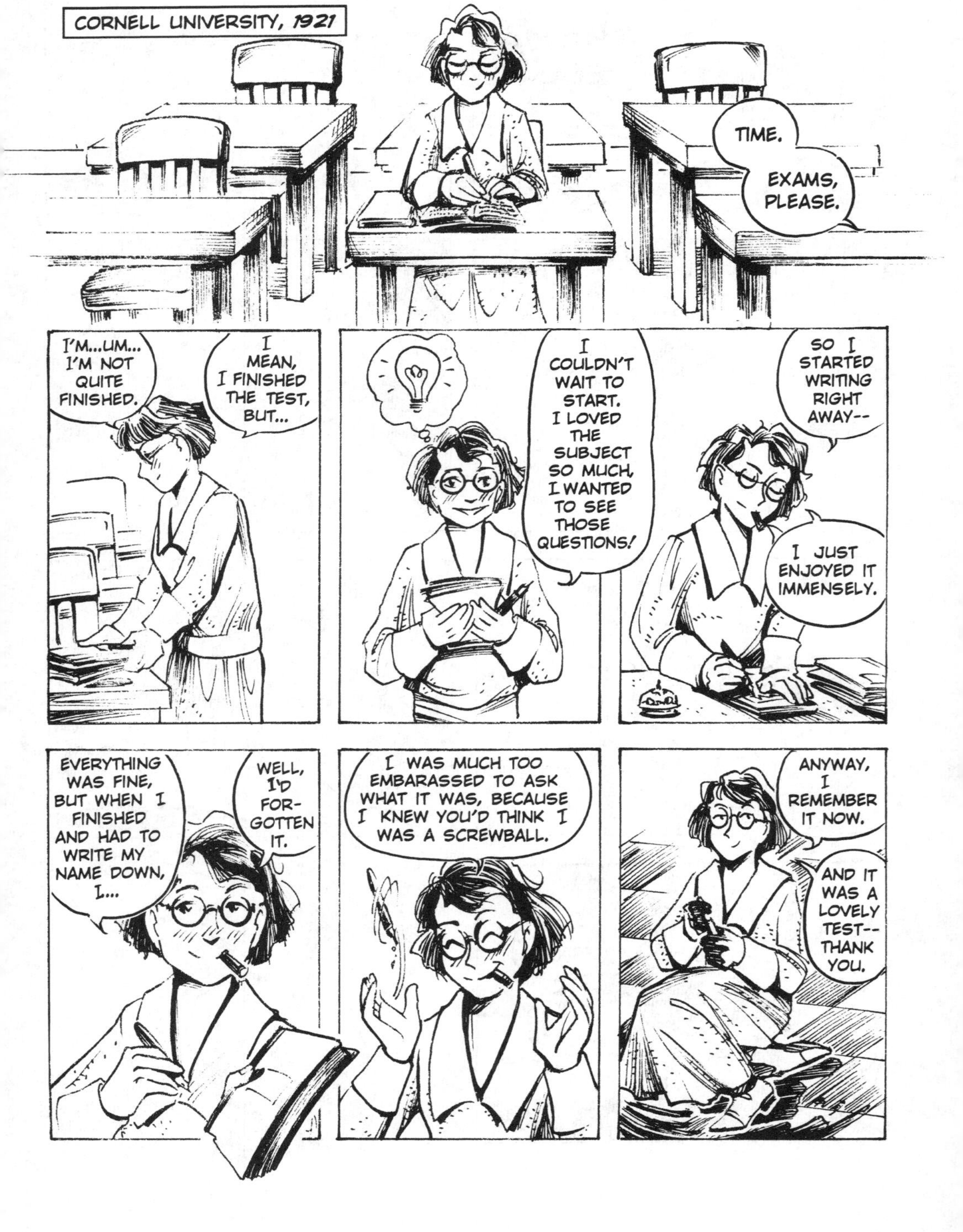
CORNELL UNIVERSITY, 1921
TIME.
EXAMS, PLEASE.
I'M...UM... I'M NOT QUITE FINISHED.
I MEAN, I FINISHED THE TEST, BUT...
I COULDN'T WAIT TO START. I LOVED THE SUBJECT SO MUCH, I WANTED TO SEE THOSE QUESTIONS!
SO I STARTED WRITING RIGHT AWAY--
I JUST ENJOYED IT IMMENSELY.
EVERYTHING WAS FINE, BUT WHEN I FINISHED AND HAD TO WRITE MY NAME DOWN, I...
WELL, I'D FOR-GOTTEN IT.
I WAS MUCH TOO EMBARASSED TO ASK WHAT IT WAS, BECAUSE I KNEW YOU'D THINK I WAS A SCREWBALL.
ANYWAY, I REMEMBER IT NOW.
AND IT WAS A LOVELY TEST--THANK YOU.

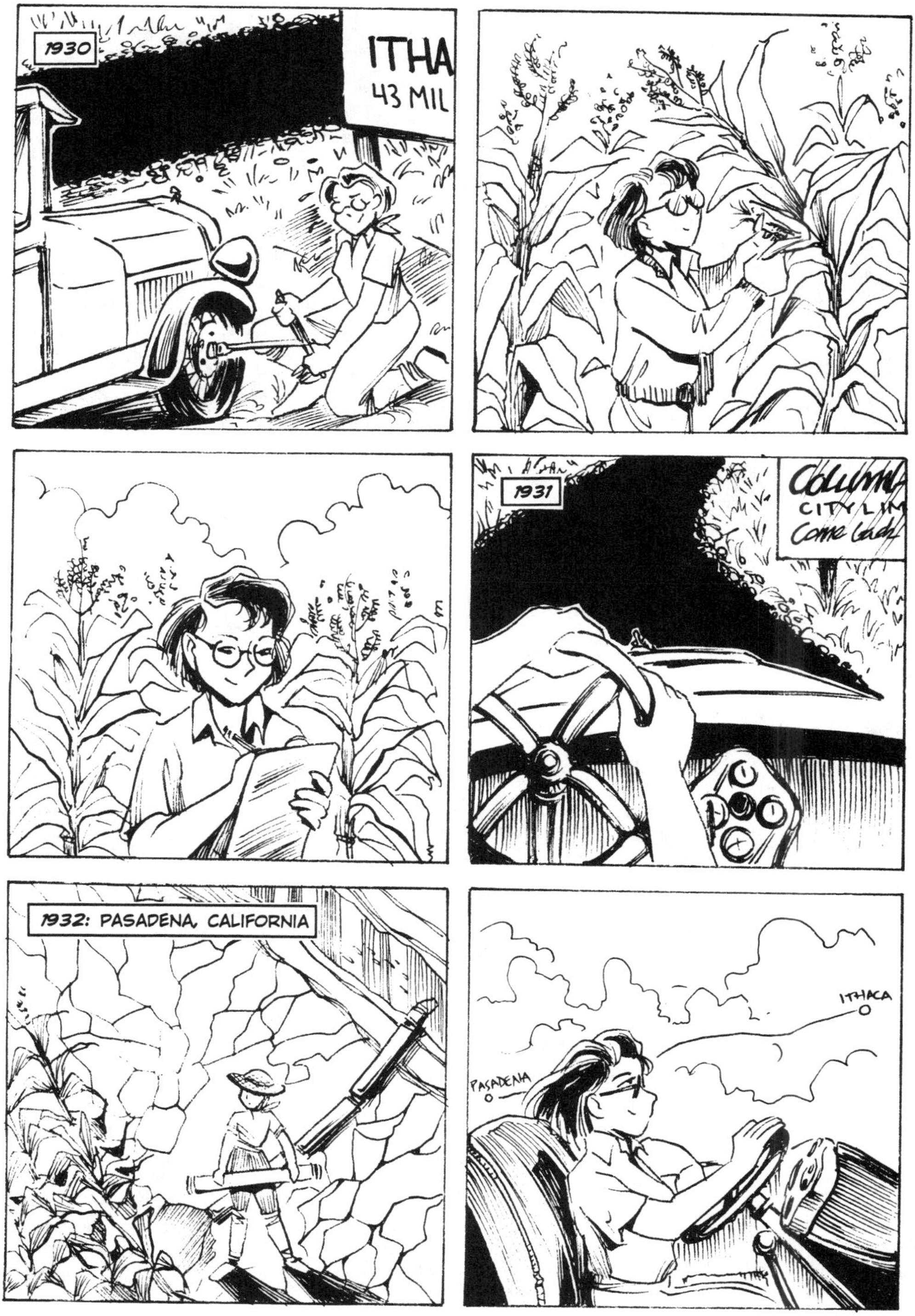
1930
ITHA
43 MIL
1931
CITY LIM
1932: PASADENA, CALIFORNIA
ITHACA
PASADENA

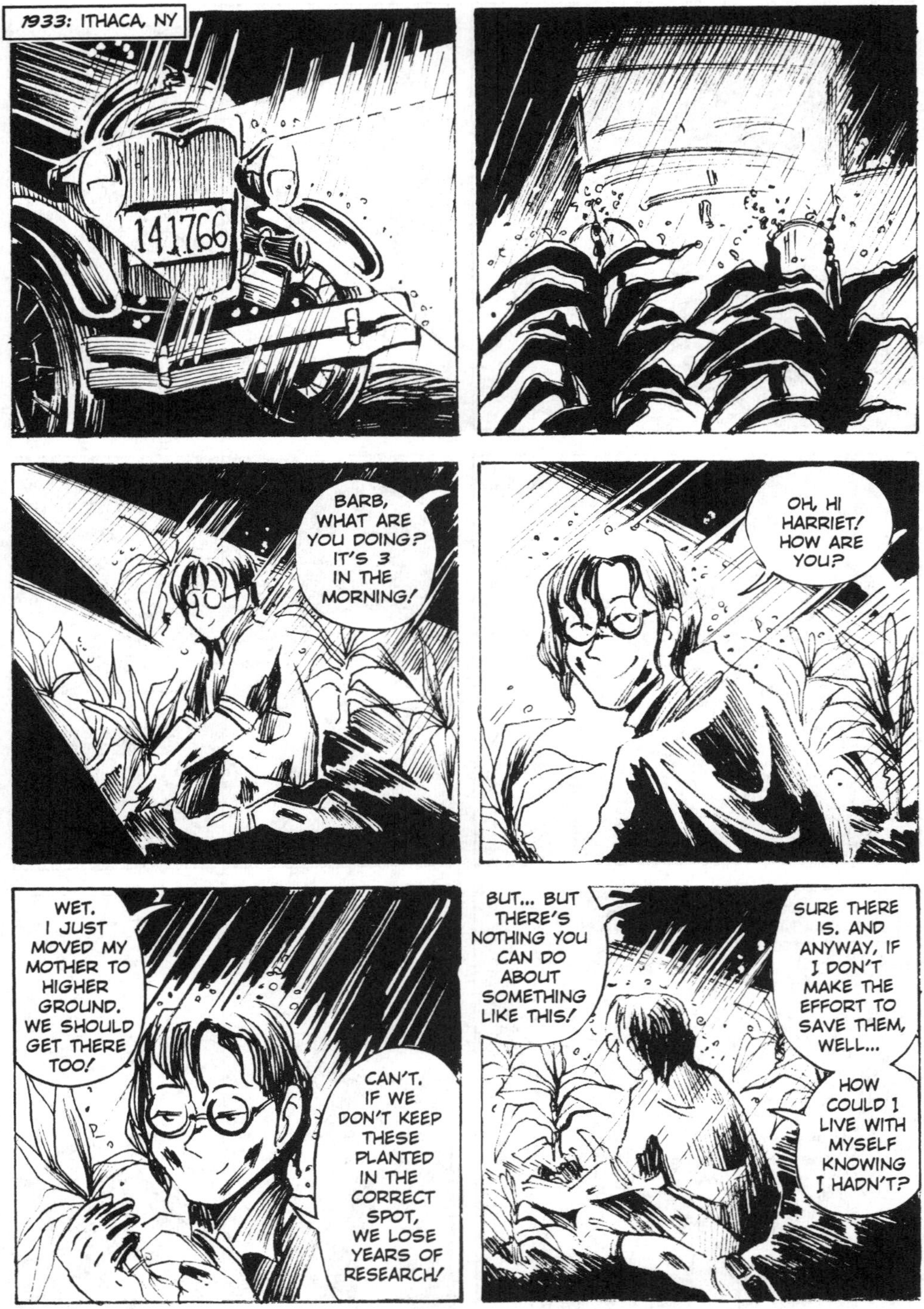
1933: ITHACA, NY
141766
BARB, WHAT ARE YOU DOING? IT'S 3 IN THE MORNING!
OH, HI HARRIET! HOW ARE YOU?
WET. I JUST MOVED MY MOTHER TO HIGHER GROUND. WE SHOULD GET THERE TOO!
CAN'T. IF WE DON'T KEEP THESE PLANTED IN THE CORRECT SPOT, WE LOSE YEARS OF RESEARCH!
BUT... BUT THERE'S NOTHING YOU CAN DO ABOUT SOMETHING LIKE THIS!
SURE THERE IS. AND ANYWAY, IF I DON'T MAKE THE EFFORT TO SAVE THEM, WELL...
HOW COULD I LIVE WITH MYSELF KNOWING I HADN'T?

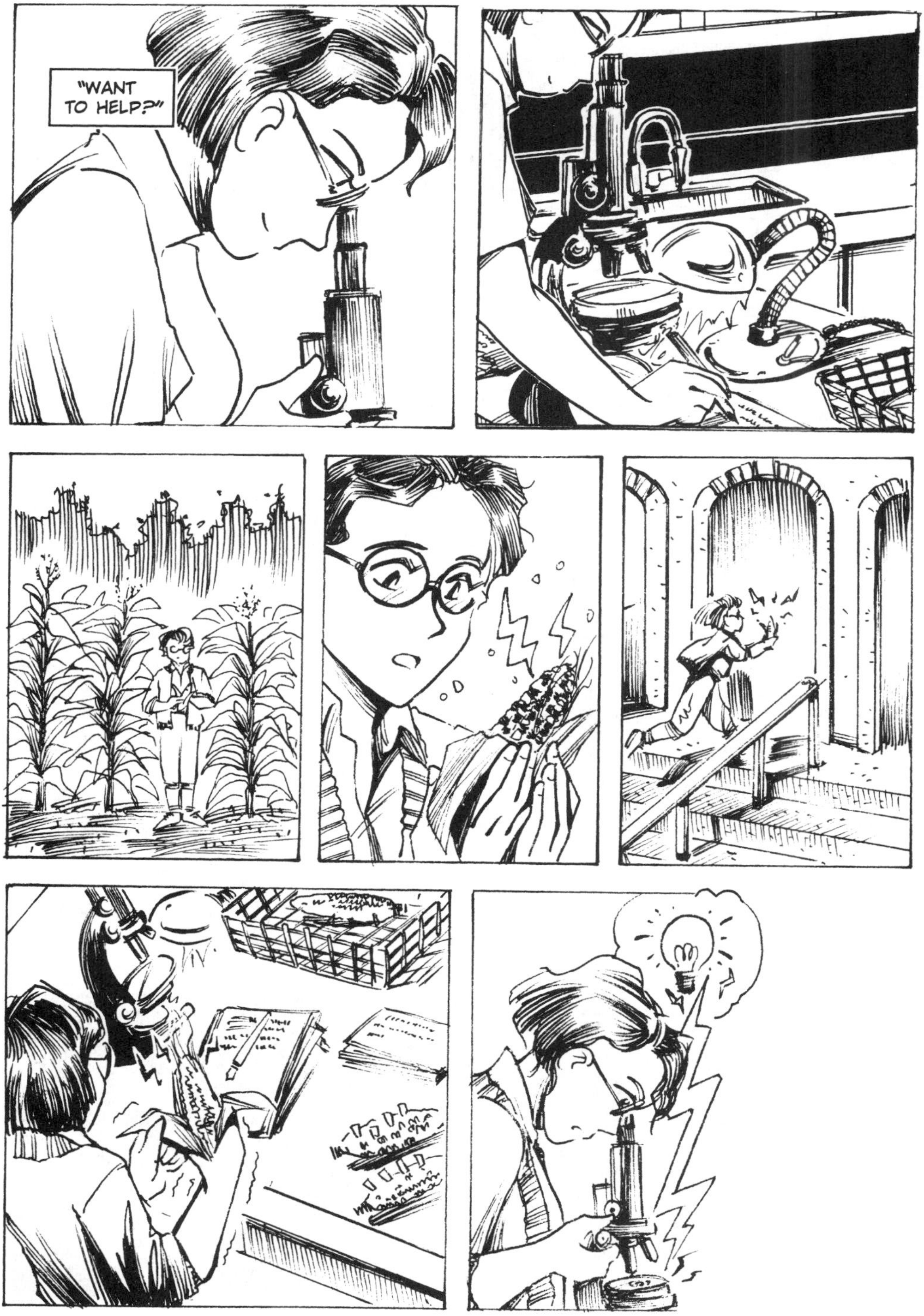
"WANT TO HELP?"

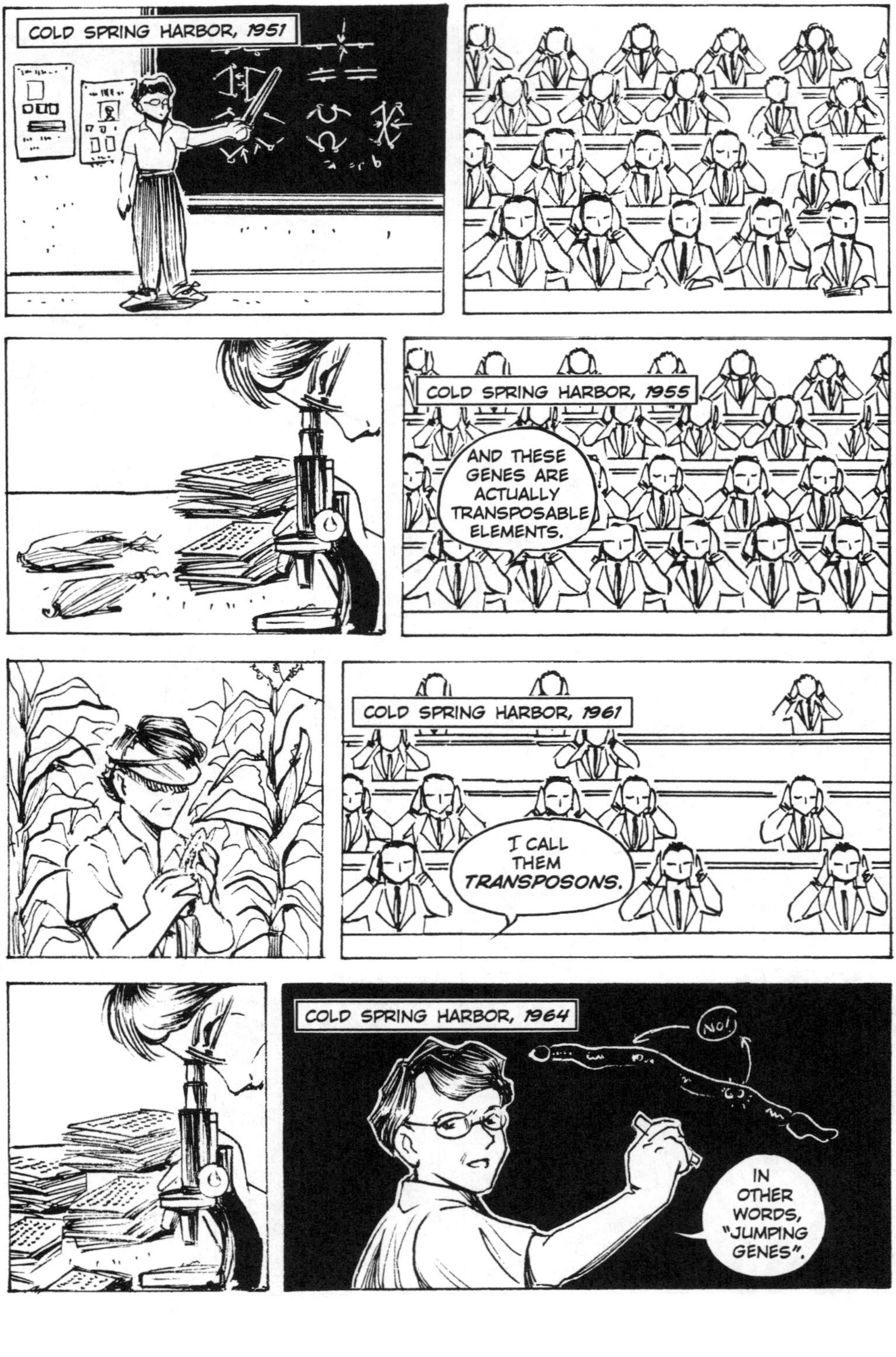
COLD SPRING HARBOR, 1951
COLD SPRING HARBOR, 1955
AND THESE GENES ARE ACTUALLY TRANSPOSABLE ELEMENTS.
COLD SPRING HARBOR, 1961
I CALL THEM *TRANSPOSONS.*
COLD SPRING HARBOR, 1964
NO!
IN OTHER WORDS, "JUMPING GENES".

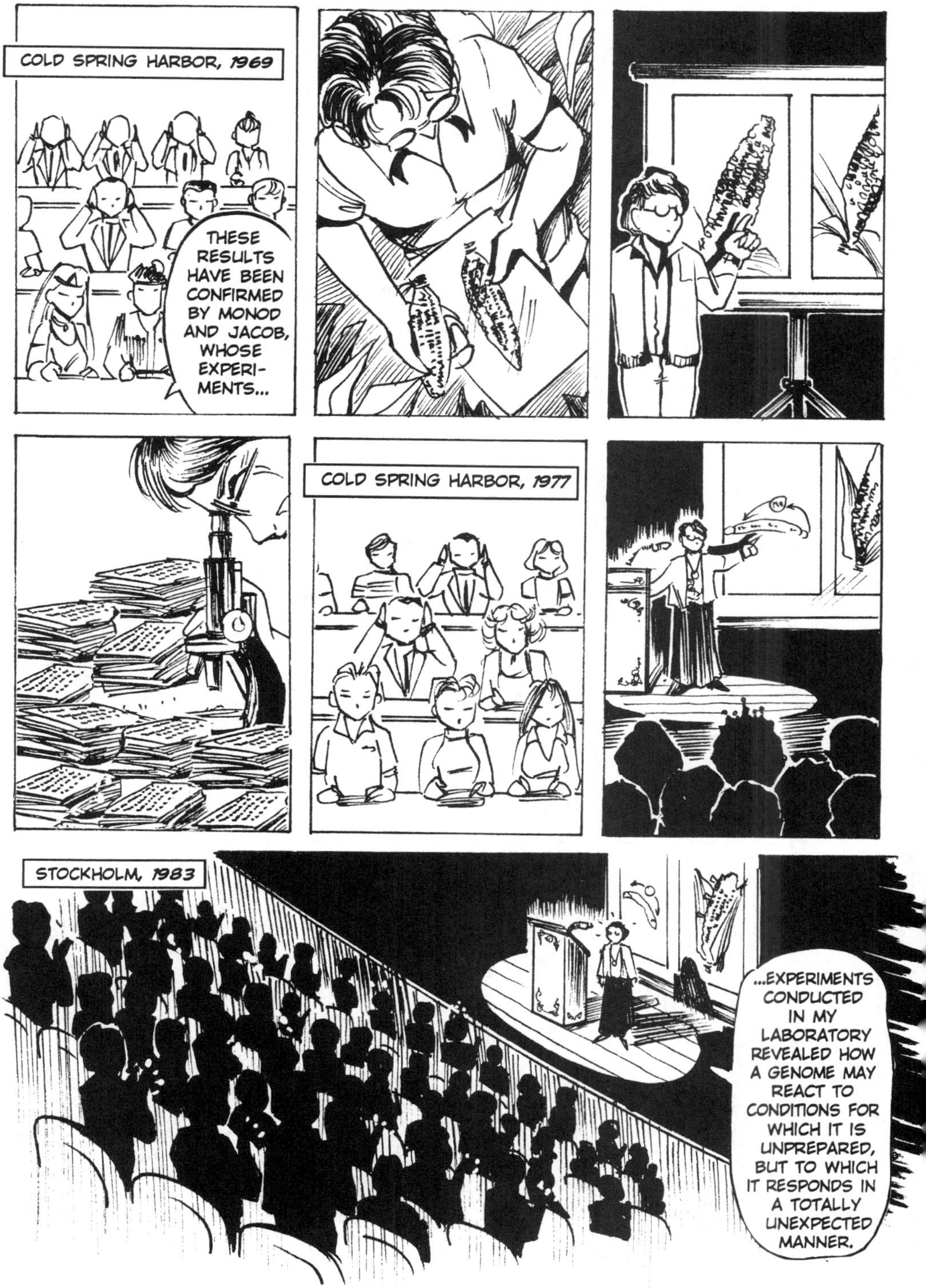
COLD SPRING HARBOR, 1969
THESE RESULTS HAVE BEEN CONFIRMED BY MONOD AND JACOB, WHOSE EXPERI- MENTS...
COLD SPRING HARBOR, 1977
STOCKHOLM, 1983
...EXPERIMENTS CONDUCTED IN MY LABORATORY REVEALED HOW A GENOME MAY REACT TO CONDITIONS FOR WHICH IT IS UNPREPARED, BUT TO WHICH IT RESPONDS IN A TOTALLY UNEXPECTED MANNER.

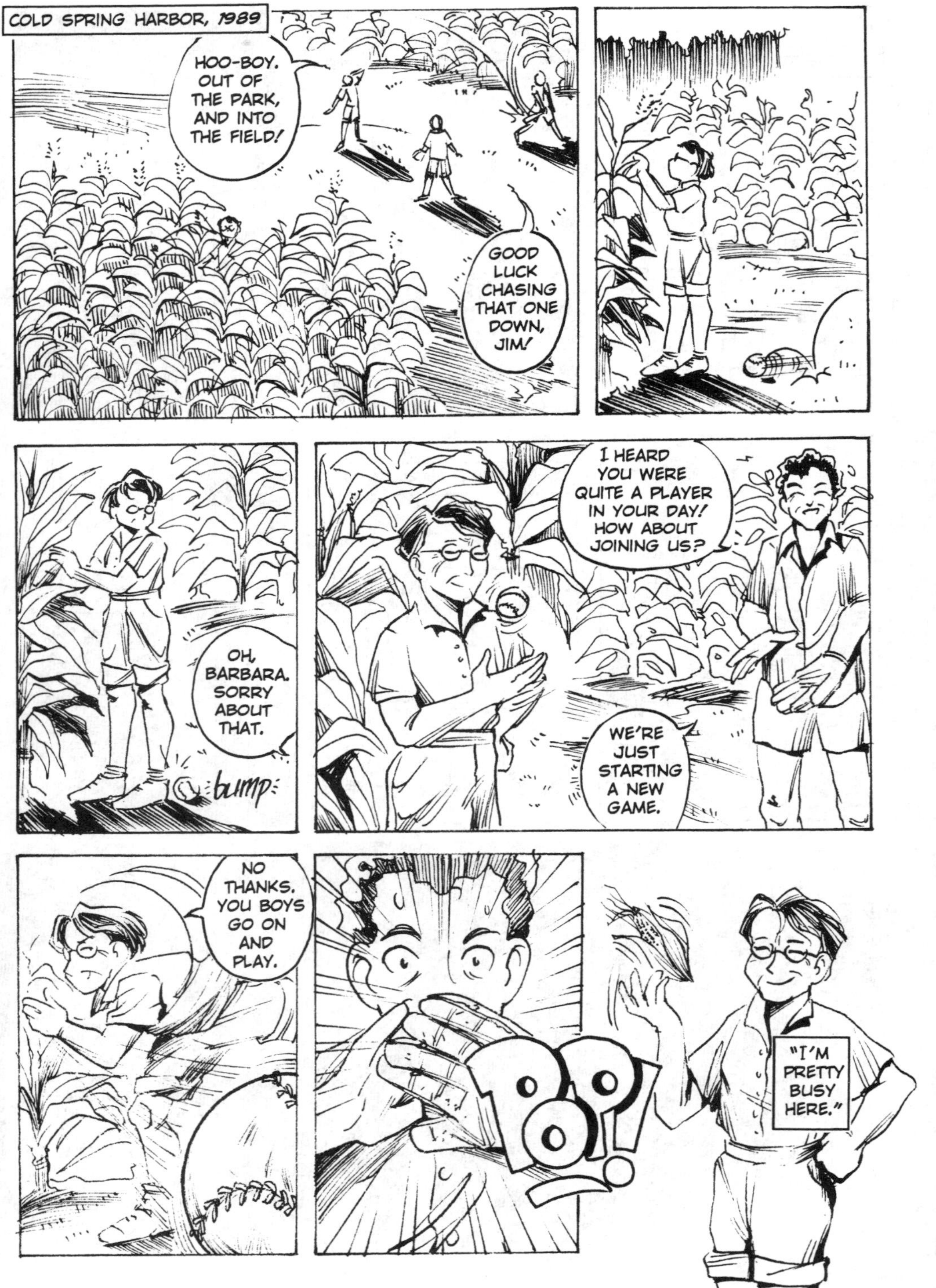
COLD SPRING HARBOR, 1989
HOO-BOY. OUT OF THE PARK, AND INTO THE FIELD!
GOOD LUCK CHASING THAT ONE DOWN, JIM!
OH, BARBARA. SORRY ABOUT THAT.
bump
I HEARD YOU WERE QUITE A PLAYER IN YOUR DAY! HOW ABOUT JOINING US?
WE'RE JUST STARTING A NEW GAME.
NO THANKS. YOU BOYS GO ON AND PLAY.
POP!
"I'M PRETTY BUSY HERE."

BIRUTÉ GALDIKAS

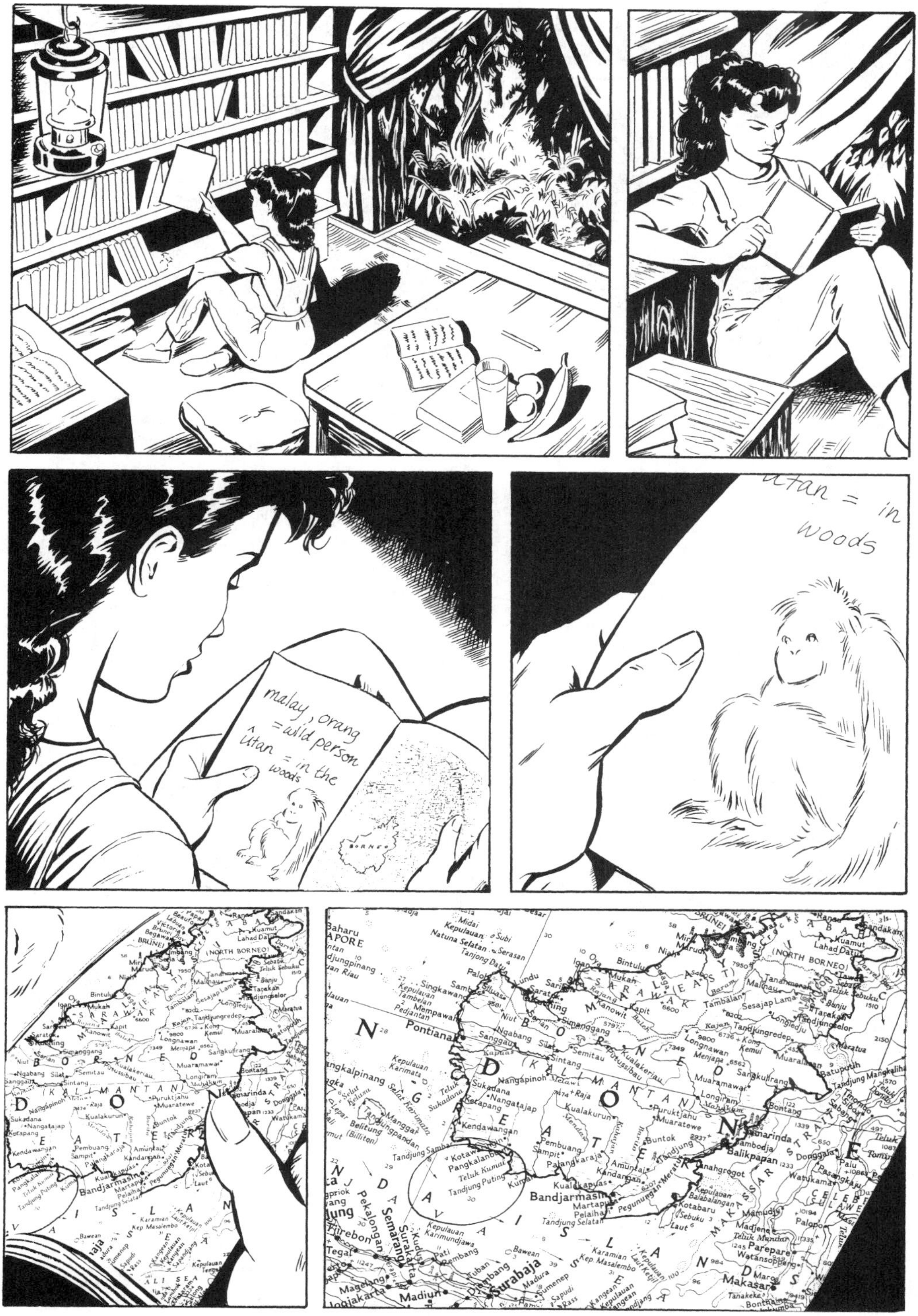
malay, orang
= wild person
ûtan = in the
woods
BORNEO
utan = in
woods
BORNEO
KALIMANTAN
SARAWAK
(NORTH BORNEO)
INDONESIA
Pontianak
Bandjarmasin
Balikpapan
Samarinda
Surabaja
Semarang
Makasar
Teluk Kumai
Tandjung Puting
Pangkalanbun
Kotawaringin
JAVA SEA
MAKASAR STRAIT

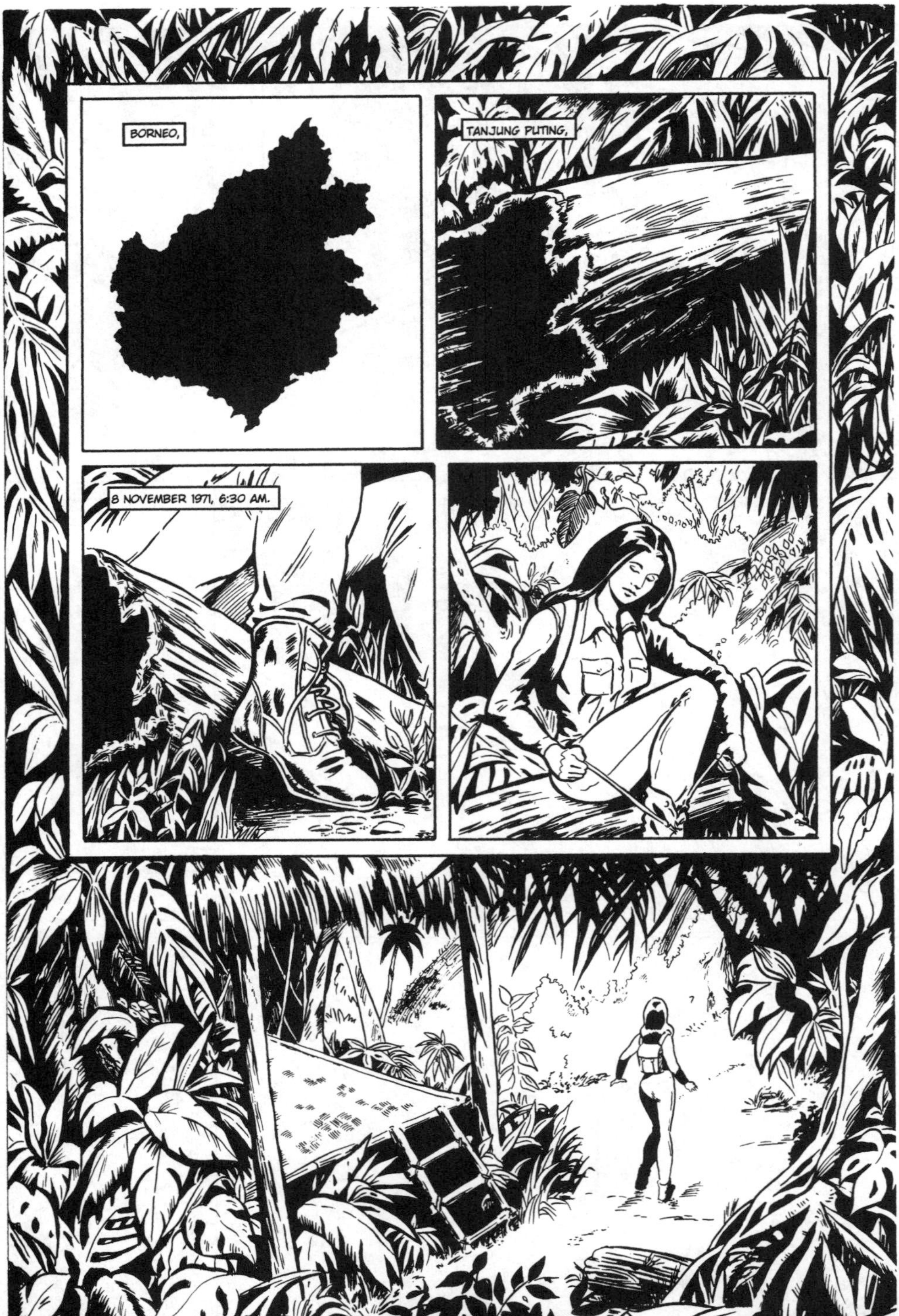
BORNEO,
TANJUNG PUTING,
8 NOVEMBER 1971, 6:30 AM.

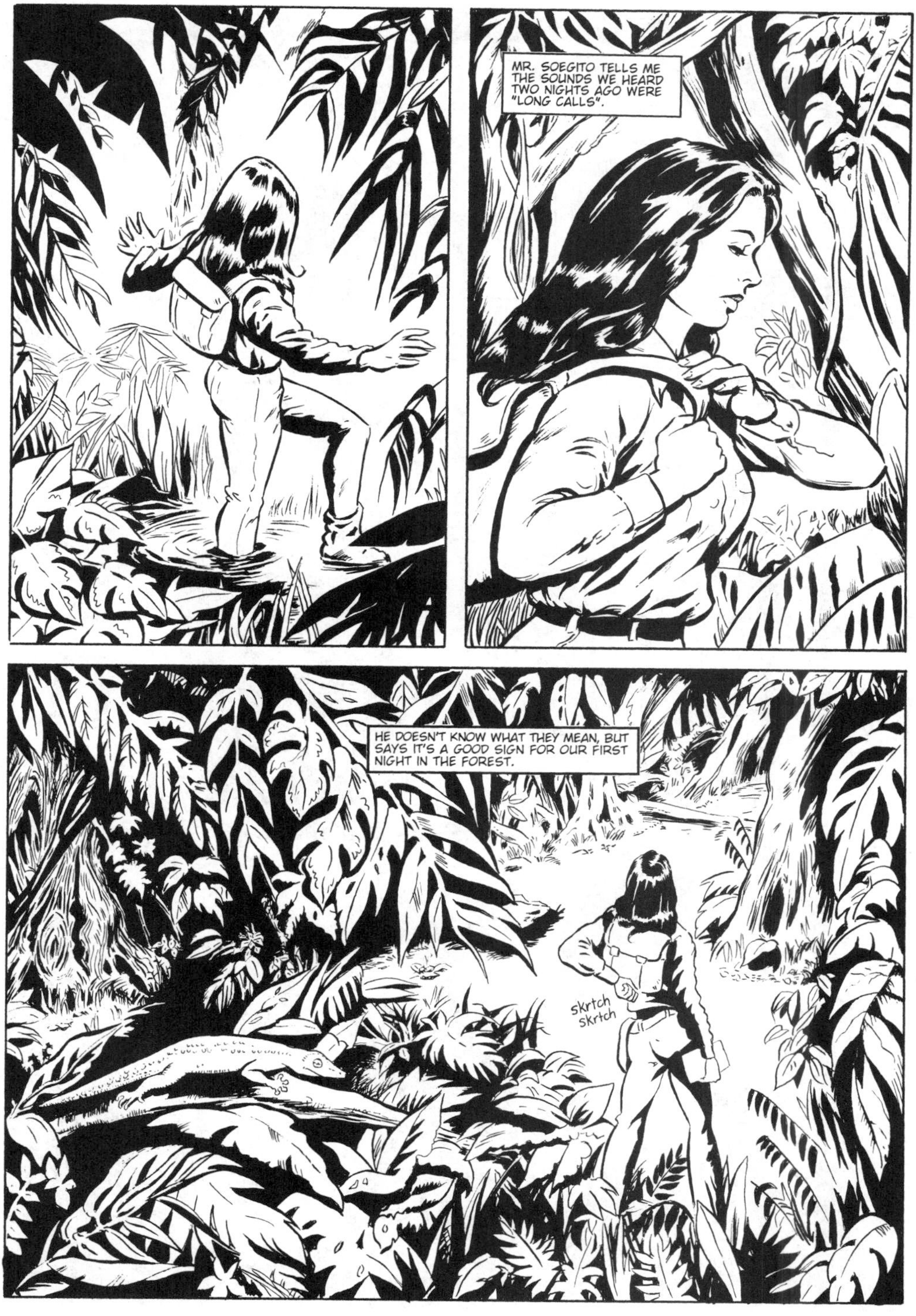
MR. SOEGITO TELLS ME THE SOUNDS WE HEARD TWO NIGHTS AGO WERE "LONG CALLS".
HE DOESN'T KNOW WHAT THEY MEAN, BUT SAYS IT'S A GOOD SIGN FOR OUR FIRST NIGHT IN THE FOREST.
skrtch skrtch

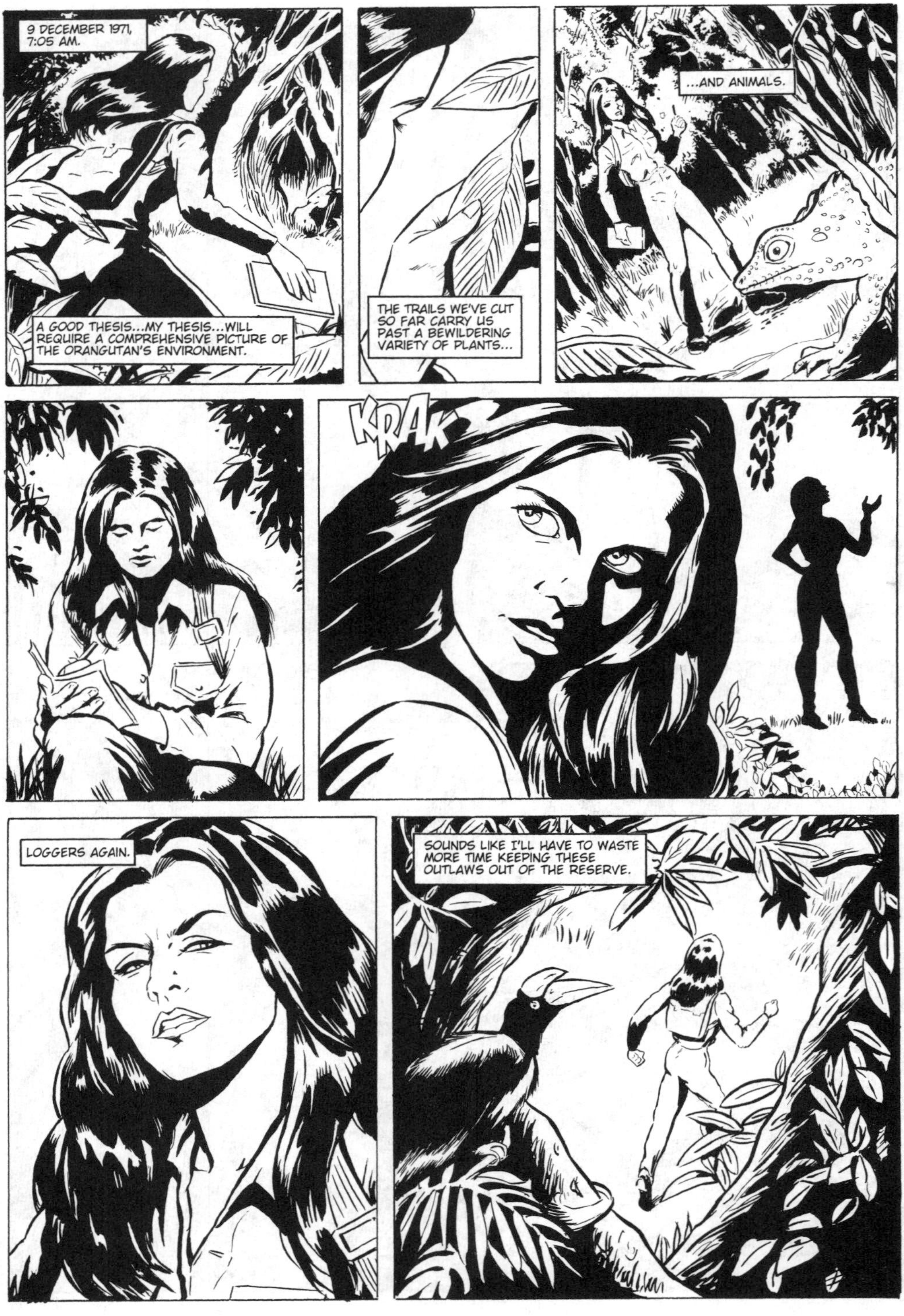
9 DECEMBER 1971, 7:05 AM.
A GOOD THESIS...MY THESIS...WILL REQUIRE A COMPREHENSIVE PICTURE OF THE ORANGUTAN'S ENVIRONMENT.
THE TRAILS WE'VE CUT SO FAR CARRY US PAST A BEWILDERING VARIETY OF PLANTS...
...AND ANIMALS.
KRAK
LOGGERS AGAIN.
SOUNDS LIKE I'LL HAVE TO WASTE MORE TIME KEEPING THESE OUTLAWS OUT OF THE RESERVE.

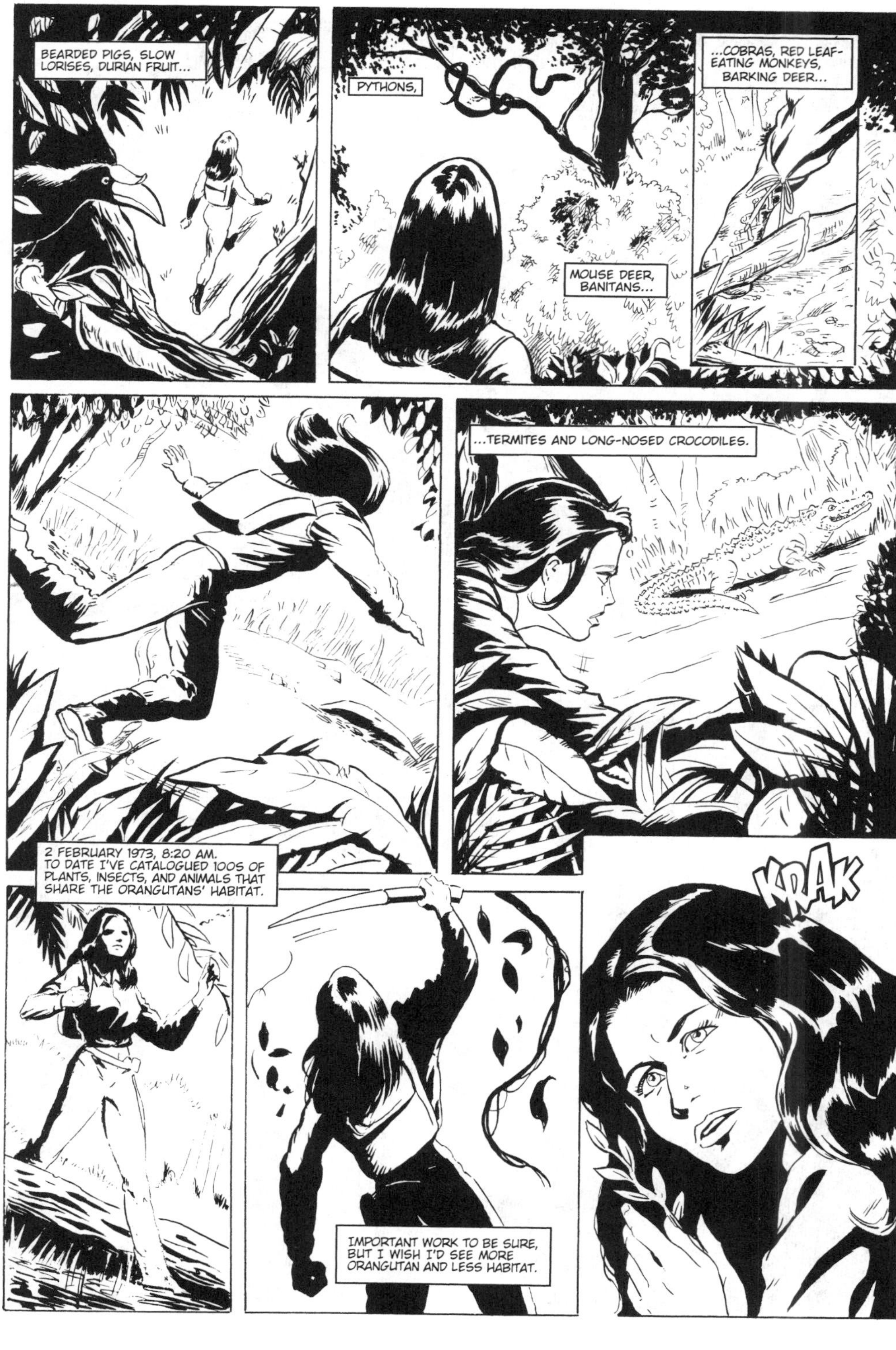
BEARDED PIGS, SLOW LORISES, DURIAN FRUIT...
PYTHONS,
MOUSE DEER, BANITANS...
...COBRAS, RED LEAF-EATING MONKEYS, BARKING DEER...
...TERMITES AND LONG-NOSED CROCODILES.
2 FEBRUARY 1973, 8:20 AM. TO DATE I'VE CATALOGUED 100S OF PLANTS, INSECTS, AND ANIMALS THAT SHARE THE ORANGUTANS' HABITAT.
KRAK
IMPORTANT WORK TO BE SURE, BUT I WISH I'D SEE MORE ORANGUTAN AND LESS HABITAT.

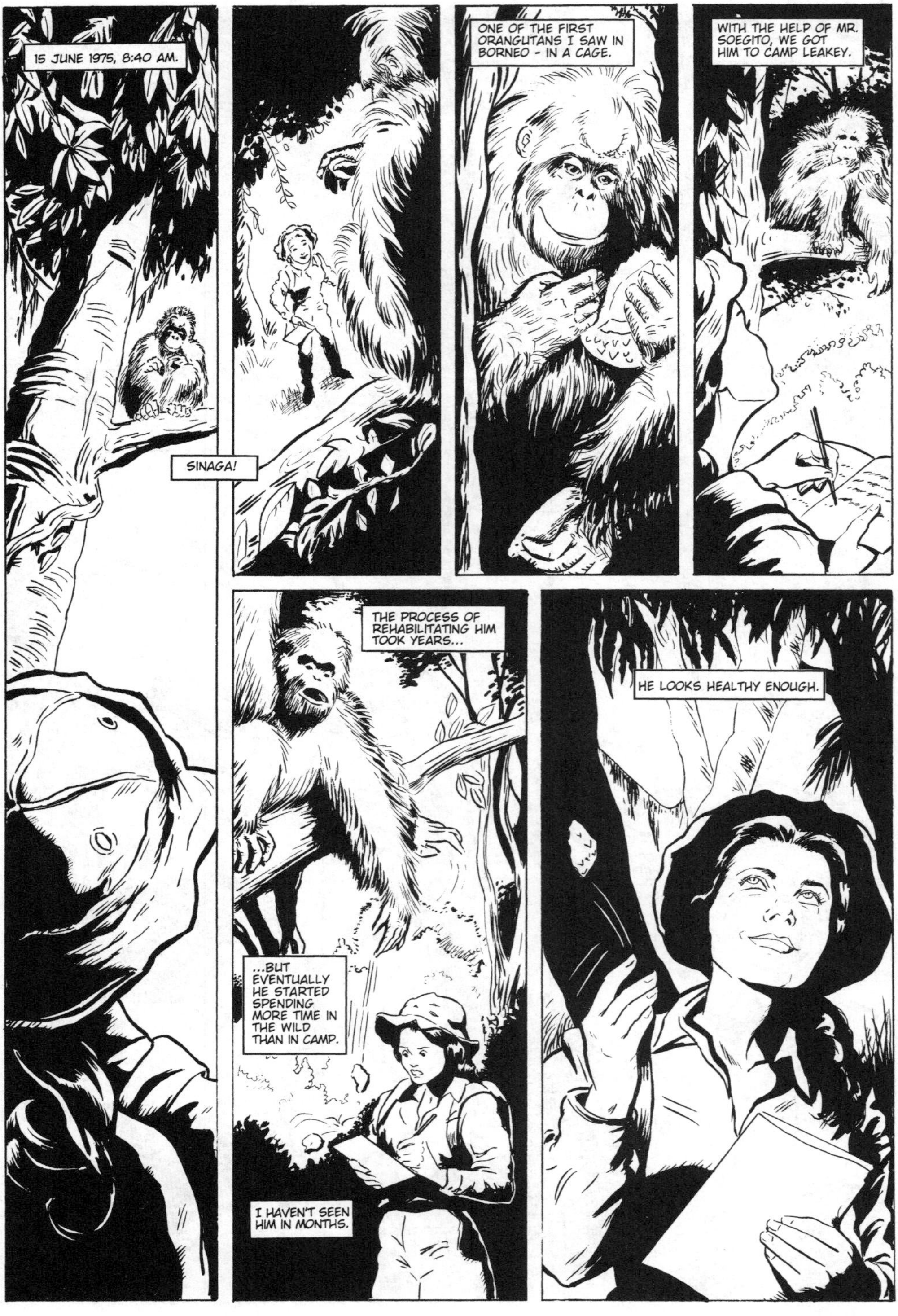
15 JUNE 1975, 8:40 AM.
SINAGA!
ONE OF THE FIRST ORANGUTANS I SAW IN BORNEO - IN A CAGE.
WITH THE HELP OF MR. SOEGITO, WE GOT HIM TO CAMP LEAKEY.
THE PROCESS OF REHABILITATING HIM TOOK YEARS...
...BUT EVENTUALLY HE STARTED SPENDING MORE TIME IN THE WILD THAN IN CAMP.
I HAVEN'T SEEN HIM IN MONTHS.
HE LOOKS HEALTHY ENOUGH.

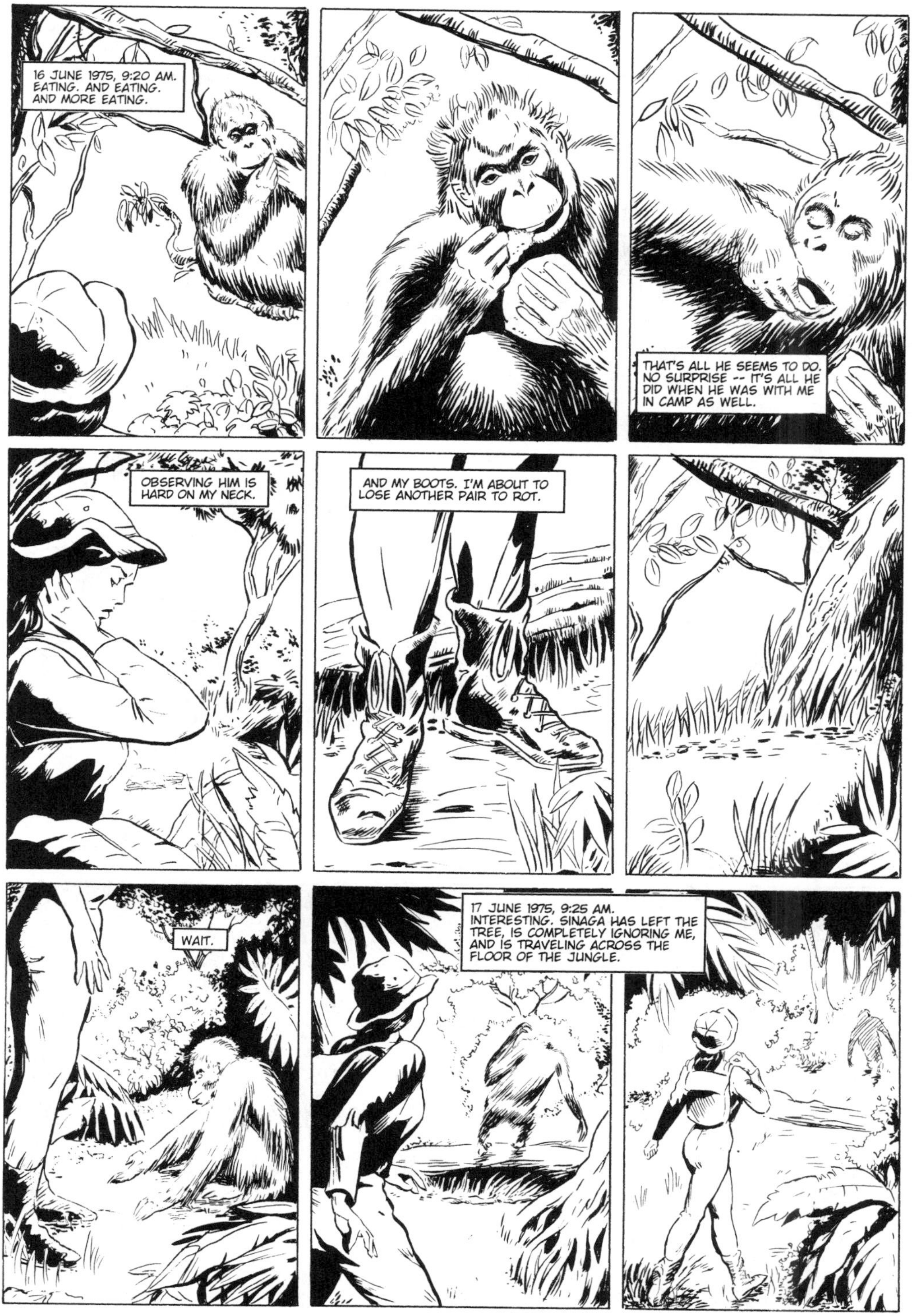
16 JUNE 1975, 9:20 AM.
EATING. AND EATING.
AND MORE EATING.
THAT'S ALL HE SEEMS TO DO. NO SURPRISE -- IT'S ALL HE DID WHEN HE WAS WITH ME IN CAMP AS WELL.
OBSERVING HIM IS HARD ON MY NECK.
AND MY BOOTS. I'M ABOUT TO LOSE ANOTHER PAIR TO ROT.
WAIT.
17 JUNE 1975, 9:25 AM.
INTERESTING. SINAGA HAS LEFT THE TREE, IS COMPLETELY IGNORING ME, AND IS TRAVELING ACROSS THE FLOOR OF THE JUNGLE.

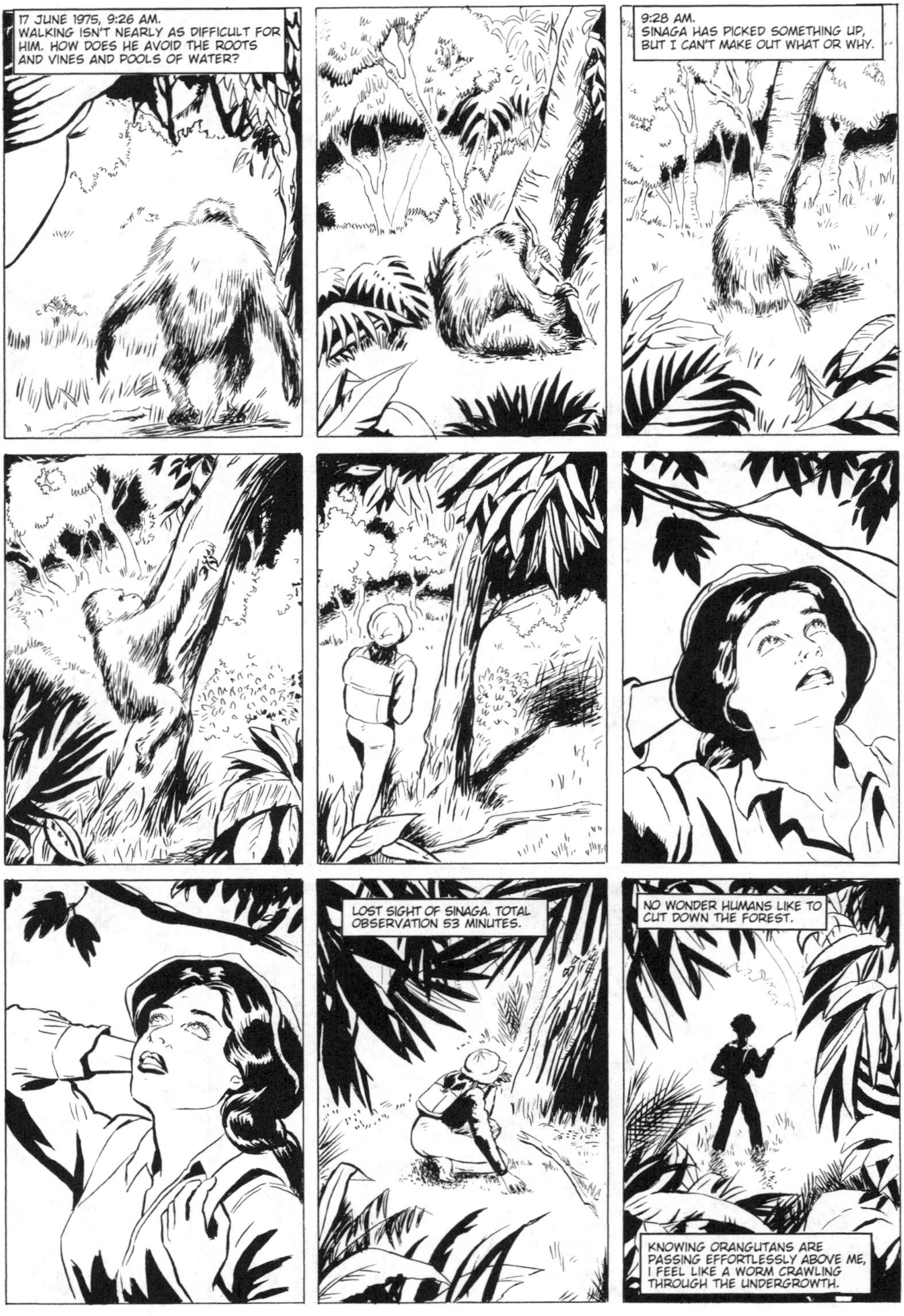
17 JUNE 1975, 9:26 AM.
WALKING ISN'T NEARLY AS DIFFICULT FOR HIM. HOW DOES HE AVOID THE ROOTS AND VINES AND POOLS OF WATER?
9:28 AM.
SINAGA HAS PICKED SOMETHING UP, BUT I CAN'T MAKE OUT WHAT OR WHY.
LOST SIGHT OF SINAGA. TOTAL OBSERVATION 53 MINUTES.
NO WONDER HUMANS LIKE TO CUT DOWN THE FOREST.
KNOWING ORANGUTANS ARE PASSING EFFORTLESSLY ABOVE ME, I FEEL LIKE A WORM CRAWLING THROUGH THE UNDERGROWTH.

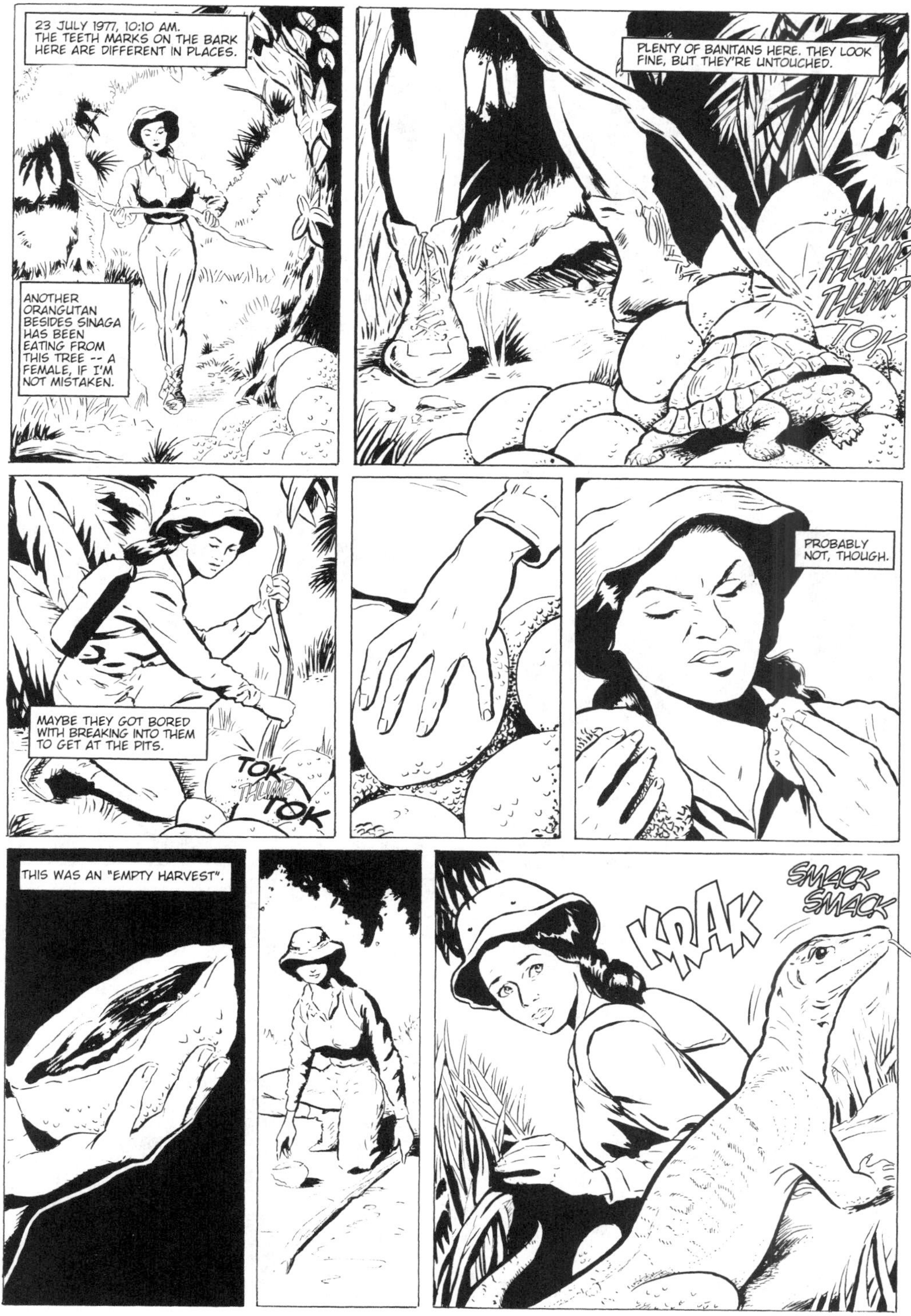
23 JULY 1977, 10:10 AM.
THE TEETH MARKS ON THE BARK HERE ARE DIFFERENT IN PLACES.
ANOTHER ORANGUTAN BESIDES SINAGA HAS BEEN EATING FROM THIS TREE -- A FEMALE, IF I'M NOT MISTAKEN.
PLENTY OF BANITANS HERE. THEY LOOK FINE, BUT THEY'RE UNTOUCHED.
THUMP THUMP THUMP TOK
MAYBE THEY GOT BORED WITH BREAKING INTO THEM TO GET AT THE PITS.
TOK THUMP TOK
PROBABLY NOT, THOUGH.
THIS WAS AN "EMPTY HARVEST".
KRAK
SMACK SMACK

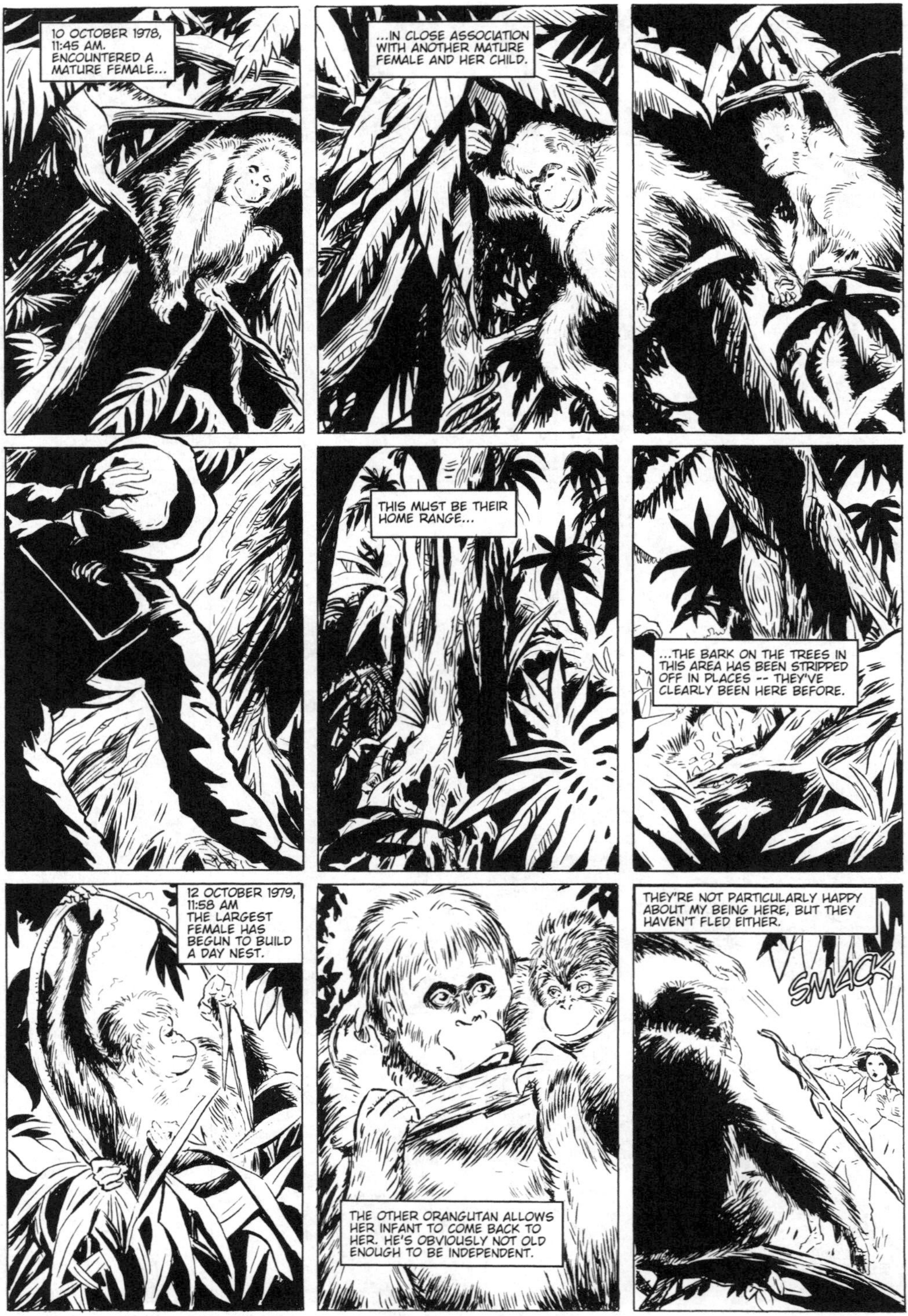
10 OCTOBER 1978, 11:45 AM. ENCOUNTERED A MATURE FEMALE...
...IN CLOSE ASSOCIATION WITH ANOTHER MATURE FEMALE AND HER CHILD.
THIS MUST BE THEIR HOME RANGE...
...THE BARK ON THE TREES IN THIS AREA HAS BEEN STRIPPED OFF IN PLACES -- THEY'VE CLEARLY BEEN HERE BEFORE.
12 OCTOBER 1979, 11:58 AM THE LARGEST FEMALE HAS BEGUN TO BUILD A DAY NEST.
THE OTHER ORANGUTAN ALLOWS HER INFANT TO COME BACK TO HER. HE'S OBVIOUSLY NOT OLD ENOUGH TO BE INDEPENDENT.
THEY'RE NOT PARTICULARLY HAPPY ABOUT MY BEING HERE, BUT THEY HAVEN'T FLED EITHER.
SMACK

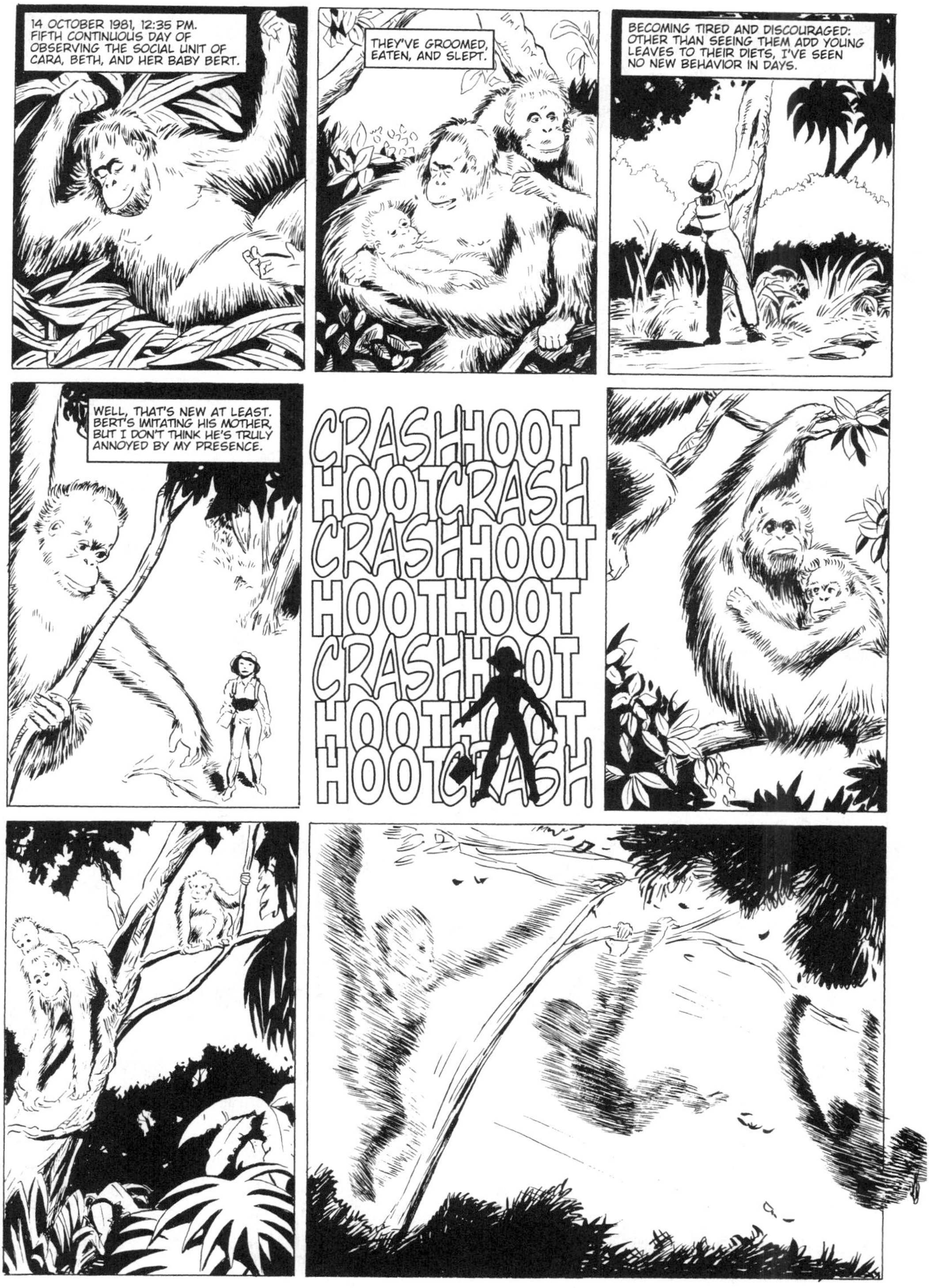
14 OCTOBER 1981, 12:35 PM. FIFTH CONTINUOUS DAY OF OBSERVING THE SOCIAL UNIT OF CARA, BETH, AND HER BABY BERT.
THEY'VE GROOMED, EATEN, AND SLEPT.
BECOMING TIRED AND DISCOURAGED: OTHER THAN SEEING THEM ADD YOUNG LEAVES TO THEIR DIETS, I'VE SEEN NO NEW BEHAVIOR IN DAYS.
WELL, THAT'S NEW AT LEAST. BERT'S IMITATING HIS MOTHER, BUT I DON'T THINK HE'S TRULY ANNOYED BY MY PRESENCE.
CRASHHOOT
HOOTCRASH
CRASHHOOT
HOOTHOOT
CRASHHOOT
HOOTHOOT
HOOTCRASH

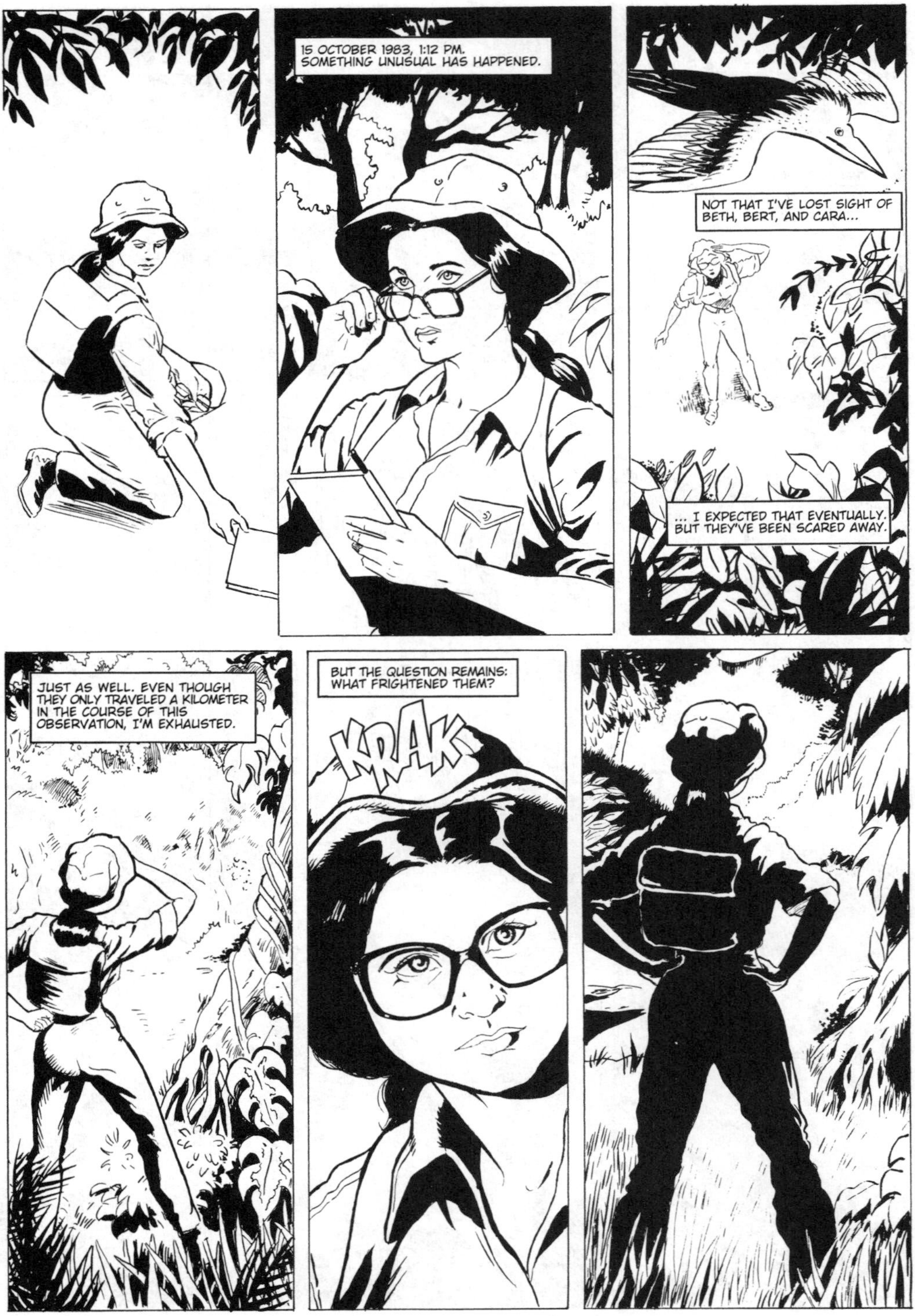
15 OCTOBER 1983, 1:12 PM.
SOMETHING UNUSUAL HAS HAPPENED.
NOT THAT I'VE LOST SIGHT OF BETH, BERT, AND CARA...
... I EXPECTED THAT EVENTUALLY. BUT THEY'VE BEEN SCARED AWAY.
JUST AS WELL. EVEN THOUGH THEY ONLY TRAVELED A KILOMETER IN THE COURSE OF THIS OBSERVATION, I'M EXHAUSTED.
BUT THE QUESTION REMAINS: WHAT FRIGHTENED THEM?
KRAK

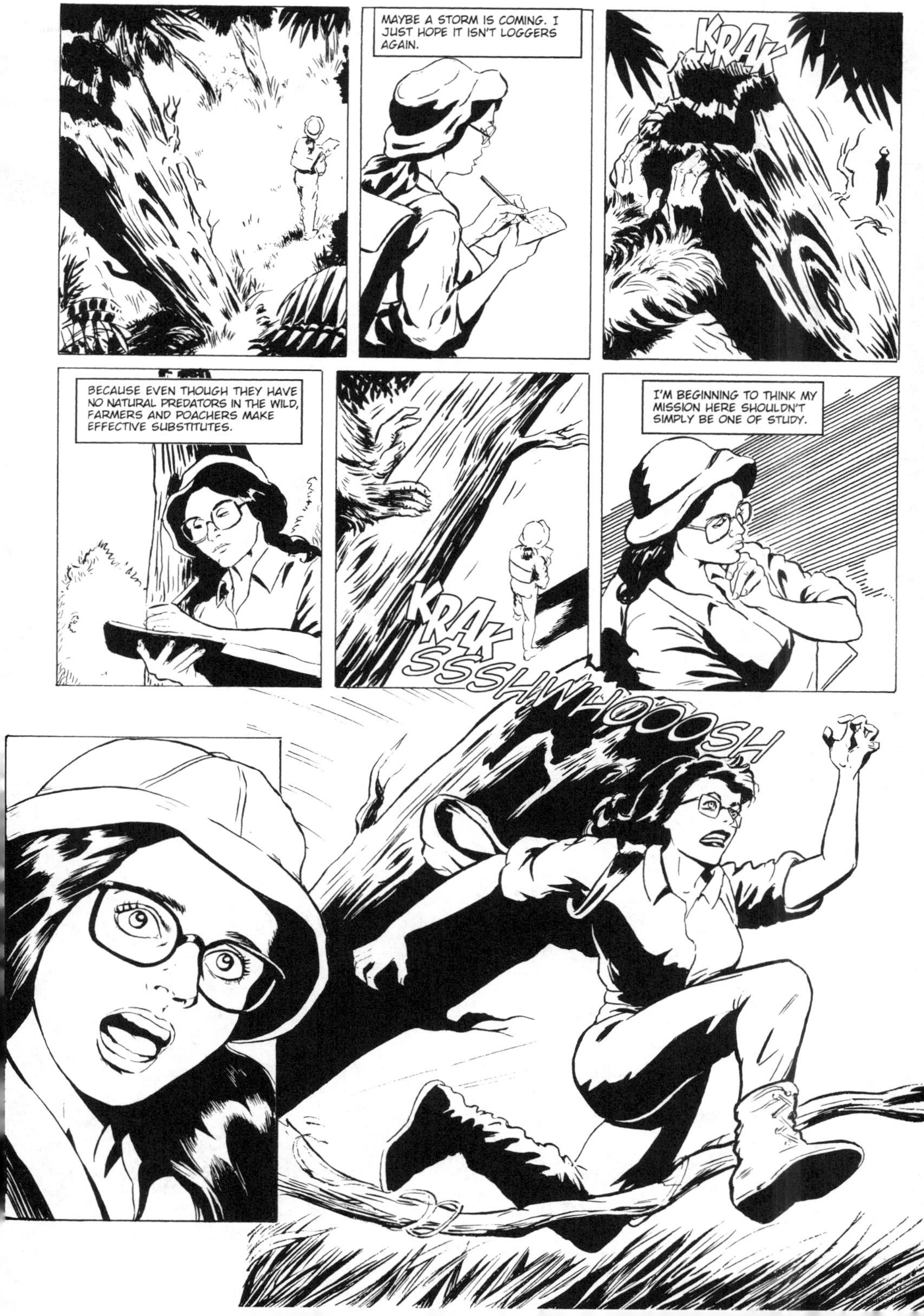
MAYBE A STORM IS COMING. I JUST HOPE IT ISN'T LOGGERS AGAIN.
KRAK
BECAUSE EVEN THOUGH THEY HAVE NO NATURAL PREDATORS IN THE WILD, FARMERS AND POACHERS MAKE EFFECTIVE SUBSTITUTES.
KRAK
SSSHWHOOOSH
I'M BEGINNING TO THINK MY MISSION HERE SHOULDN'T SIMPLY BE ONE OF STUDY.

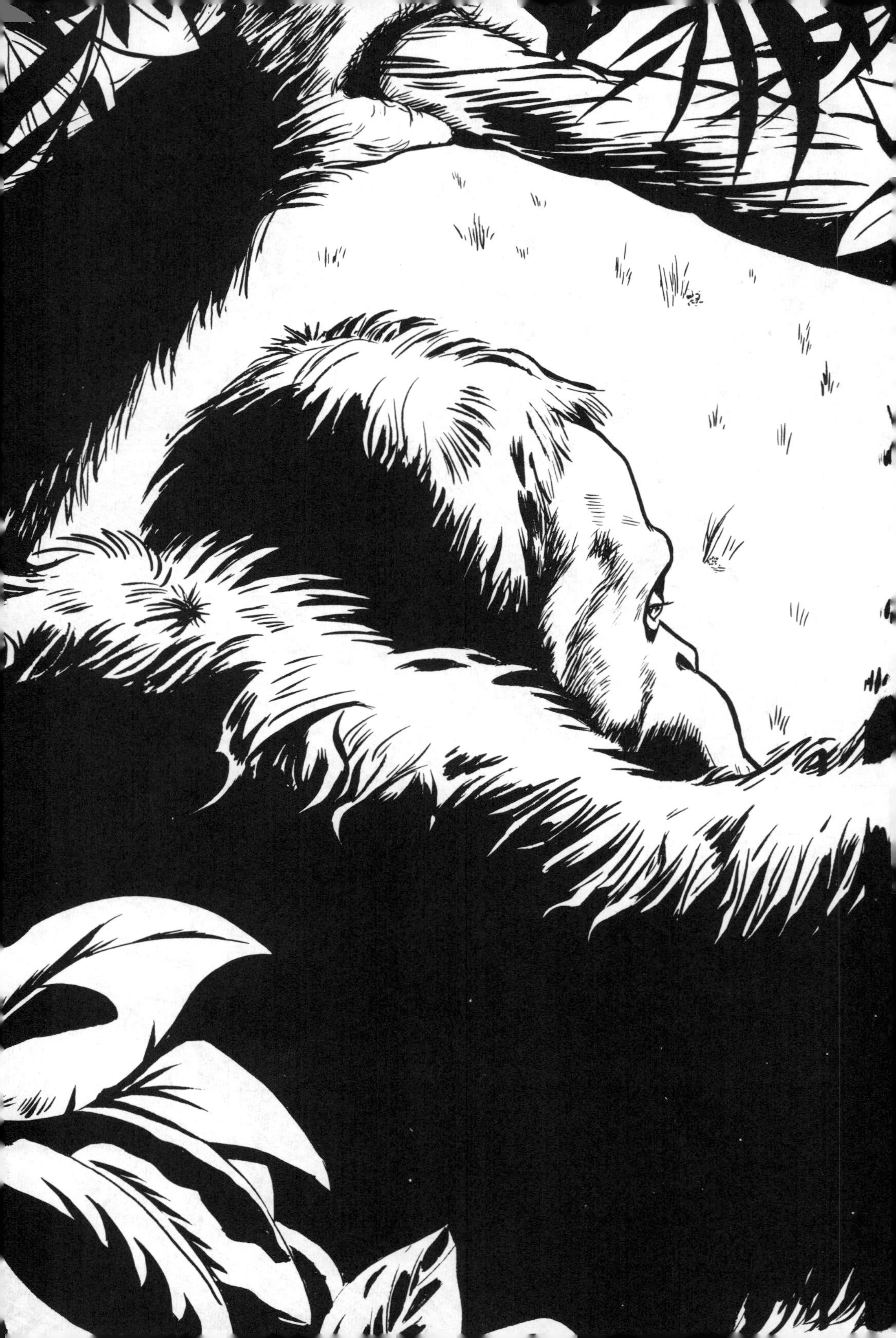

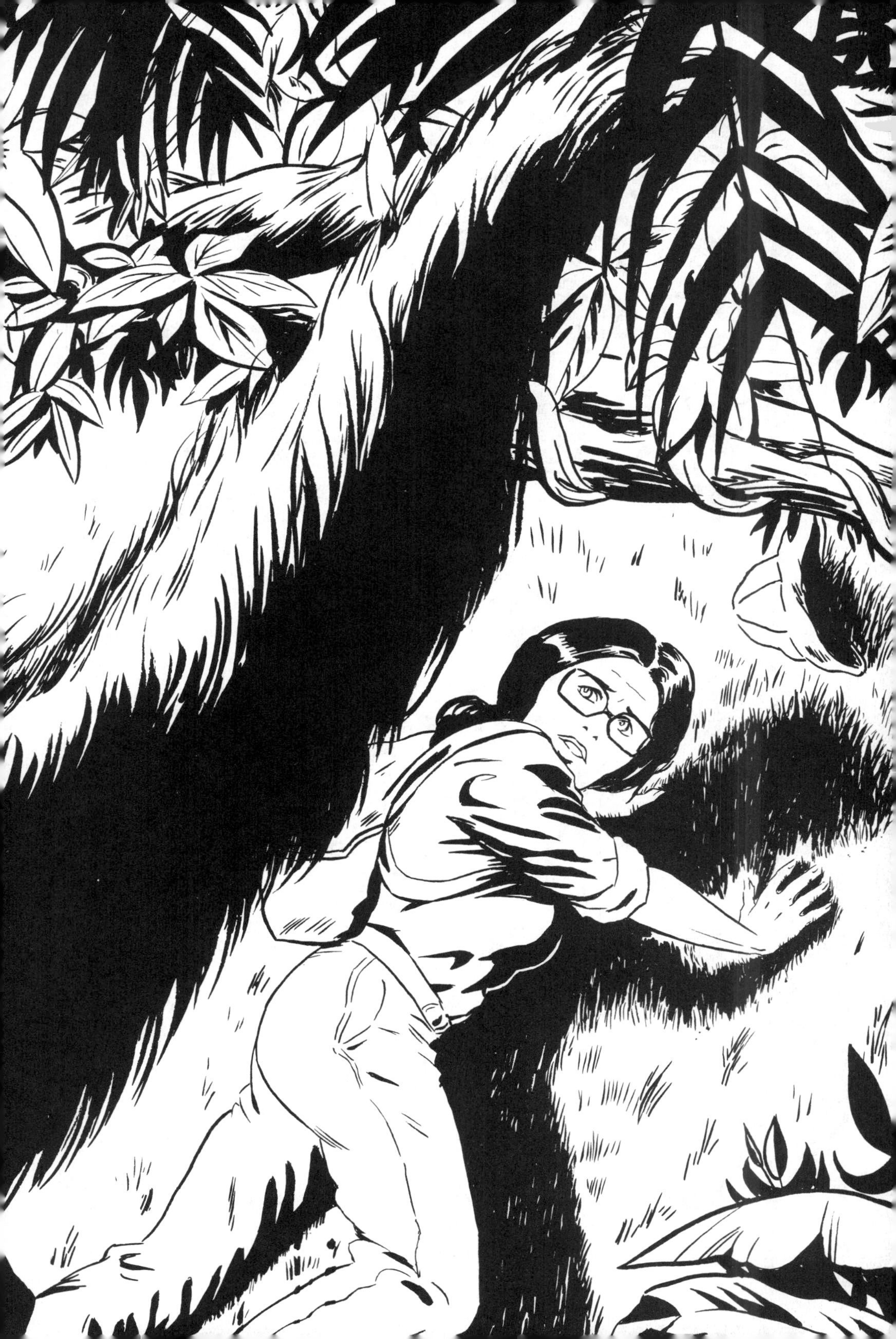

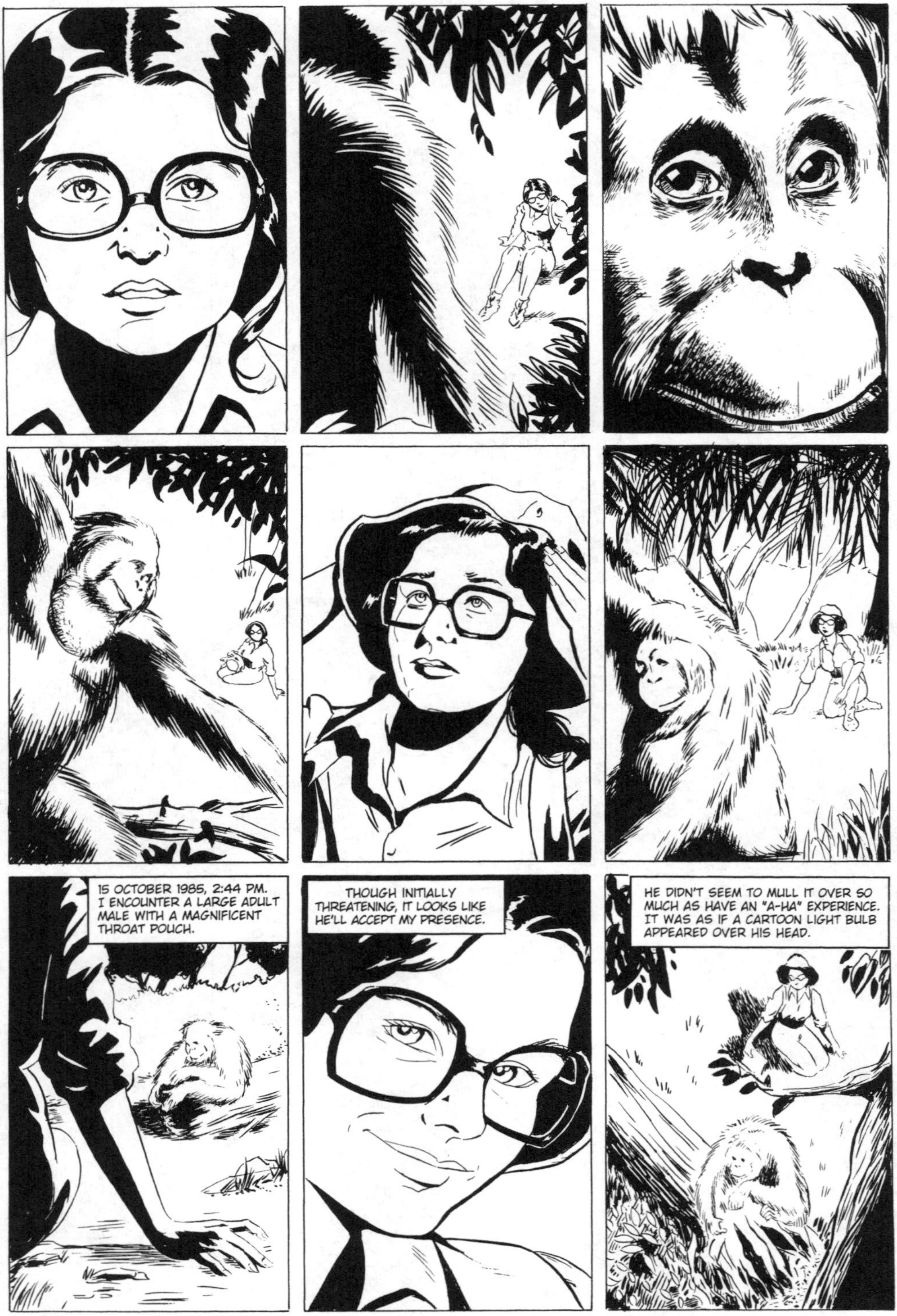
15 OCTOBER 1985, 2:44 PM. I ENCOUNTER A LARGE ADULT MALE WITH A MAGNIFICENT THROAT POUCH.
THOUGH INITIALLY THREATENING, IT LOOKS LIKE HE'LL ACCEPT MY PRESENCE.
HE DIDN'T SEEM TO MULL IT OVER SO MUCH AS HAVE AN "A-HA" EXPERIENCE. IT WAS AS IF A CARTOON LIGHT BULB APPEARED OVER HIS HEAD.

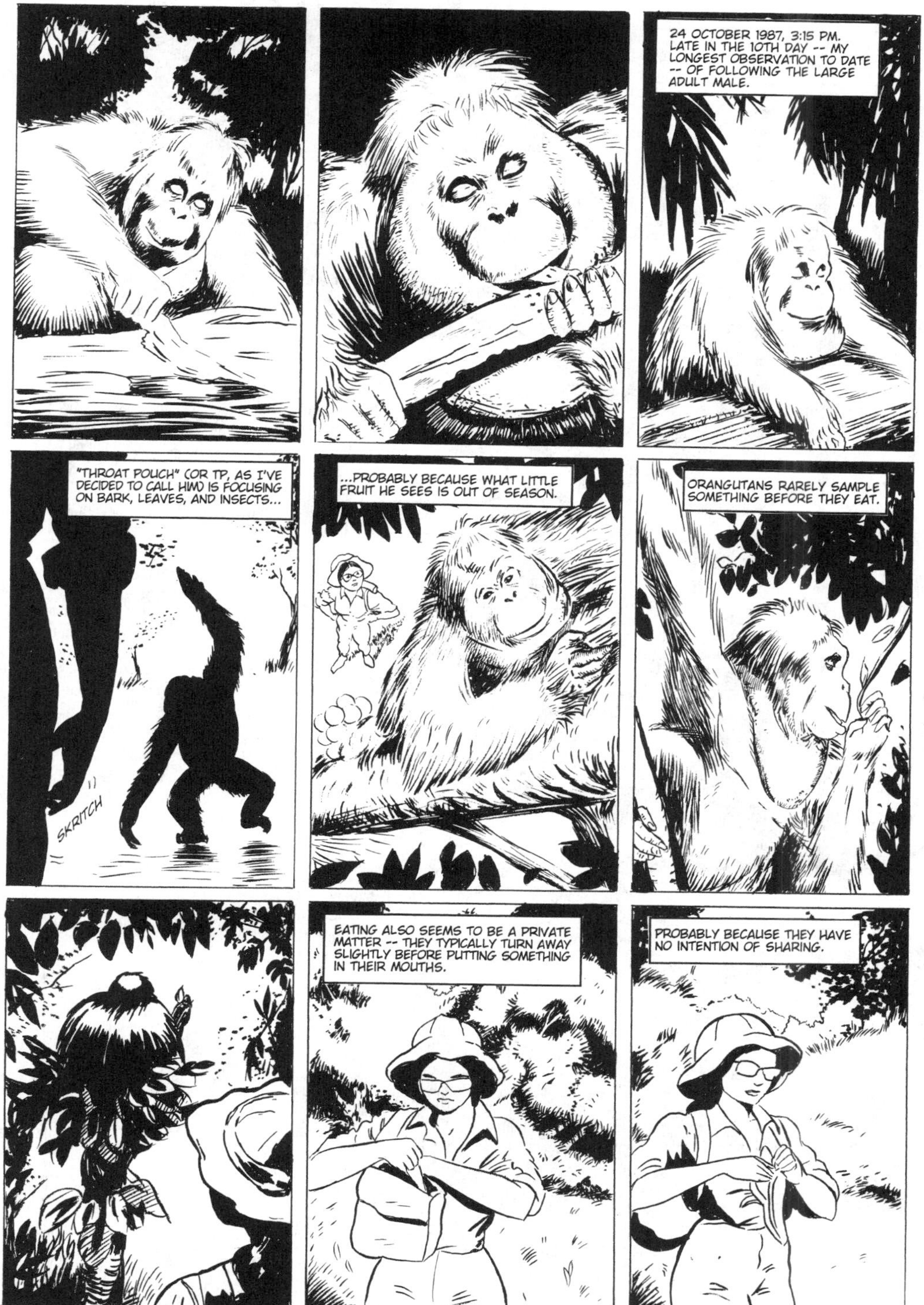
24 OCTOBER 1987, 3:15 PM. LATE IN THE 10TH DAY -- MY LONGEST OBSERVATION TO DATE -- OF FOLLOWING THE LARGE ADULT MALE.
"THROAT POUCH" (OR TP, AS I'VE DECIDED TO CALL HIM) IS FOCUSING ON BARK, LEAVES, AND INSECTS...
SKRITCH
...PROBABLY BECAUSE WHAT LITTLE FRUIT HE SEES IS OUT OF SEASON.
ORANGUTANS RARELY SAMPLE SOMETHING BEFORE THEY EAT.
EATING ALSO SEEMS TO BE A PRIVATE MATTER -- THEY TYPICALLY TURN AWAY SLIGHTLY BEFORE PUTTING SOMETHING IN THEIR MOUTHS.
PROBABLY BECAUSE THEY HAVE NO INTENTION OF SHARING.

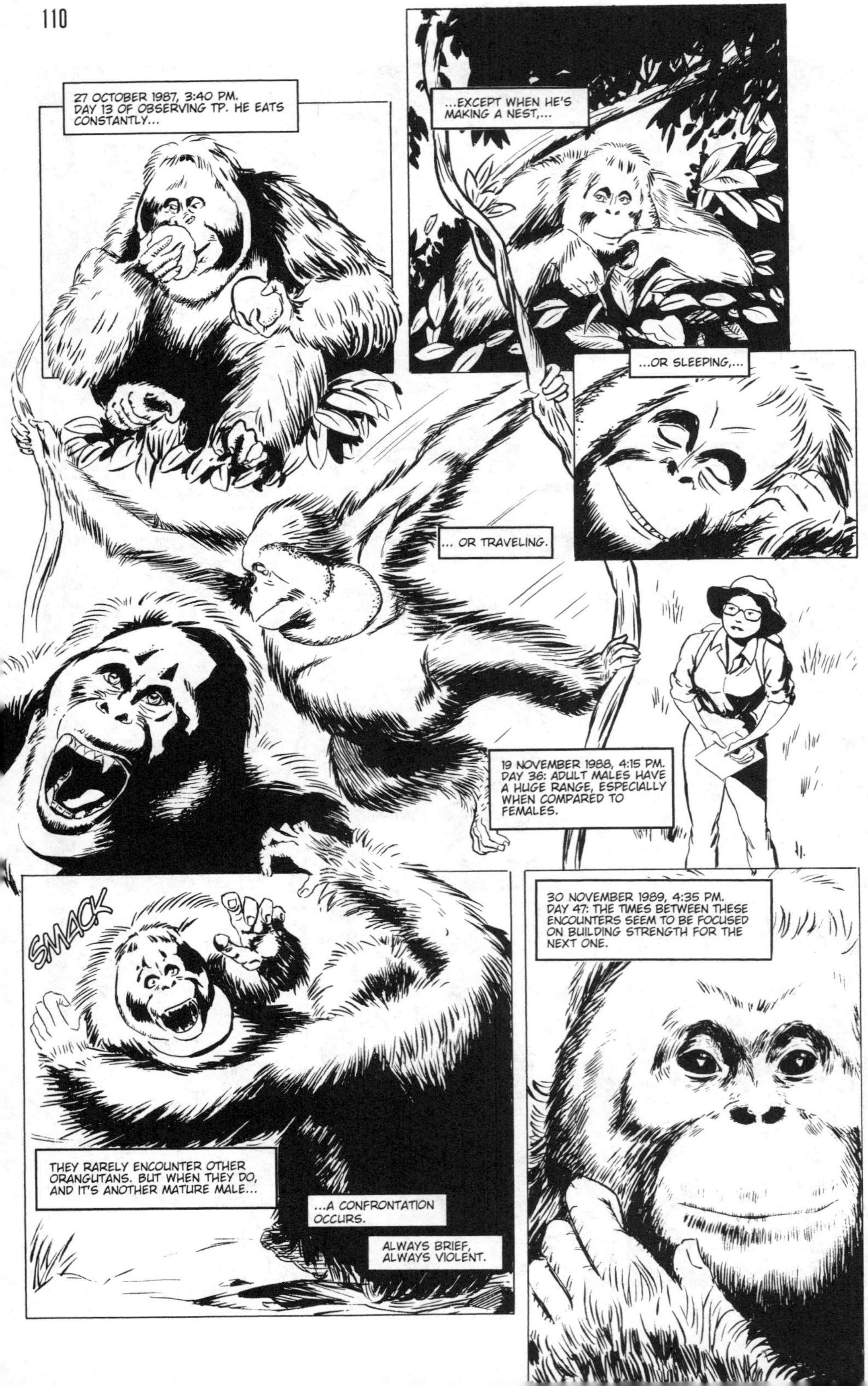
27 OCTOBER 1987, 3:40 PM.
DAY 13 OF OBSERVING TP. HE EATS CONSTANTLY...
...EXCEPT WHEN HE'S MAKING A NEST,...
...OR SLEEPING,...
... OR TRAVELING.
19 NOVEMBER 1988, 4:15 PM.
DAY 36: ADULT MALES HAVE A HUGE RANGE, ESPECIALLY WHEN COMPARED TO FEMALES.
SMACK
THEY RARELY ENCOUNTER OTHER ORANGUTANS. BUT WHEN THEY DO, AND IT'S ANOTHER MATURE MALE...
...A CONFRONTATION OCCURS.
ALWAYS BRIEF, ALWAYS VIOLENT.
30 NOVEMBER 1989, 4:35 PM.
DAY 47: THE TIMES BETWEEN THESE ENCOUNTERS SEEM TO BE FOCUSED ON BUILDING STRENGTH FOR THE NEXT ONE.

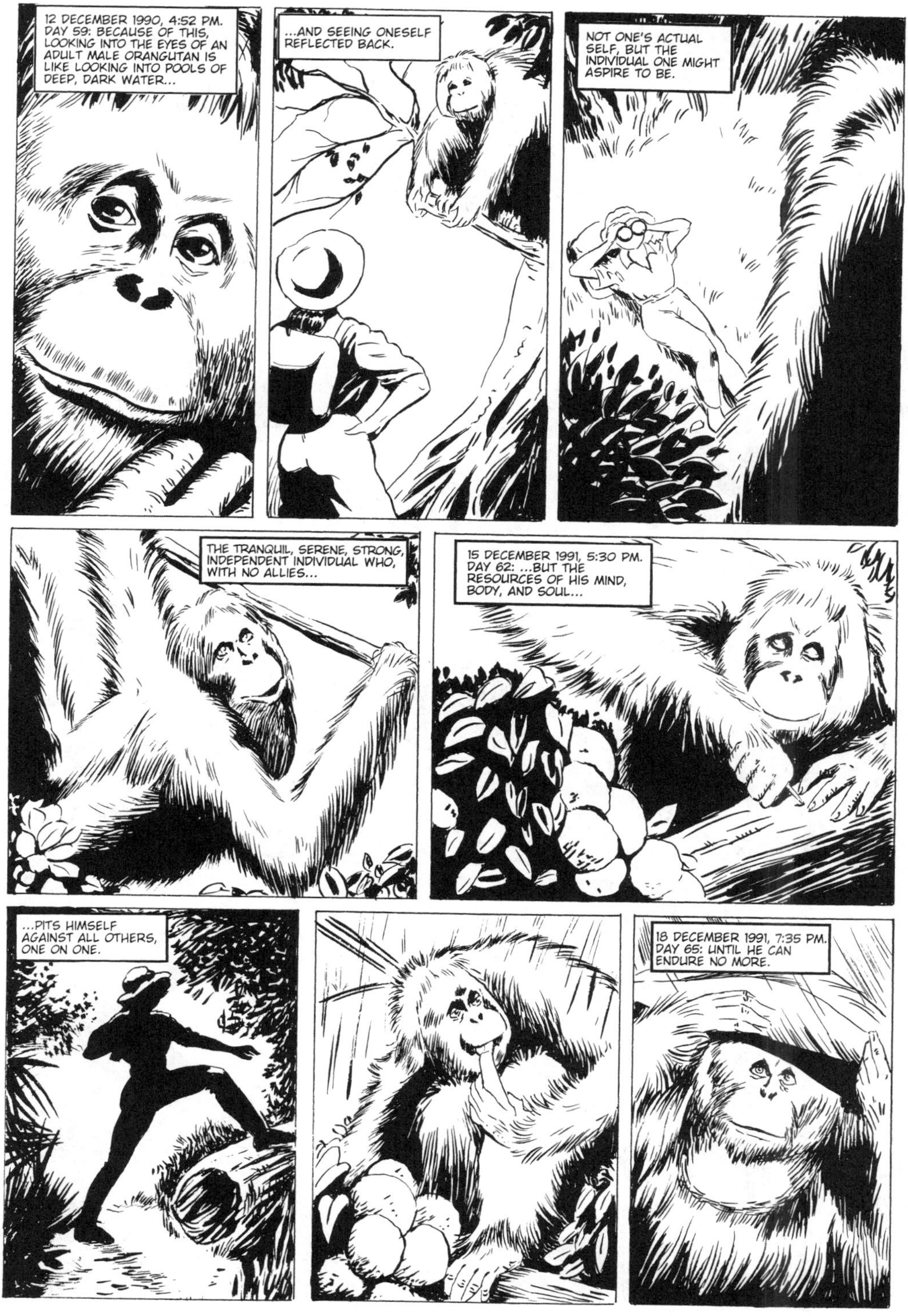
12 DECEMBER 1990, 4:52 PM. DAY 59: BECAUSE OF THIS, LOOKING INTO THE EYES OF AN ADULT MALE ORANGUTAN IS LIKE LOOKING INTO POOLS OF DEEP, DARK WATER...
...AND SEEING ONESELF REFLECTED BACK.
NOT ONE'S ACTUAL SELF, BUT THE INDIVIDUAL ONE MIGHT ASPIRE TO BE.
THE TRANQUIL, SERENE, STRONG, INDEPENDENT INDIVIDUAL WHO, WITH NO ALLIES...
15 DECEMBER 1991, 5:30 PM. DAY 62: ...BUT THE RESOURCES OF HIS MIND, BODY, AND SOUL...
...PITS HIMSELF AGAINST ALL OTHERS, ONE ON ONE.
18 DECEMBER 1991, 7:35 PM. DAY 65: UNTIL HE CAN ENDURE NO MORE.

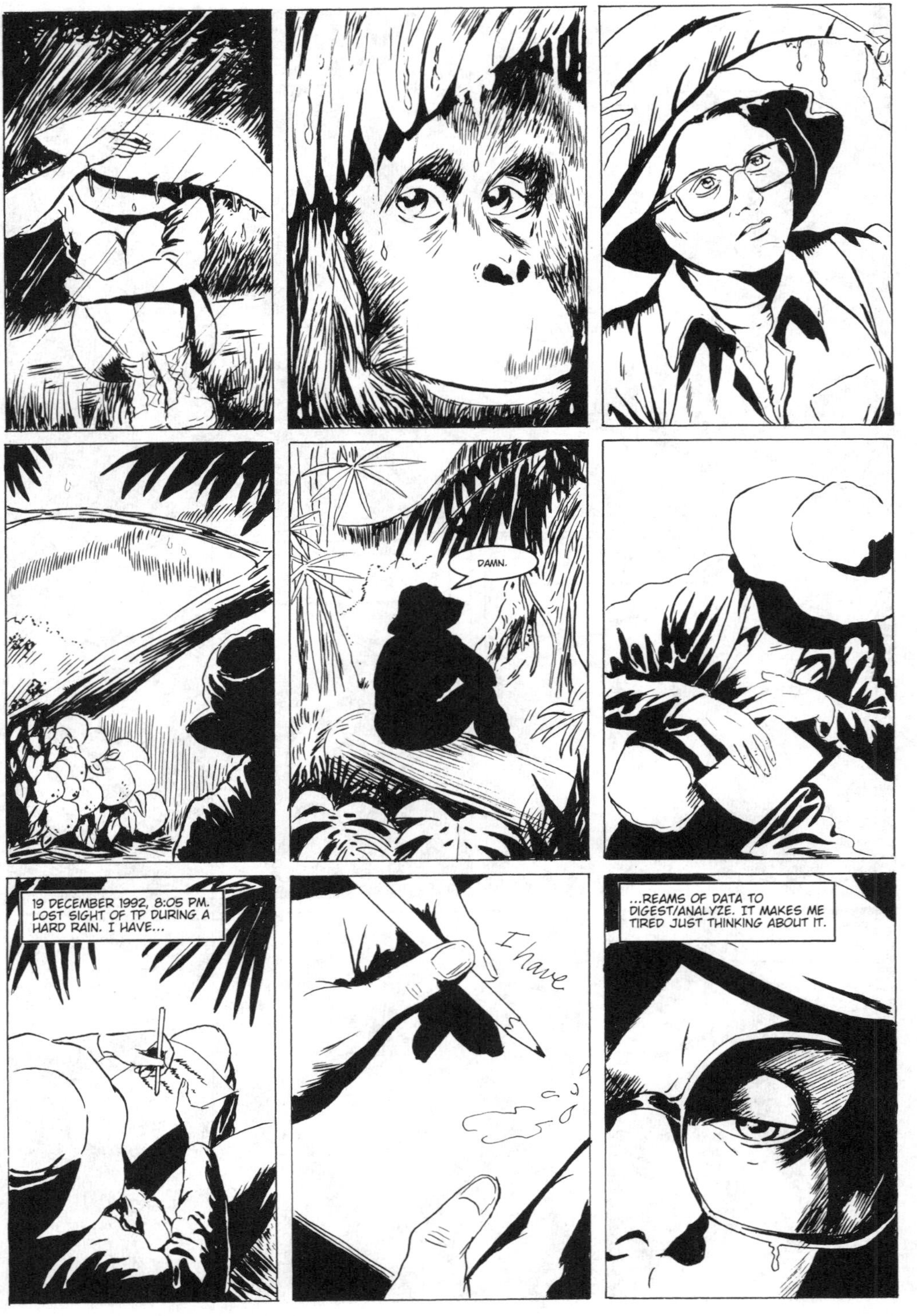
DAMN.
19 DECEMBER 1992, 8:05 PM. LOST SIGHT OF TP DURING A HARD RAIN. I HAVE...
I have
...REAMS OF DATA TO DIGEST/ANALYZE. IT MAKES ME TIRED JUST THINKING ABOUT IT.

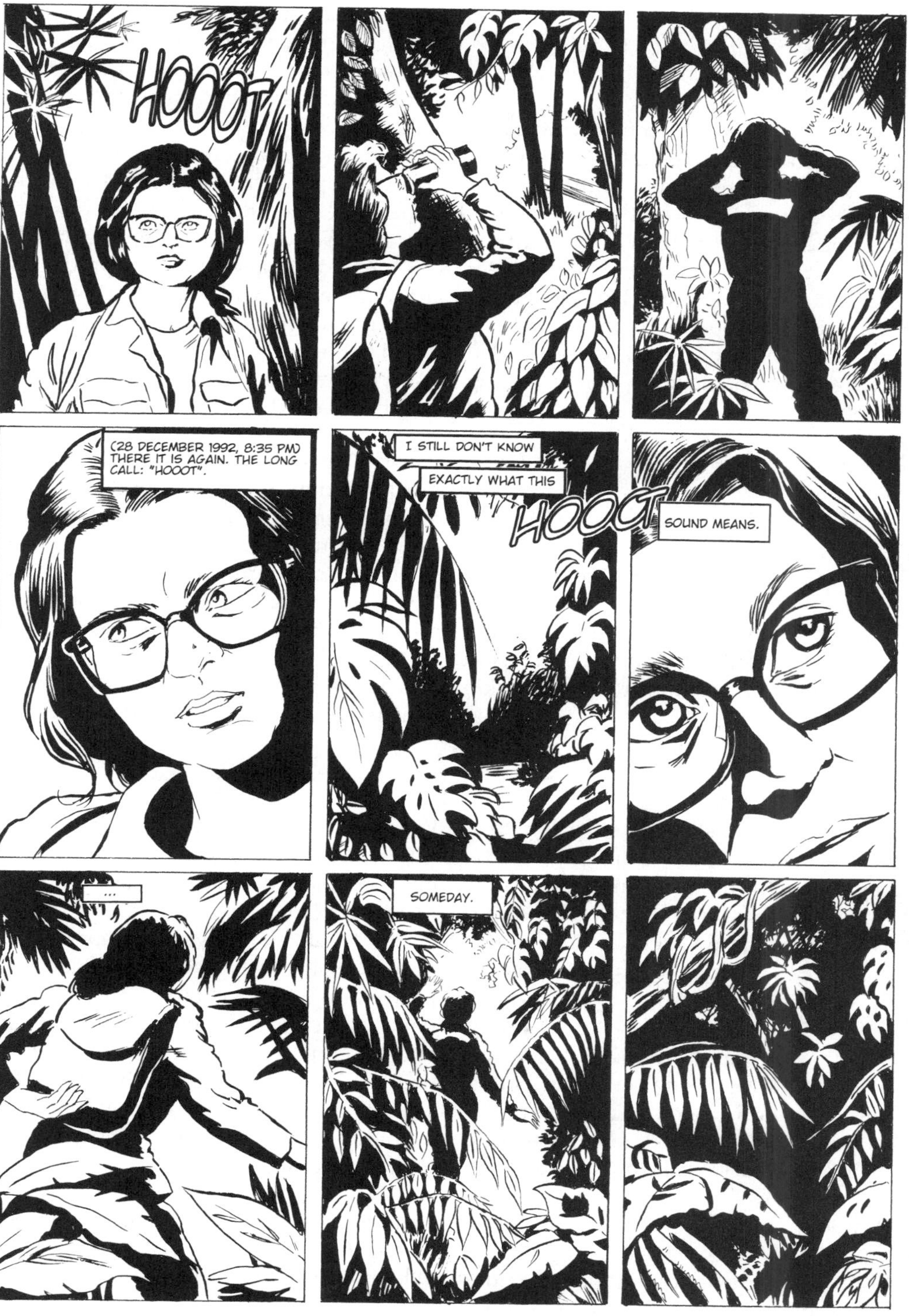
HOOOT
(28 DECEMBER 1992, 8:35 PM) THERE IT IS AGAIN. THE LONG CALL: "HOOOT".
I STILL DON'T KNOW
EXACTLY WHAT THIS
HOOOT
SOUND MEANS.
...
SOMEDAY.

NOTES

PAGE 94

Panel 3: Galdikas saw her first wild orangutans on the second day out of Camp Leakey (named for her mentor Louis Leakey). This boded well, since other researchers who attempted to study them had far less success. One two-month study went without a single sighting. During another 52 day survey a Japanese primatologist saw only one, and other studies have settled for drawing conclusions from counting empty nests.

PAGE 95

Panel 2: Mr. Soegito served as Galdikas' government liaison and became, along with his boss Mr. Sinaga, a friend and ally.

Panel 3: Acidic sap from logs and insect bites combined with the ever-present damp result in constant rashes and skin problems.

PAGE 96

Panels 2-3: While she worked on her Ph.D. thesis, Galdikas and Rod Brindamour (her husband at the time) cut and marked over 125 kilometers of trails, staked and mapped every 25 meters, through the Tanjung Puting reserve. Literally thousands of species make their home there.

Panel 6: Aboriginal farmers clear ramen trees and harvest jelung sap. Sirap (roof slat makers) cut down ironwood trees, mostly working them where they fall. Illegal foresting results in dry rice fields called ladang.

PAGE 98

Biruté Galdikas has re-introduced a number of orangutans to the wild. Though owning orangutans is technically illegal, most government officials look the other way, and some keep captive orangutans themselves. Shortly after coming to Borneo Galdikas realized that her mission would have to consist of conservation in addition to study. She has since devoted much of her time and effort to gaining respect for herself and her mission, and much less on traditional academic awards. As an example, she wrote her first book on orangutan adaptation in Indonesian (as opposed to English), and works to amass the political power needed to save orangutans and their habitat.

Panel 3: The spiky fruit Sinaga peels is the durian, a delicacy for orangutans—and daring humans. It's famous for its delicious, creamy interior and its uniquely foul smell. Patricia Martin, in an article entitled "'Never', she said, 'Not even with a gas mask'" appearing in the Costa Rican Tico Times (4/24/98, page W-12) quoted some brave diners as saying it's like a sauerkraut sundae, or eating custard in a sewer.

PAGE 99

Panels 4-5: Fatigue and illness both contribute to the difficulty of doing field work, but boredom may be the biggest problem in Borneo: Jane Goodall commented that it took Galdikas two years to observe as much social activity as Goodall could see in two hours of watching Gombe's chimpanzees. Further, the environment itself is hostile, not only to researchers but to their equipment. Boot leather isn't the only thing that decays — the intense heat and humidity rots clothing and enables fungi to bloom in cameras.

Panels 7-9: Initially, researchers believed orangutans to be completely arboreal. While this is largely true of females, who spend on average only 3 minutes of each day on the ground, males spend a little over an hour a day out of the trees.

Panel 8: By turning his back, Sinaga was showing her the height of orangutan respect. When describing a similar encounter with another rehabilitated orangutan named Ralph, Galdikas wrote: "What I [took] as indifference and rejection was the orangutan expression of acceptance. I had measured orangutans by human standards of sociability, and had misunderstood… Irrationally, I had joined the mothers who complain, 'They never call, they never write.'"

Creating conditions where observations can proceed without conflict or fear (on the part of either party) is one of the most challenging aspects of field research.

PAGE 100

Panel 2: At the time of her initial study, tool use was virtually unknown among orangutans. It took Galdikas five years to observe it in the wild. She had seen it in camp, but mostly in terms of her ex-captives dismantling things like her water pump.

Panel 8: Over the course of her thesis research, Galdikas' contact with target animals ranged from one minute to 65 consecutive days, resulting in almost 7,000 hours of direct observation. In contrast with her work, which has lasted more than 26 years at the time of this writing, the only Westerners to do long-term studies in Borneo were David Horr (who observed orangutans for a little over two years) and John MacKinnon (who did 1,200 hours of observation).

PAGE 101

Panel 1: Galdikas can indeed tell from the teeth marks if a male or female has eaten from a branch.

Panel 3: Though banitan pits have sweet tasting meats inside, they are difficult to get to. Orangutans don't get impatient with cracking them, though. In fact, Galdikas found her own impatience at odds not only with her subjects, but with the local people as well. As she describes it: "The Javanese believe that time is infinite. Time never runs out. Since there is always enough, time has little meaning."

Panel 6: 'Mast fruiting', when all of the trees bear fruit at the same time, offers high times to orangutans. But as Galdikas notes: "[A]lthough the forests look lush, there actually is very little to eat in any one place. This is why the tropics have been called a 'counterfeit paradise'." One instance of this is the so-called empty harvest: sometimes fruit will look perfect on the outside, but will be unripe, inedible, or perhaps even empty or rotten inside.

PAGE 102

Panels 1-3: Close association for traveling orangutans means they stay within 10-20 meters of each other. Bigger groups of any sort are rare—the largest Galdikas has observed is nine, and the most she has ever seen traveling together is five.

Panel 5: Both males and females have home ranges, though a male's is typically larger and more complex. These ranges relate to the scarcity of food in the jungle, since even though orangutans eat more than 300 types of plants and insects, the density of good food is low.

Panel 8: Baby orangutans cling to their mothers constantly for the first 18 months of their lives.

PAGE 103

Panels 1-2: Like chimpanzees, orangutans

only form temporary associations. They differ from chimps mainly in the behavior of the adult males. The only close associations adult male orangutans form are with females, and even these are fairly rare. (It's a wonder they mate at all!) Chimpanzee males form more close bonds with other males than with females. Gorillas, like humans, organize into permanent groups.

Panel 4: Lip-smacking is an expression of anger. Though it is speech, scientists don't consider it language. Galdikas says orangutans "...don't need phonemes, words, and sentences. Quite simply, they have nothing to say to one another that can't easily be communicated through facial expressions, gestures, movements, and vocalizations."

Panel 8: The fact that close association between orangutans is usually 10-20 meters relates not only to the scarcity of food, but also to how they travel: they bend the tops of trees and ride them like pole vaulters.

PAGE 104

Panel 5: Orangutans — females especially, since males will occasionally fight with each other, sometimes to the death — have no natural predators, so it's rare to see them frightened.

PAGE 108

Panels 1-3: Making direct eye contact is both aggressive and dangerous. The Melayu people have many stories about people fighting with orangutans. In these stories the orangutans always win.
Panel 4: Mature male orangutans look very different from females and sub-adult males. In fact, their appearance is so different that some aboriginal people consider the adult male orangutan an

entirely separate species.

Panels 7-9: Unlike humans, orangutans do not appear to use trial and error. Instead, they seem to contemplate problems and suddenly (insightfully) arrive at a solution. Laboratory researchers call the *a-ha!* experience TP has here 'insight learning'.

PAGE 109

Panel 6: Wild orangutans don't taste, but do inspect, handle, and sniff new food. This is mainly because they almost never *try* new foods. Their behavior in captivity is another matter, and in some respects all too human. According to Galdikas: "Given a choice between a juicy, sun-ripened, golden pineapple and a gooey, fat-laden milk chocolate bar or a Tootsie Pop, I have never known an ex-captive orangutan to choose the former."

Page 110

Mature males appear to be totally intolerant of each other. Aggressive encounters with other males can lead to fights to the death.

Page 111

This journal entry is quoted, almost verbatim, from Galdikas' book *Reflections of Eden*.

Page 113

Though Galdikas has studied orangutans longer than anyone else, to this day much of their behavior remains a mystery. The combination of human population pressure and recent drought (resulting in fires that have done even more damage to their habitat) makes continued research and discovery, not to mention conservation, all the more challenging.

UM...
following a straight
line along the
path I thought
and listened. In
WELL...AND THEN WHAT HAPPENED?

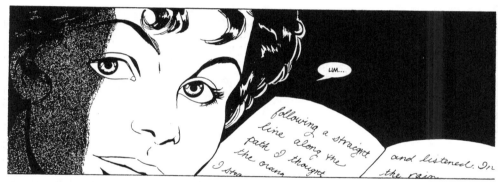

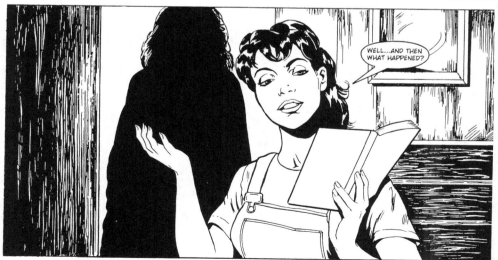

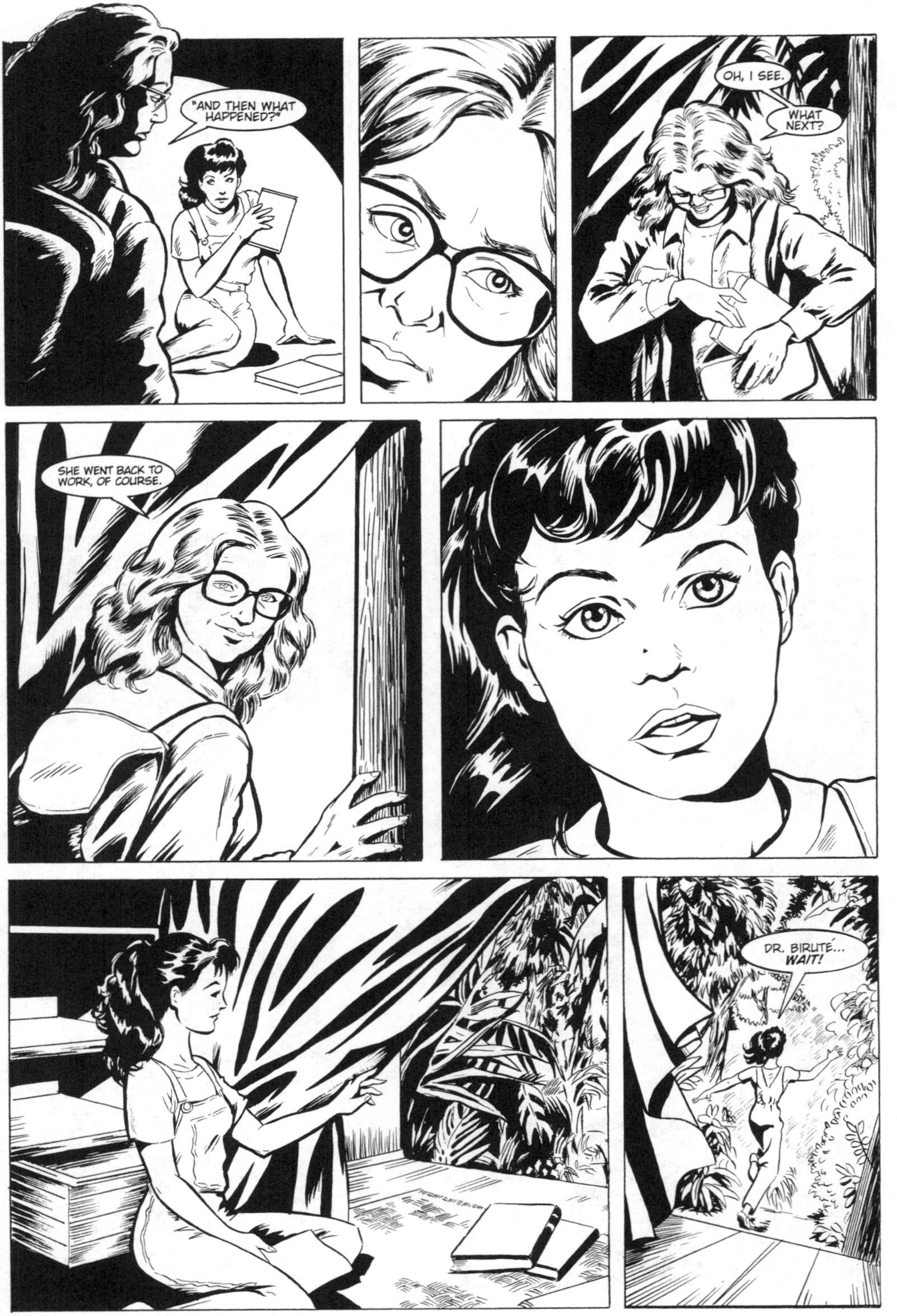
"AND THEN WHAT HAPPENED?"
OH, I SEE.
WHAT NEXT?
SHE WENT BACK TO WORK, OF COURSE.
DR. BIRUTÉ... WAIT!

NOTES AND REFERENCES

Before offering suggestions for further reading in the guise of acknowledging the sources for these stories, two books in particular deserve notice above all others.

The first is *Nobel Prize Women in Science,* by Sharon Bertsch McGrayne (NY: Birch Lane Press, 1993). If you only read one other book as a result of *Dignifying Science,* please make it this one. It's enjoyable, succinct, and you'll recognize many of the people you just read about. Further, it will introduce you to many more important figures. A newer, expanded edition became available in 1998.

Women in science are not a historical curiosity, of course. For personal accounts by today's working scientists, read *Journeys of Women in Science and Engineering: No Universal Constant,* by Susan A. Ambrose, Kristin L. Dunkle, Barbara B. Lazarus, Indira Nair, and Deborah A. Harkus (Philadelphia: Temple University Press, 1997). History in the making told by the people making it.

PROLOGUE: MARIE SKLODOVSKA

The motivation to *not* include Mme. Curie (née Sklodovska) in a book about women scientists is strong — if people know about anybody, she's the one. Better to focus on lesser known figures, perhaps. But reading her correspondence proved enough to force my reluctant hand, and the image of a scientist trying to trick herself into feeling warm by using the weight of furniture in place of blankets struck me as heartbreaking and funny in equal measure.

REFERENCE

Madame Curie, by Eve Curie, translated by Vincent Sheean (NY: Garden City Publishing, 1940).

The letter to her brother used as (con)text for the prologue comes from this affectionate biography written by her youngest daughter. Eve Curie's description of her mother's early years of deprivation and optimism are particularly inspiring. The book is full of quotes that seemed like they ought to fit in a book of this sort but somehow didn't. They're too good to omit, though, so here they are:

> "Marie Curie is, of all celebrated beings, the only one whom fame has not corrupted."
> — Albert Einstein

> "In science we must be interested in things, not in persons."
> — Mme. Curie to a reporter who tracked her down during a vacation

HEDY LAMARR

Hedy Lamarr might seem an awkward or forced choice for inclusion in this book. Unlike the others featured here, she clearly did not devote her life to science. (In fact, her contribution was limited, and more along the lines of engineering than the pure science of all the others.) But besides her story being unusual, interesting, and so unlikely *vis-à-vis* her public persona as a film star, I think her appropriate to include for one important reason: She's sadly typical. At almost every turn others actively discouraged her from pursuing her talents in this 'male' direction. Though it only occupied a small part of her life, her aptitude for invention was important to her. Further, her co-inventor George Antheil asserts that she was rather indifferent to her acting career by the time of their work together. There's no telling what she might have accomplished had she devoted her efforts to the National Inventor's Council. She might not have created anything else as important as her first patent, but then again…

In more recent times she might have been encouraged (or at least permitted) to pursue her interest in invention. Today Hollywood would make a big deal of her affinity for science, especially since her patent is a fundamental part of that most important of all movie-making tools, the cellular phone. She got no support or acclaim from the studio system of the 1940s, though. But long after her films stop appearing on screens we'll dial up friends using the technology she invented to knock out Nazi U-boats.

NOTES

PAGE 15

Panel 1: Fritz Mandl, Lamarr's handsome but cruel (sounds like something out of the Brothers Grimm, doesn't it?) first husband, spent two years and much of his fortune trying to wipe out the film. The negative was actually destroyed much later when the Russians invaded Budapest.

PAGE 17

Though *Ecstasy* is the first movie she became known for, Lamarr (Hedy Kiesler at the time) had her first bit part in the ironically titled *The Weaker Sex*. Most people recall *Ecstasy* as being scandalous because it showed Lamarr (from a great distance) running naked through the woods, but what really got everybody all riled at the time was the scene of her character in the

throes of passion. The U.S. Commissioner of Customs report objected (in part) to "[t]hat portion of the film beginning with the engineer placing the girl on the couch and ending with the girl caressing his head as he sits on the floor…" Tame by today's standards — little would be cut even for television — it was banned in the U.S. until 1940, and until even later in Great Britain, as we'll see in the Rosalind Franklin story.

PAGE 18

Panels 5-6: Mussolini and Mandl refer to both Mandl's former wife Hella Strauss (a Viennese beauty) and to the affair he had with Eva May, a famous German actress who committed suicide when Mandl wouldn't marry her. Lamarr herself was engaged twice before this marriage. Her first fiancé (Ritter Franz von Hochestetten) killed himself when she broke the engagement because she was more interested in pursuing a career in drama. The same sort of situation (*sans* suicide) occurred between her and Count Blucher von Wahlstatt.

PAGE 19

Panels 7-9: Mandl did indeed have great difficulty controlling torpedoes, and it seems likely that he would have edited out misses from the infomercials he showed prospective buyers.

PAGE 20

Panel 5: This scene, and particularly this panel, is pure fiction. At this point in their relationship Lamarr wouldn't have offered her husband her ideas, and there's no evidence that Lamarr was thinking about much besides escape. But Mandl's jealousy, which led to her being at his side night and day, coupled with Lamarr's native intelligence, probably started her thinking about the problem at about this time.

PAGE 21

Panel 6: Mandl did indeed keep Lamarr under guard and had her followed for much of their marriage. He viewed her more as a possession than a person: Mandl, rifle in hand, burst in on a (mostly) innocuous encounter she had with a nobleman who was kissing her fingers in the Hapsburg Palace. She dove out the window to escape and landed head first in the snow bank. Looking down at her from the window, Mandl simply said "Get her out of the snow…she'll catch her death of a cold."

PAGE 24

This sequence makes reference to Milton Caniff's Sunday 7/9/39 *Terry and the Pirates* comic strip. Is it coincidence that this classic page from a classic strip came out at roughly the same time as Lamarr made her escape from pre-WWII Europe?

Well, yes.

PAGE 27

Panel 1: Lamarr escaped to the U.S. on the *Normandie*, a ship with the same name as Pat Ryan's unrequited love in Caniff's *Terry and the Pirates*. This too is a coincidence — I wrote page 24's nod to Caniff before learning this.

Lamarr did indeed get a divorce from Mandl on the charge of desertion! She argued that she was so in love that she couldn't stand his business trips. In fact, she applied to the Holy Rota for an annulment, which was granted thanks in part to pressure put on the church by some of Lamarr's reluctant but influential friends.

PAGE 29

Panel 9: This line is similar to the famous "Play it again, Sam" in that even though everyone remembers it, it isn't in the movie. (Nor was Lamarr — in *Casablanca*, that is. She turned down the role that Ingrid Bergman made famous.)

PAGE 30

Panel 1: Gene Markey, though he was her husband for only eight months, has his surname immortalized on Lamarr's patent.

PAGE 32

Panel 3: Antheil's avant garde piece called "Ballet Méchanique" featured 16 player pianos, two electrically driven airplane propellers, four xylophones, four bass drums, and a siren. It caused quite a sensation, and din.

PAGE 33

In fairness to the Navy, Lamarr's patent couldn't be used for reasons in addition to the short-sightedness of military brass. The mechanical device proposed in the patent, though theoretically workable, would have been difficult to construct with enough precision in the 1940s. But by 1962 solid-state technology had caught up with her and frequency-hopping was part of the secure communications systems used during the Cuban Missile Crisis. Today, wireless communications for the Internet and cellular phones depend on the technique. As her son John Loder — who owns a Los Angeles phone store — said, "It's in every other phone system I sell." In 1997, the Electronic Frontier Foundation awarded her its Pioneer Award for "blazing new trails on the electronic frontier."

PAGE 34

Panel 2: The National Inventor's Council, in place to promote ideas helpful to the war effort, existed until 1974. In its time it generated over 600,000 suggestions for inventions, but only a few became patents.

PAGE 36

Even at $50,000 a kiss, if you do the math you'll come up with a lot of frogs that didn't turn into princes.

REFERENCES

Ecstasy and Me: My Life as a Woman, by Hedy Lamarr (NY: Bartholomew House, 1966).
    Lamarr has denied writing this, and at the very least it seems unlikely that she wrote all of it. My suspicion is that much of the book comes from conversations with a ghostwriter, who took liberties when filling in details. (Considerable liberties is my guess, especially where descriptions of bedroom antics and passages that purport to be actual psychiatric transcripts are concerned.) Lamarr and the publisher settled out of court.

The Films of Hedy Lamarr, by Christopher Young (Secaucus, NJ: Citadel Press, 1978).
    Though its tone lends it more believability than *Ecstasy and Me*, this book is mostly a love-letter from a fan. And like the "autobiography," it makes no mention of her interest in invention.

Bad Boy of Music, by George Antheil (Garden City, NY: Doubleday, 1945).
    Like *Ecstasy and Me*, Antheil's stories are too overtly candid (in a conspiratorial "now don't let anybody know I told you this, but..." sense) and his prose style is too breathless to take at face value. But this book appears to be the only source of first hand facts about their meeting and collaboration, and his respect and admiration for Lamarr as a person and an intellect come across as genuine.

The Great Movie Stars, by David Shipman (NY: Hill and Wang, revised edition 1979).
    This encyclopedic book on film personalities provided the kernel of the idea for the last scene with Louis B. Mayer and some insights into his character, from which I imagined his and Lamarr's interactions.

"A sultry screen star who didn't just act — she invented," by Elizabeth Weise (The Associated Press, March 9, 1997).
    This wire service report appeared in dozens of U.S. newspapers, and gives the basic facts on the history of Lamarr's life

and patent.

"Advanced weaponry of the stars," by Hans-Joachim Braun, in *American Heritage of Invention & Technology*, vol. 12, no. 4, Spring 1997, 10-17.

If you read only one other piece about Lamarr, I would recommend this one. It comes complete with photos, conjecture, narration, and more history than you get from Weise's article. A related article called "Celebrity is the mother of invention" by Travis Brown provides intriguing glimpses of inventors who were famous for things other than their ingenuity. Additional perspectives on Lamarr's invention appear in *Forbes* ("I guess they just take and forget about a person," by Fleming Meeks, vol. 145, no. 10, May 14, 1990, 136-138) and *Scientific American* ("Spread-spectrum radio," by David R. Hughes and Dewayne Hendricks, vol. 278, no. 4, April 1998, 94-96).

"Secret Communication System," U.S. Patent #2,292,387 issued to Hedy Kiesler Markey and George Antheil, August 11, 1942.

Though we've attempted to give the gist of the invention in the story, if you want all the details about how to control torpedoes from a distance without your enemies jamming the signal, start here. Lamarr and Antheil sent their idea in to the National Inventor's Council in December 1940 and chairman Charles F. Kettering (the research director for General Motors) encouraged them to write it up as a patent.

Meitner's was another life profoundly affected by World War II. Like Lamarr, she too was thwarted by an irrelevant trait she could do nothing about: her

LISE MEITNER

Jewish background. Leaving Germany was a hardship for her, but on balance the likely alternatives — execution in a concentration camp or forced labor on nuclear weapons — make exile sound better. She enjoyed more success and certainly more longevity in her field than Lamarr, though, and had a productive and respected career in science that lasted all her life.

NOTES

PAGE 39

Panel 1: Niels Bohr was perhaps the second most famous physicist of his day, eclipsed only by Albert Einstein. Unlike Einstein, though, Bohr enjoyed interacting with students, and he was a mentor to many scientists who later won Nobel Prizes.

Panel 2: James Franck and Gustav Hertz went on to share the Nobel Prize for ex- perimentally demonstrating one of the fundamental ideas behind quantum mechanics: that atoms could absorb energy only in discrete amounts.

Panel 3: Fritz Haber was one of the most famous chemists of his day, and considered a great patriot for his work on chemical weapons during World War I. He was also Jewish, and died in exile in Switzerland after leaving Germany. A few bold scientists defied the Nazis to hold a memorial service in his name.

PAGE 40

Panel 1: The German economy was devastated by the war. Inflation was so bad that many received their wages daily, some in wheelbarrows, and all rushed to spend the rapidly devalued currency before its worth decreased further the next day…or hour.

Panel 4: It's impossible to summarize Max Planck's contributions to modern physics in a footnote. He was the first to explain hitherto baffling experimental results with his early attempt at a quantum theory. One of the fundamental constants of the modern theory is now named for him. He also liked foot races.

PAGE 42

Panels 3-4: Meitner's early experiments were similar to her friends Franck and Hertz's. She (along with Otto Hahn) bombarded atomic nuclei with electrons and then studied what kind of radiation they produced as a result.

PAGE 43

Panel 2: Meitner and Bohr became good friends, and she visited Bohr's institute in Copenhagen often. They got along well, and he was one of the first people she saw after her exile. There he demonstrated his newest ideas about atomic nuclei, teasing her (Meitner's approach to physics was less playful than Bohr's) by introducing his model using billiard balls he'd had manufactured especially for this purpose.

Panels 4-5: Beta rays are, for all practical purposes, just like the electrons orbiting the atom's nucleus. Magnets deflect charged particles, so you can tell how energetic an electron is by how much a magnet bends its path as it speeds by. Think about driving a car (electron) over a pothole (magnet): If you're going slow your wheel will dip into it and you'll feel quite a jolt. The faster you go, the less the pothole will deflect the path of your tire, and the less you'll bounce.

PAGE 44

Panel 2: Atoms are made up of small electrons, which surround a nucleus made of much larger (~2000 times as massive as electrons) protons and neutrons. Radioactive atoms decay by emitting particles (protons, neutrons, electrons, and photons) from their nuclei, where the protons and neutrons are. If you have a bunch of these atoms, their "half-life" is the time in which half of the atoms emit their particles.

Panel 6: Ida Noddack and Irene Curie both had theories about what would happen if you bombarded heavy elements like uranium with neutrons. Their ideas, though wrong in important ways, were very close to Meitner's correct interpretation (fission).

PAGE 45

Panel 2: An alpha particle is made up of two neutrons and two protons, so it's roughly four times as massive as a neutron. If you think of a nucleus as a big pile of bowling balls (alpha particles), then Meitner's skepticism makes sense: You wouldn't expect that lobbing a softball (a slow neutron) into this pile of bowling balls would knock two out!

Panel 6: Meitner's Jewish background made staying in Germany impossible. Though she held on longer than many, she eventually accepted that she'd have to leave. (If Haber wasn't safe from persecution, how could she expect to be?) By the time she got out it was difficult for even someone as respected as she to find a position abroad — there were simply more refugees than jobs. So though her appointment in Stockholm wasn't ideal, in many ways she was fortunate to get it.

Panel 7: Surface mail moved a *lot* faster in those days. Letters got delivered daily between Stockholm and Berlin, which even in this era of email doesn't sound too bad.

PAGE 46

Panel 5: An isotope is an element with an atypical number of neutrons in its nucleus. Because chemical properties of atoms are determined by their charged particles (the protons and electrons), isotopes are chemically identical to their parents. For instance, we mentioned earlier that hydrogen usually has no neutrons. Deuterium is an isotope of hydrogen with one neutron. Water made with this isotope is called "heavy water", and in most respects it behaves chemically just like regular old H_2O.

Panel 6: Remember when we said that knocking off alpha particles with slow neutrons is like knocking out bowling balls with softballs? Well, a barium atom is much larger than an alpha particle. So this seems even more unlikely. But that's only if we assume a "pile of bowling balls" model of the nucleus...

Panel 8: ...a model that Bohr (and Meitner) didn't think told the whole story. When they thought of large nuclei as having some of the properties of a drop of water—specifically, a wobbly and unstable nature balanced by forces that had a cumulative effect a lot like surface tension—they could more easily picture it breaking apart. And that's what Meitner and Frisch did!

PAGE 47

Panel 5: It's tough to explain why the sum of the masses of the two pieces of a uranium nucleus is less than the nucleus it came from in a short footnote, so let's trust that Lise and Otto know what they're talking about here.

Panel 8: Both Meitner and Frisch understood the physical implications of their calculations almost immediately.

PAGE 48

Panels 6-7: Bohr loved a good solution even when he didn't think of it himself, and the more visual (and less buried in equations) that solution, the better. He would often say "You're not thinking; you're just being logical!" if his colleagues got too abstract and mathematical with their arguments.

REFERENCES

What Little I Remember, by Otto Frisch (London: Cambridge University Press, 1979).

Frisch actually remembered plenty, and writes about his work with many famous physicists with verve and humor.

"Looking back," by Lise Meitner, in *Bulletin of the Atomic Scientists*, vol. 20, no. 11, November 1964, 2-7.

Meitner's good-natured recollections in this short article prompted the humorous touches in this story. Though disappointed (and perhaps briefly embittered) by the Nobel Prize committee's decision to award their prize for the discovery of fission only to Hahn and Strassman, she didn't let those feelings dominate her life.

Lise Meitner: A Life in Physics, (Berkeley: University of California Press, 1996); "Lise Meitner in Sweden 1938-1960: Exile from physics," in *American Journal of Physics*, vol. 62, no. 8, August 1994, 695-701; "A Nobel tale of postwar injustice," in *Physics Today*, vol. 50, no. 9, September 1997, 26-32; and

"Lise Meitner and the discovery of nuclear fission," in *Scientific American*, vol. 278, no. 1, 80-85.

Ruth Lewin Sime wrote all of the above (working with Elisabeth Crawford and Mark Walker in the *Physics Today* article), and they combine to form a comprehensive look at Meitner, and though heavily footnoted, they are readable as well. Though she sometimes focuses on the negative (she is particularly hard on Otto Hahn and his post-war posture), Sime does a thorough and convincing job of making the case that Meitner was treated poorly by both Hahn and the Nobel Prize committees.

Lise Meitner, Atomic Pioneer, by Deborah Crawford (NY: Crown Publishers, 1969).

Crawford aims her book at less scholarly, and certainly younger, readers. Because of this, she concentrates more on fictitious dialogue (not that I can fault her for that, of course!) and a lightweight and optimistic take on Meitner's career and relationship with Otto Hahn. Still, this is an engaging introduction, and includes a transcript of a radio conversation Meitner had with Eleanor Roosevelt just after the first atomic bomb fell.

Otto Hahn: My Life, by Otto Hahn, translated by Ernst Kaiser and Eithne Wilkins (NY: Herder and Herder, 1970); and *Otto Hahn: A Scientific Biography*, by Otto Hahn, translated by Willy Ley (NY: Scribner's, 1966).

From Hahn's perspective, the discovery (or perhaps the Nobel Prize) resulted from work he did alone and/or with Fritz Strassman. The second book reprints a paper he published in the journal *Die Naturwissenschaften* that gives much more credit to Meitner than he does in these books.

ROSALIND FRANKLIN

"Never attribute to malice what you can explain with incompetence." An old saying, and often true. Nobody here was incompetent, though, including the Nobel Prize committee — off camera but almost always in many of our characters's peripheral vision. Nor was anyone malicious, actually. All merely looked for and saw different things in the data and each other. So how can we explain Rosalind Franklin's comparative lack of fame for her role in the discovery of DNA's structure? She earned better, both in terms of respect from her colleagues during their crucial work and during her lifetime. Like Adrienne Weill says at the end, we'll never know for sure whether this was because of her gender or her temperament.

NOTES

PAGE 51

Adrienne Weill ties together the beginning, middle, and end of this story and this book in more ways than one. She was not only a close friend and correspondent of Franklin's, but also one of Marie Curie's co-workers. A noted French-Jewish scientist, she was instrumental in getting Franklin her job studying holes in coal in Paris.

PAGE 52

Panel 1: According to many accounts, this analysis is just the sort of thing Franklin was likely to do.

PAGE 53

Panel 1: The lab was a mixture of physicists and biologists — an experiment in biophysics arranged by John T. Randall, a famous physicist and co-inventor of radar.

Panel 3: Though Randall (working in the role of an administrator here, so he's no longer overly concerned with the science or personalities involved) seems to dismiss Gosling's work, it was first rate given his equipment. The whole purpose of hiring Franklin was to take things to the next level, and Gosling bore her no animosity. He became her friend as well as her colleague.

PAGE 54

Panel 3: Franklin did seminal work on coal, and later on the tobacco mosaic virus. If she'd had no role in the discovery of DNA she would still be remembered today (by scientists, at least) for this crucial research.

PAGE 58

This page is told from Maurice Wilkins' perspective, and is the first alternate take on Franklin as a person and (less so) as a scientist. Wilkins and Franklin got off on the wrong foot immediately, in part because of a misunderstanding regarding the terms of her employment, and in part because they simply had incompatible personalities. Their relationship never moved beyond this, and most of the time didn't even reach a level of professional courtesy. They simply didn't get along. This may have been the main reason why her contributions to the discovery of DNA's structure were given short shrift.

PAGES 59-60

Franklin's decision to focus on "dry" DNA may have been an important factor in her lack of involvement in the subsequent discovery. Though solving dry DNA's structure may have been the harder problem to solve, it wasn't necessarily the *right* problem to solve. DNA in action exists in its wet form, after all. Why did she do it, then? We'll never know, but as Francis Crick has put it: "Just as important as having ideas is getting rid of them." Franklin would have done well to get rid of this one.

In her notes to herself she acknowledged "evidence for [a] spiral structure" but was unwilling to talk about a helical structure with Wilkins. She concluded that there was a "big helix or several chains, phosphates on the outside, phosphate-phosphate bonds, disrupted by water ... The results suggest helical structures ... capable of absorbing water in large quantities [of eight molecules per nucleotide] ..."

PAGE 61

Panel 1: This scene, completely imagined, is intended to make the point that the tea room Boy's Club was so ingrained and natural to the male scientists that it probably took even a sensitive and guileless fellow like Gosling a while to notice.

PAGE 62

This section, told from James Watson's perspective, focuses on his initial failure to pay attention to, learn from, and do more than stereotype Rosalind Franklin (physically and intellectually) during their first encounter. Though he quite candidly acknowledged most of these (and other) mistakes in his famous book *The Double Helix*, he does so in a rather offhand "aren't I a charming and brutally honest fellow anyway" manner. Because his book is so popular, and tells such a compelling story, it propagated a misleading view of Franklin and her work for years. Regarding panel 8, Watson was indeed a good tennis player.

Page 66

Francis Crick, Watson's partner in writing their famous paper describing the structure of DNA, became closer to Franklin in her later years. So, unlike in the Watson section above, we show Crick seeing her much more as she is. In fact, he's the closest we come in the story to a fair witness, other than Adrienne Weill (who you may have forgotten about by now). Sir Lawrence Bragg is another famous physicist who, like Randall, ended up working in biology after World War II.

Page 68

Panels 3-5: Franklin did write a memo to this effect and deliver it to her lab partners.

Page 70

This section, told from Watson's and Wilkins' perspectives, depicts the OK Corral-esque showdown between Franklin and Watson, which Watson made into one of the high points of his book *The Double Helix*. I hope this reads as a bit of a farce here, since a violent confrontation between the two was pretty much unthinkable according to both Wilkins and Crick. Watson clearly overreacted at the time and dramatized it in his book, presumably for the sake of an exciting anecdote.

Page 72

Panel 7: Wilkins: "DNA, you know, is Midas' gold. Everybody who touches it goes mad."

Panel 9: Watson and the rest of the audience found *Ecstasy* disappointing: "Before the film was half over we joined the violent booing of the disgusted undergraduates as the dubbed voices uttered words of uncontrolled passion."

Page 73

Panels 4-6: Though it looked easier (or at least more fun) than what Franklin was doing, the model building Watson and Crick did here required a great deal of intellectual effort. Their work was rigorous and scientific — and successful.

Francis Crick's thoughts on her (and their) approach says a lot about how, and why, science gets done the way it does: "I believe that one reason for [her reluctance to build or use physical models], apart from the marked difference in temperament, was because she felt that a woman must show herself to be fully professional. Jim had no such anxieties about his abilities. He just wanted the answer, and whether he got it by sound methods or flashy ones did not bother him one bit. All he wanted was to get it *as quickly as possible*."

Page 75

Francis Crick narrates the final section not told by Adrienne Weill, in large part because he, more than the other two Nobel Prize winners, seems to have had a mature, truly professional, and personal relationship with Franklin. He and his wife Odelle eventually became good friends with Franklin, and helped her (and put her up in their home) during one of the brief convalescences preceding Franklin's death from cancer.

REFERENCES

The Double Helix, by James D. Watson (originally published in 1968, but seek out the Norton Critical Edition edited by Gunther Stent, NY: W.W. Norton & Company, 1980).

Start here, but don't stop with what Watson accurately calls "A personal account of the discovery of the structure of DNA." If it were mine to subtitle, I would change that to "A very personal account..." This book caused an uproar in both its draft and published forms, and may have been the main (though inadvertent) reason why many began to pay attention to Franklin's role in the discovery. It's fascinating.

Rosalind Franklin & DNA, by Anne Sayre (NY: W.W. Norton & Company, 1975).

Clearly a reaction to Watson's book and an important and essential source. I couldn't put a finger on why this left a bad taste in my mouth until reading Vivian Gornick's description of it in *Women in Science* (NY: Touchstone, 1990 edition): "...its tone is so defensive the reader comes to distrust its account and interpretation of the crucial events it is describing." An important book, but because of its overt agenda and tendency towards speculation about motives, it doesn't read as any more objective than Watson's.

Rosalind Franklin, the Dark Lady of DNA, by Brenda Maddox (NY: HarperCollins, 2002).

This book presents a much more balanced account of Rosalind Franklin than Sayre's. If you read only one book about Rosalind Franklin, make it this one.

What Mad Pursuit, by Francis Crick (NY: Basic Books, 1988).

Not at all a reaction to Watson's book (though its subtitle—"A personal view of scientific discovery" — is similar enough to make the idea plausible), this is a more measured and philosophical look at how one scientist approaches science. It's by no means dry, however, and offers lively insights into Crick's views of how science is best done. It also recounts the making of a BBC docudrama (which I've still not seen) called *Life Story*, about the quest for DNA's structure and mentions an unsuccessful attempt at a Hollywood movie, for which the script failed to find a backer. Just as well that it didn't appear and I didn't see it either, since Crick specifically mentions that he and Watson retained rights to any comic book adaptation!

"An interview with Nobel Laureate Maurice Wilkins," by Stephanie Johnson and Thomas R. Merten, in *The American Biology Teacher*, vol. 51, no. 3, March 1989, 151-153.

This interview typifies for me how little Wilkins cares to reveal about himself. Perhaps I didn't look hard enough, but I found very few sources outside of Judson's book (below) that gave a sense of Wilkins either as a flesh-and-blood person or scientist. Interestingly, for all their enmity, Wilkins is the only one of the three Nobel Prize winners who mentioned Franklin in his Nobel lecture. *The World of Physics*, by Jefferson Hane Weaver (Vol. 2, NY: Simon & Schuster, 1987) reprints part of his and Crick's lectures.

"Molecular structure of nucleic acids: A structure for deoxyribose nucleic acid," by James Watson and Francis Crick, in *Nature*, vol. 171, no. 4356, April 25, 1953, 737-738.

A surprisingly accessible paper, even for a lay audience, considering its contents earned them a Nobel Prize.

The Eighth Day of Creation, by Horace Freeland Judson (NY: Simon and Schuster, 1979).

Judson's detailed but accessible account of the history of biochemistry draws on both published accounts and extensive interviews with the principals involved. Part I in particular covers similar ground to Olby and Watson's books, but from a different (and in the case of Watson, at least, a more balanced and rigorous) perspective.

"The legend of Rosalind Franklin", by Horace Freeland Judson, in *Science Digest*, vol. 94, no. 1, January 1986, 56-59; 78-83.

Judson apparently wrote this condensed version of *The Eighth Day of Creation*, with its emphasis on the question of Franklin's contribution, at least in part as a reaction to the books by Sayre and Gornick. He goes to great lengths and presents much evidence (drawing on interviews with her fellow scientists) to refute the idea that Franklin's isolation was a result of sexual discrimination.

The Path to the Double Helix, by Robert Olby (NY: Dover Publications, 1994).

This book presents a thorough, detailed scientific history of the path to the double helix. The players in the story you just read don't even appear until the book is well past the halfway point! It offers little in terms of the personalities involved, which played a key part in who made the final discovery, but does feature many direct quotes by Crick, Watson, Wilkins, and Bragg.

Finally, Wilkins, Watson, and Crick all cite Erwin Schrödinger's *What is Life?* (London: Cambridge University Press, 1944) as influential in their early thinking about the problems of the genetic code. This is a slender volume, but more than fifty years later Schrödinger's book still fascinates both for what it says and for being one of the first examples of a world class physicist venturing into the life sciences.

The last line of the story is also the last line of *The Sun Also Rises* by Ernest Hemingway (NY: P.F. Collier, 1926).

BARBARA McCLINTOCK

I hope this book (and all the other G.T. Labs books) shows that the community of scientists is made up of honest-to-goodness people. As such, scientists can succumb to trends. Perhaps not as often or as extreme as the ones we see in pop music and *haute couture*, but there's hip science and there's unfashionable science. McClintock resisted the fad of molecular biology (which began with the discovery of DNA's structure and continues to this day), stuck with her research on corn genetics when other organisms were more popular, and eventually won the Nobel Prize for her discoveries.

Talking about her life's work, McClintock once said: "You may think [chromosomes] are small when I show you pictures of them. But when you look at them, they get bigger and bigger and bigger." This applies to her life as well. She considered herself an anomaly, shunned the idea of being a role model for others, and was "plainly miserable" with all the attention she began to receive in the 1970s. But though her life is certainly unique, she gives us a worthy and joyous model.

NOTES

PAGE 81

Panel 1: Your basic building block of life, about which McClintock said: "Well, you know, when I look at a cell [in a micro-scope], I get down in that cell and look around." This is in fact a corn cell, but not of the type she would usually look at.

Panel 3: McClintock studied corn through-out her scientific career, staying out of the more *chic* areas of research in molecular biology. Prompted by the discovery of DNA's structure, most of her colleagues began to focus on the more easily quanti-fied chromosome in smaller organisms like *E. coli*. McClintock stuck with the far more elusive genes, in the vastly more complicated corn. Her ability to grasp this complexity where others couldn't led many to call her a mystic. She didn't like that, but was probably too modest to say that what others called mysticism was sim-ply smarter, more painstaking, and more dedicated science. She wasn't so enamored with science that she couldn't speak at least a little mystically, though: "[The scientific method] gives us relationships which are useful, valid, and technically marvelous… [It's] lots of fun…but you don't get the truth. Things are much more marvelous than the scientific method allows us to conceive."

PAGE 84

We've left the class and the test McClintock found so engrossing ambiguous, so you probably assumed it was biology that en-thralled her to the point of forgetting her own name. In fact, it was geology. But the rest of this anecdote is true. She would later say the following about scientific work: "As you look at these things, they become part of you. And you forget yourself. The main thing about it is you forget yourself."

PAGE 85

Panel 7: Wait…there is no panel 7 on page 85! After graduating with a Ph.D. in 1927, she traveled extensively across the U.S. At the time, geneticists were either breeders (working in the field to create new strains of plants) or people who worked on chro-mosomes. The two never mixed. Except in the person of McClintock, who because of this (and because she was a woman) never found a position that suited her, or a faculty that would accept her. She also trav-eled briefly to Germany on a Guggenheim Fellowship in 1933, but returned quickly, shaken by the political situation there.

PAGE 87

Panel 4: "Animals can walk around, but plants have to stay still to do the same things… For instance, if you pinch a leaf of a plant you set off electric pulses. You can't touch [one] without setting off an electric pulse… There is no question that plants have all kinds of sensitivities."

PAGES 88-89

McClintock slowly convinced her col-leagues of the correctness of her theories, in part by sheer force of will. It took most of them a long time to get it, though, and confirming results by Monod and Jacob proved essential for her work's acceptance. "The logic was compelling. The logic made itself, the logic was it. What's compelling in these cases is that the problem is sharp and clear. The problem is not something that's ordinary, but it fits into the whole picture, and you begin to look at it as a whole… It isn't just a stage of this, or that. It's what goes on in the whole cycle. So you get a feeling for the whole situation of which this is [only] a component part."

PAGE 89

Panel 6: It wasn't easy to find pictures of McClintock in a dress. In fact, the one taken at the Nobel Prize ceremony is the only one I've seen.

PAGE 90

She continued to work alone after receiving the Nobel. In fact, her colleagues said she "was plainly miserable" with all the attention. And James Watson (Jim in the previous story) did indeed play ball near her corn field, and later became Cold Spring Harbor's successful and respected director.

REFERENCES

A Feeling for the Organism, by Evelyn Fox Keller (NY: W.H. Freeman, 1983).

Though McClintock stopped cooperating with Keller before she had finished the book, it still reads as an authoritative account of her work.

The Dynamic Genome, edited by Nina Federoff and David Botstein (Plainview, NY: Cold Spring Harbor Laboratory Press, 1992).

Definitive and surprisingly accessible to all readers, this collection of scientific papers, reminiscences, and original articles by McClintock and others will give you a well-rounded picture of her as both a person and a scientist.

"Two genes, no enzyme: A second look at Barbara McClintock and the 1951 Cold Spring Harbor Symposium," by Nathaniel C. Comfort, in *Genetics*, vol. 140, no. 4, August 1995, 1161-1166.

An interesting perspective on why McClintock's first "jumping gene" talk didn't connect with the vast majority of her audience, from one of those audience members. (Who "got it" sooner than many.)

"A naturalist of the genome," by Roger Lewin, in *Science*, vol. 222, no. 4622, October 28, 1983, 402-404; and "Barbara McClintock (June 16, 1902 – September 2, 1992)," by Nina Federoff, in *Genetics*, vol. 136, no. 1, January 1994, 1-10.

If *The Dynamic Genome* gets too technical (it did for me), try these summaries of McClintock's accomplishments. One was written soon after her Nobel Prize was announced and the other upon her death.

BIRUTÉ GALDIKAS

We aged Dr. Galdikas throughout the story because her work continues to this day, and the story we've told here gives only a glimpse of the complex nature of a field researcher and her life. Compressing more than 20 years of work into roughly 20 pages of comics means we had to leave out details and background information.

That scientific and conservation work is by no means finished. Fortunately, as Galdikas says, "Orangutans are what conservationists call 'charismatic megafauna': large, extremely appealing animals." In other words, they're ideal tourist attractions. In part because of this, volunteers, many from Earthwatch, have helped her gather the data and preserve the orangutans (who are threatened by poachers) and their fragile habitat (threatened by loggers, farmers, and the wildfires that spread easily because of their activities).

If you would like to learn more about this important work you can contact the Orangutan Foundation International by messaging *ofi@orangutan.org*, visiting their website at *http://www.orangutan.org/*, or by writing

Orangutan Foundation International
824 S. Wellesley Ave.
Los Angeles, CA 90049 USA

REFERENCES

Orangutan Adaptation at Tanjung Puting Reserve, Central Borneo, by Biruté M.F. Galdikas (Ph.D. thesis, University of California, Los Angeles, 1978); and *Reflections of Eden: My Years with the Orangutans of Borneo*, by Biruté M.F. Galdikas (Boston: Little, Brown and Company, 1995).

If all dissertations were this readable scientists would probably have an easier time getting grant funding. Her book offers even more accessible prose and I found its personal focus on individual orangutans and stories engrossing and entertaining.

"Orangutans, Indonesia's 'People of the forest'," by Biruté Galdikas with photographs by Rod Brindamour, in *National Geographic*, vol. 148, no. 4, October 1975, 444-473; "Living with the great orange apes," by Biruté Galdikas and Rod Brindamour, in *National Geographic*, vol. 157, no. 6, June 1980, 830-853; and "Orangutans in the wild," by Cheryl Knott with photographs by Tim Laman, in *National Geographic*, vol. 194, no. 2, August 1998, 30-57.

The two articles by Galdikas don't add a great deal to her thesis or book. They do feature many more pictures, though, all of the consistently high quality *National Geographic* is famous for.

Watching the Wild Apes, by Bettyann Kevles (NY: E.P. Dutton, 1976) and *Walking with the Great Apes*, by Sy Montgomery (Boston: Houghton Mifflin, 1991).

Kevles' book planted the seed of the idea for presenting a fictionalized day in the life of a researcher, and provides a fine introduction to all three of Louis Leakey's protégés (Galdikas, Dian Fossey, and Jane Goodall). As for Montgomery, after reading the introduction I was prepared to dislike the rest, anticipating an "Aren't they wonderful because they're women?" tone to mar the book. Fortunately, the conclusion I jumped to was wrong. Hers isn't the objective journalism that people (especially scientists) pretend exists, but is instead intelligent advocacy writing.

Finally, if you like the story's pictures more than its words, have a look at *Orangutan Odyssey* by Biruté Galdikas and Nancy Briggs, with photographs by Karl Ammann (NY: Harry N. Abrams, 1999), *The Nature of Borneo*, by Steven Yates (NY: Facts on File, 1992) or seek out the National Geographic videos *Search for the Great Apes* (Executive Producer Dennis Kane, 1975) and *Creatures of the Mangrove* (Executive Producers Dennis Kane and Thomas Skinner, 1986).

EPILOGUE: MARIE CURIE

I hope that this epilogue, though at first glance sad, instead reads as ironic in light of the quotes reproduced in the prologue section. Like many of the others in this book, Marie Curie found that even though she disdained it, fame had many rewards, and that she could use her position to help others. Unfortunately, and also like many of the scientists featured here, she also found that fame came at a high personal price.

REFERENCE

Marie Curie, by Robert Reid (London: William Collins Sons & Co. Ltd., 1974).

This provided the source and context for the title of the book, which appears here in the epilogue as well. The complete letter appears (along with many others to and from her daughter Irene) in *Correspondence; choix de lettres, 1905-1934 de Marie et Irène Curie. Présentation par Gillette Ziegler*, by Marie Curie (Paris: Èditeurs Francais Réunis, 1974).

EMMY NOETHER

Hermann Weyl, a noted mathematician in his own right, put it best: "She was not clay, pressed by the artistic hands of God into a harmonious form, but rather a chunk of human primary rock…" As for the German on the back cover, Mist = crap, and Formelngestrüpp = a jungle of formulas—words Noether often used to describe her doctoral dissertation.

REFERENCES

Women and Numbers, by Teri Perl (San Carlos, CA: Wide World Publishing/Tetra, 1993).

A nifty book for teachers, this all-ages illustrated book contains biographical anecdotes, classroom activities, and plenty of mathematical games.

Emmy Noether: A Tribute to Her Life and Work, edited by J.W. Brewer and M.K. Smith (NY: Marcel Dekker, 1981); and *Emmy Noether, 1882-1935*, by Auguste Dick (Boston, MA: Birkhäuser, 1981).

For a brief biography either book will serve, though Brewer and Smith give a more complete mathematical picture of her career.

THE ARTISTS

DONNA BARR is the award-winning, acclaimed author of such works as *The Desert Peach*, *Stinz, Hader and the Colonel, Bosom Enemies,* and many others. Her work can be found at *www.stinz.com* and at *Moderntales.com*.

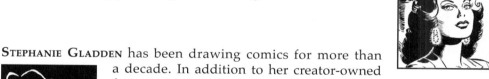

MARY FLEENER writes and draws *Fleener* (published by Zongo Comics), does illustration for lotsa magazines, exhibits her paintings at the La Luz de Jesus gallery in Los Angeles, makes ceramic pottery, and rarely sleeps. You can reach her via *www.maryfleener.com*.

Brenda Starr, Plastic Man, Metamorpho, and *Batman* are just a few of the titles **RAMONA FRADON**'s art has graced over a career in illustration more than fifty years long, and counting.

STEPHANIE GLADDEN has been drawing comics for more than a decade. In addition to her creator-owned funny animals in *Hopster's Tracks* and *Cricket & Plato*, Steph has worked on characters as diverse as The Powerpuff Girls, The Simpsons, Bugs Bunny, Pepper Ann, Ren & Stimpy, The Flintstones, Tex Avery's Wolf & Red and many others. You can see more of her work at *www.stephaniegladden.com* ask her about comics, animation, sushi, and even science.

ROBERTA GREGORY has been inflicting her unique comics on an unsuspecting populace since 1974. She is best known for *Naughty Bits* (featuring Bitchy Bitch) and also for *Winging It, Artistic Licentiousness*, and many others… Check out her website at *www.robertagregory.com* or send a self-addressed, stamped envelope to P.O. Box 27438, Seattle, WA 98125.

LEA HERNANDEZ is the multiple-Eisner nominated creator of *Killer Princesses* (with Gail Simone, Oni Press), *Rumble Girls*, the Texas Steampunk graphic novels *Cathedral Child*, *Clockwork Angels* and *Ironclad Petal* (*ModernTales.com*). Find out more by visiting *divalea.livejournal.com*.

CARLA SPEED MCNEIL was shocked to discover that turning thirty was no big deal. She writes/draws/everythings the acclaimed science fiction comic series *Finder* published on the web at *www.lightspeedpress.com*.

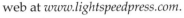

Though best known in the comics world for her award-winning series *Castle Waiting*, **LINDA MEDLEY** has also illustrated children's books (including Kipling's *The Elephant's Child* and stories by Isaac Bashevis Singer and the Brothers Grimm) and comics for many publishers.

MARIE SEVERIN actually got her start in the 1950s with the legendary E.C. Comics group. Her longest affiliation was with Marvel Comics, where she was best known for her work as artist on the humorous *Not Brand Ecch!* and on the popular *Dr. Strange, Incredible Hulk,* and *Kull* titles.

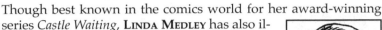

JEN SORENSEN is the creator of *Slowpoke*, which you can read in a number of alternative weekly newspapers or in the collection (published by Alternative Comics) called *Slowpoke: Cafe Pompous*. When she's not doodling and lollygagging she also draws for *Nickelodeon* and *National Geographic Kids*. See more at *www.slowpokecomics.com*.

ANNE TIMMONS currently draws the Lulu Award winning *GoGirl!* She has also done covers and interior art for magazines ranging from *Comic Book Artist* to *Wired*. Visitors to the Cartoon Art Museum, the Secession gallery in Vienna, and the permanent collection of the Library of Congress have all enjoyed her illustrations…and if you drop by *http://homepage.mac.com/tafrin* you can see more too.

EPILOGUE: MARIE CURIE

EPILOGUE: Marie Curie

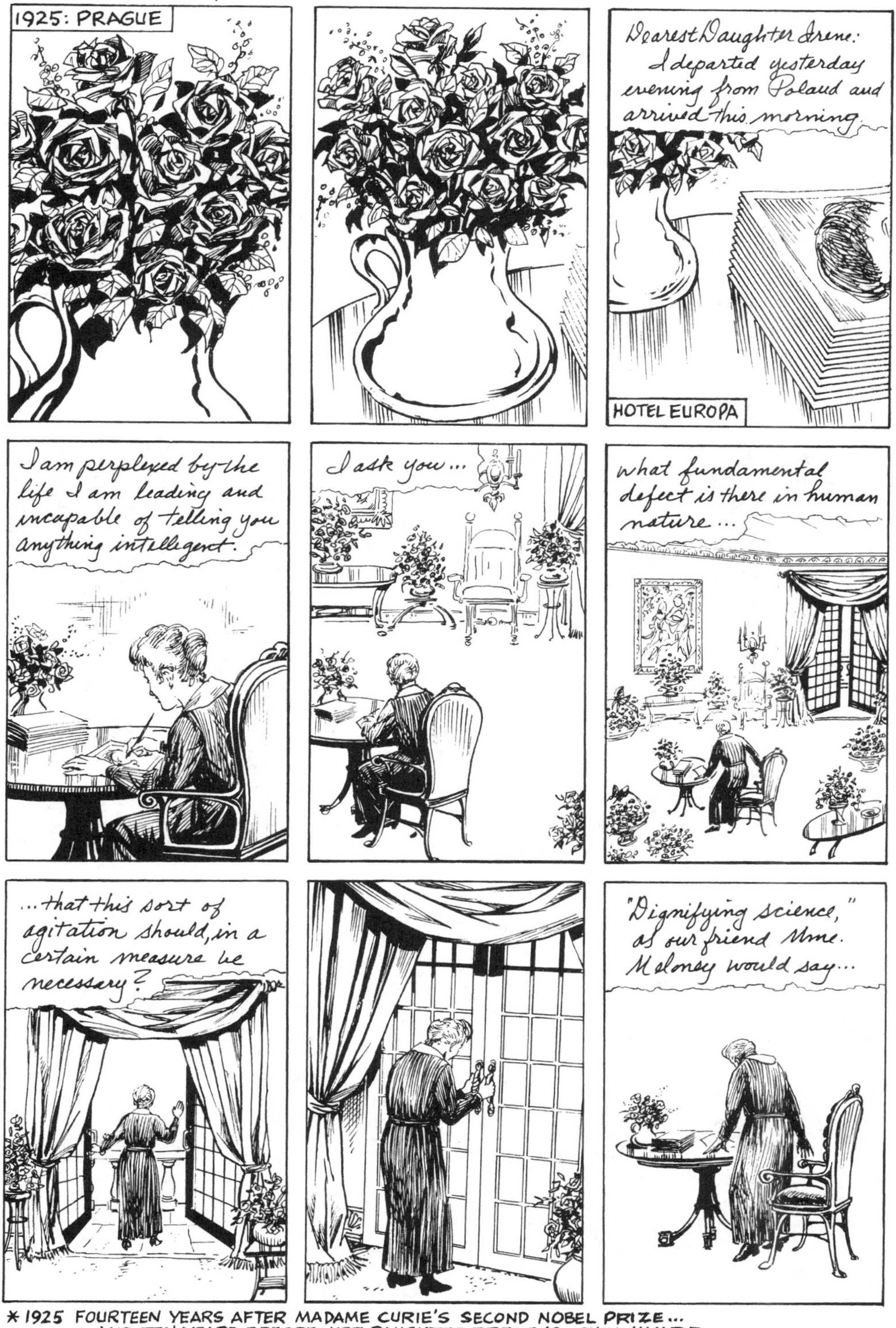
1925: PRAGUE
Dearest Daughter Irene: I departed yesterday evening from Poland and arrived this morning.
HOTEL EUROPA
I am perplexed by the life I am leading and incapable of telling you anything intelligent.
I ask you...
what fundamental defect is there in human nature...
...that this sort of agitation should, in a certain measure be necessary?
"Dignifying science," as our friend Mme. Meloney would say...

* 1925 FOURTEEN YEARS AFTER MADAME CURIE'S SECOND NOBEL PRIZE...
... AND TEN YEARS BEFORE HER DAUGHTER IRENE'S OWN AWARD.

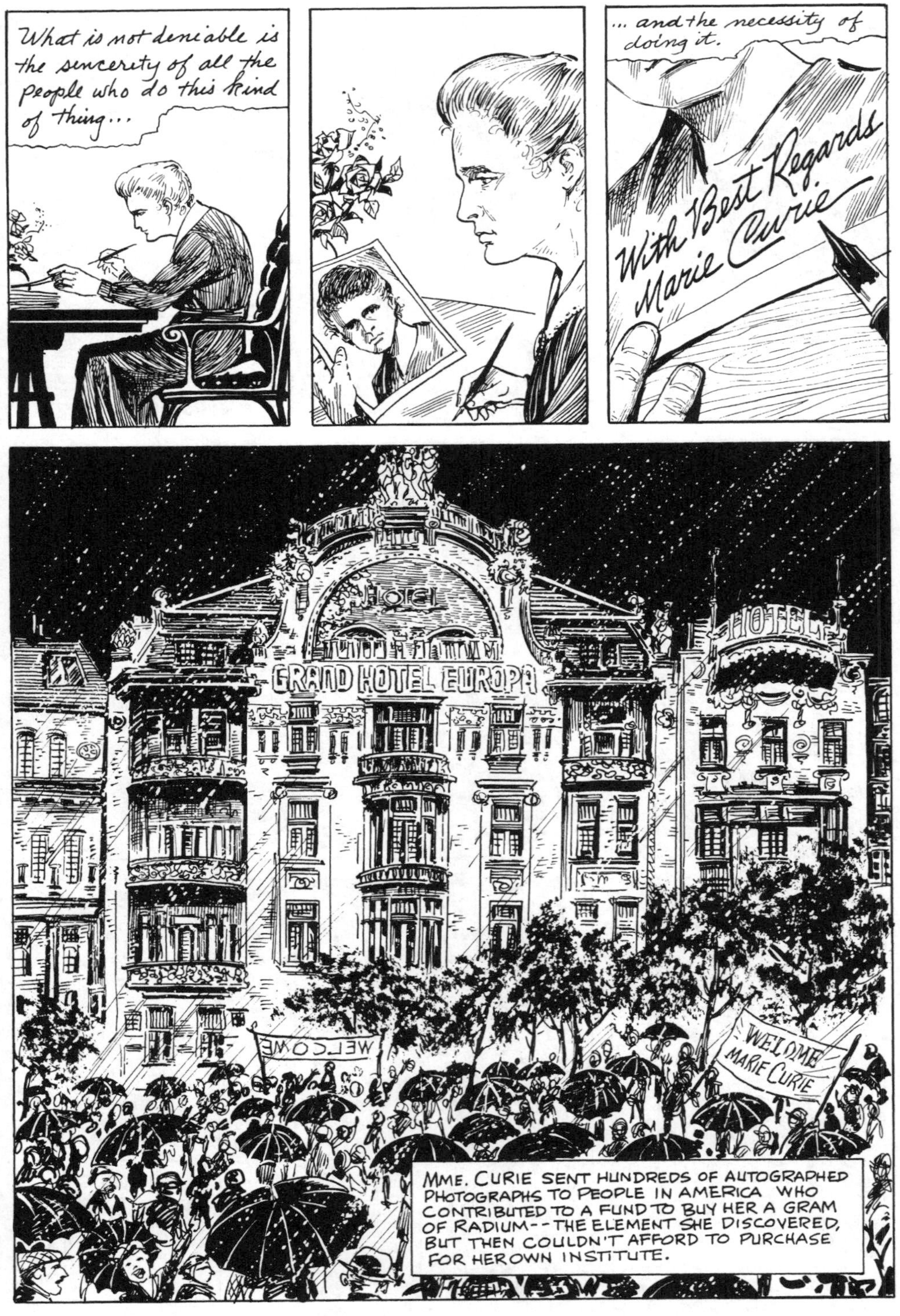
What is not deniable is the sincerity of all the people who do this kind of thing...
...and the necessity of doing it.
With Best Regards
Marie Curie
HOTEL
GRAND HOTEL EUROPA
HOTEL
WELCOME
MARIE CURIE
MME. CURIE SENT HUNDREDS OF AUTOGRAPHED PHOTOGRAPHS TO PEOPLE IN AMERICA WHO CONTRIBUTED TO A FUND TO BUY HER A GRAM OF RADIUM--THE ELEMENT SHE DISCOVERED, BUT THEN COULDN'T AFFORD TO PURCHASE FOR HER OWN INSTITUTE.

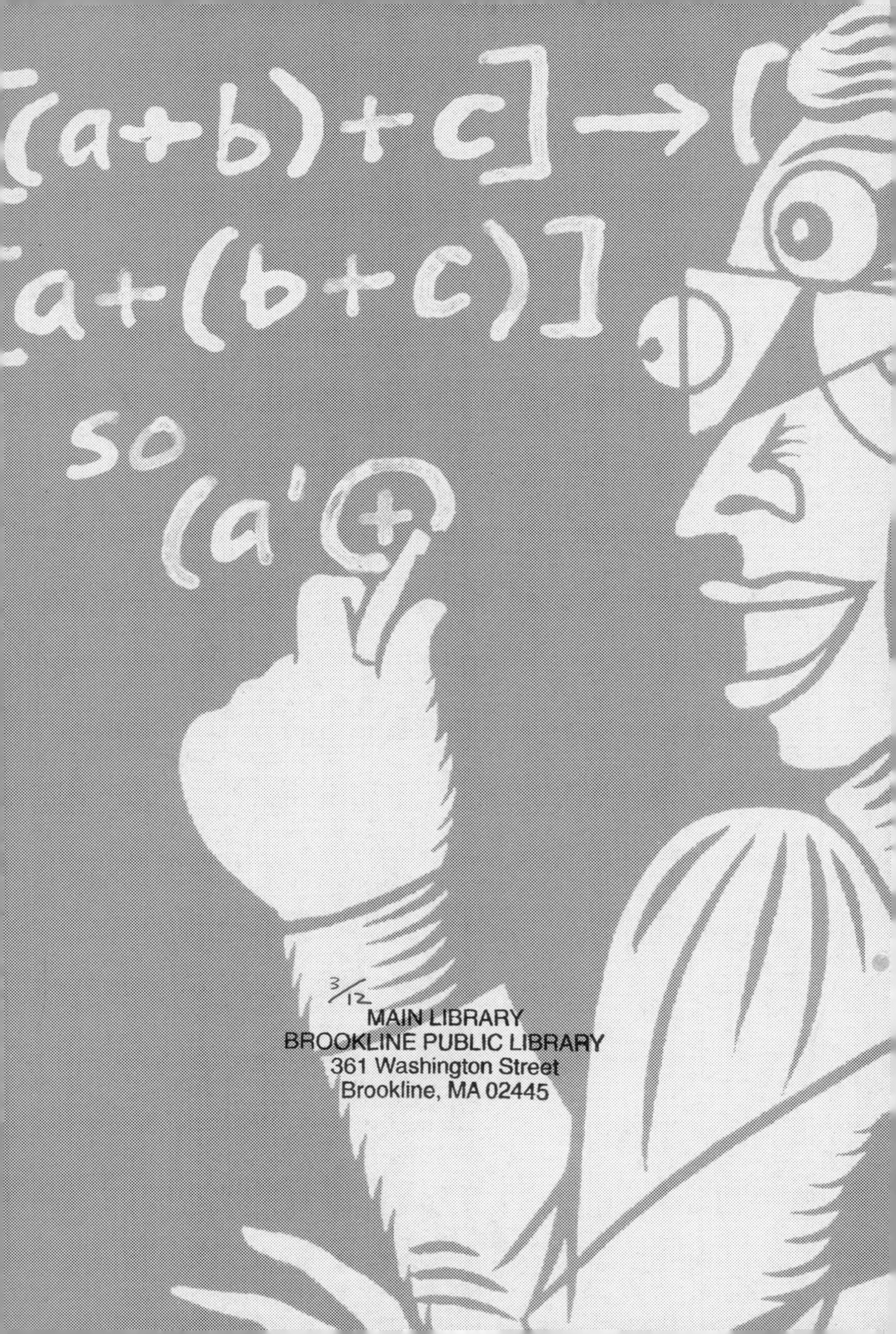
(a+b)+c] →
a+(b+c)]
so